JF Patterson

Pg 71
Eleanor became an
unofficial ombudsman

ELEANOR ROOSEVELT

Recent Titles in Greenwood Biographies

ELEANOR ROOSEVELT

A Biography

Cynthia M. Harris

GREENWOOD BIOGRAPHIES

GREENWOOD PRESS
WESTPORT, CONNECTICUT • LONDON

Library of Congress Cataloging-in-Publication Data

Harris, Cynthia M., 1937–
    Eleanor Roosevelt : a biography / Cynthia M. Harris.
        p. cm. — (Greenwood biographies, ISSN 1540–4900)
    Includes bibliographical references and index.
    ISBN–13: 978–0–313–33166–4 (alk. paper)
    ISBN–10: 0–313–33166–9 (alk. paper)
    1. Roosevelt, Eleanor, 1884–1962.   2. Presidents' spouses—United States—
Biography. I. Title.
E807.1.R48H37   2007
973.917092—dc22   2007017643
[B]

British Library Cataloguing in Publication Data is available.

Library of Congress Catalog Card Number: 2007017643
ISBN–13: 978–0–313–33166–4
ISBN–10: 0–313–33166–9
ISSN: 1540–4900

First published in 2007

Greenwood Press, 88 Post Road West, Westport, CT 06881
An imprint of Greenwood Publishing Group, Inc.
www.greenwood.com

Printed in the United States of America

The paper used in this book complies with the
Permanent Paper Standard issued by the National
Information Standards Organization (Z39.48–1984).

10 9 8 7 6 5 4 3 2 1

CONTENTS

Photo essay follows page 78

SERIES FOREWORD

In response to high school and public library needs, Greenwood developed this distinguished series of full-length biographies specifically for student use. Prepared by field experts and professionals, these engaging biographies are tailored for high school students who need challenging yet accessible biographies. Ideal for secondary school assignments, the length, format and subject areas are designed to meet educators' requirements and students' interests.

Greenwood offers an extensive selection of biographies spanning all curriculum-related subject areas including social studies, the sciences, literature and the arts, history and politics, as well as popular culture, covering public figures and famous personalities from all time periods and backgrounds, both historic and contemporary, who have made an impact on American and/or world culture. Greenwood biographies were chosen based on comprehensive feedback from librarians and educators. Consideration was given to both curriculum relevance and inherent interest. The result is an intriguing mix of the well known and the unexpected, the saints and sinners from long-ago history and contemporary pop culture. Readers will find a wide array of subject choices from fascinating crime figures like Al Capone to inspiring pioneers like Margaret Mead, from the greatest minds of our time like Stephen Hawking to the most amazing success stories of our day like J. K. Rowling.

While the emphasis is on fact, not glorification, the books are meant to be fun to read. Each volume provides in-depth information about the subject's life from birth through childhood, the teen years, and adulthood. A thorough account relates family background and education, traces personal and professional influences, and explores struggles, accomplishments, and contributions. A timeline highlights the most significant life events against a historical perspective. Bibliographies supplement the reference value of each volume.

PREFACE

An astute politician, dedicated feminist, and champion of the rights of minorities, especially African Americans, and of the poor, Eleanor Roosevelt was one of the most powerful women in twentieth-century America. In an age when proper ladies were expected to supervise the household, dine with the right people, entertain elegantly, and perhaps acknowledge the poor by volunteering at a settlement house, she established careers as a teacher, social worker, and reformer, set up a furniture factory, and became a successful journalist. Forming a unique political alliance with her husband, she was a key figure in FDR's political career, playing a role in the Democratic Party, traveling extensively throughout the United States to serve as his eyes and ears, and playing a major role in the shaping of many New Deal programs. Always she fought for the inclusion of women and African Americans in New Deal projects. As her journalism career soared with the creation of "My Day," her not insignificant income went to projects for helping the disadvantaged and unemployed. Ultimately, in postwar America she became an official delegate to the newly formed United Nations, where, as chair of the Commission on Human Rights, she used her diplomatic skills to steer the creation and approval of the Universal Declaration of Human Rights through difficult political terrain.

Yet Eleanor Roosevelt was not always the confident woman admired today. A timid, shy child orphaned at the age of 10, she was acutely aware of her own awkwardness and inadequacies, especially as a child, teenager, and young wife and mother. Her personal life was often troubled, her family relations strained. Increasingly, as an adult she devoted her time to causes she felt passionate about, developing a public persona that belied her innate insecurity. Becoming a skilled politician and diplomat, she was, by the time of her death in 1962, dubbed the first lady of the world.

This book is a concise biography of Eleanor Roosevelt. It does not aim to put forth or disprove any new theories, but rather to introduce students to an extraordinary woman whose life and legacy had a major impact on American life as it is known today.

ACKNOWLEDGMENTS

After wearing an editor's hat for many years, moving to the author's role has been an interesting and rewarding experience. My thanks go especially to my Greenwood editor and former colleague Michael Hermann for his insightful comments. He always hit on exactly the items that were bothering me as I wrote. Thanks also to Gary Kuris, editorial vice president, and Emily Birch, formerly managing editor at Greenwood, for agreeing that my writing this book would be a good retirement project. Maurine Beasley of the University of Maryland read the penultimate version of the manuscript, and I thank her for her comments and suggestions.

Thanks also to Sarah Hostetter for reading the early chapters and assuring me of their readability and to Catherine and William Brennan for giving me a teenager's perspective on Chapter 1. I'd like to thank my hiking friends for showing an interest in my writing project, as I'm sure some of them must have wondered if I would ever finish. As I read for this book, I was surprised to realize how much of what my mom liked to quote as I grew up came from Eleanor Roosevelt. This book is dedicated in loving memory to my mom, Rachel Mead.

TIMELINE: EVENTS IN THE LIFE OF ELEANOR ROOSEVELT

1884   Anna Eleanor Roosevelt (called Eleanor) was born on October 11 in New York City.

1892   Eleanor's mother, Anna Hall Roosevelt, died. Eleanor went to live with her grandmother, Mary Hall.

1894   Eleanor's father, Elliott, died.

1899   Eleanor went to Allenswood, a boarding school in England.

1902   Eleanor made her debut in New York, began seeing Franklin D. Roosevelt.

1903   Eleanor began volunteer work at Rivington Street Settlement House.

1905   Eleanor and Franklin married, March 17.

1906   Daughter Anna born May 3.

1907   Son James born December 23.

1909   Son Franklin Jr. (the first) born March 18 and died in November.

1910   Son Elliott born on September 23. Franklin elected to the New York State Senate.

1911   Family moved to Albany, New York.

1913   Franklin appointed assistant secretary of the navy. Family moved to Washington, D.C.

1914   Son Franklin Jr. (the second) born August 17.

1916   Son John was born March 17.

1917   The United States entered World War I.

1917–1918   Eleanor visited naval hospitals and volunteered at
            Red Cross canteens.
1918   Eleanor became aware of Franklin's affair with
            Lucy Mercer.
1920   Franklin defeated as Democratic candidate for
            vice president. Family moved back to New York.
            Eleanor joined the League of Women Voters.
1921   Franklin was afflicted with polio.
1922   Eleanor joined the Women's Trade Union League and
            began working with the Women's Division of the
            New York State Democratic Committee.
1925   Eleanor became editor of *Women's Democratic News*. She,
            Nancy Cook, and Marion Dickerman built a cottage at
            Val Kill.
1927   Eleanor began teaching at Todhunter School in
            New York and opened the Val Kill furniture factory.
1928   Eleanor co-chaired the Women's Division of the
            Democratic National Committee. Franklin elected
            governor of New York. Family moved back to Albany.
1929   Eleanor continued to teach part-time and wrote magazine
            articles. Stock market crashed in October.
            The Great Depression began.
1932   Franklin elected president.
1933   Family moved back to Washington. Eleanor began weekly
            press conferences for women reporters, began fact-finding
            trips for Franklin, initiated Arthurdale homestead in
            West Virginia, and began writing a monthly column for
            Woman's Home Companion.
1934   Eleanor began promoting African American civil rights.
1935   Eleanor worked with National Youth Administration,
            began publishing her "My Day" column on December 30.
1936   Eleanor began speaking tours. Val Kill furniture factory
            closed and was converted into a cottage for Eleanor and
            Tommy Thompson. Franklin elected to second term as
            president.
1937   Eleanor's first autobiographical book, *This Is My Story*,
            published.
1940   Eleanor's speech at the Democratic National Convention
            united the party behind Franklin's choice for vice
            president, Henry Wallace. Franklin elected to third term as
            president.

1941   Eleanor appointed assistant director of Office of Civilian
        Defense. Her brother Hall died September 25. The
        Japanese bombed Pearl Harbor December 7. United
        States entered World War II.

1942   Eleanor resigned from Office of Civilian Defense, made a
        wartime visit to England.

1943   Eleanor visited troops in South Pacific, played a role in
        the creation of day care centers.

1944   Eleanor visited troops in Latin America. Franklin elected
        to fourth term as president.

1945   Franklin died of a stroke April 12. Germany surrendered
        three weeks later. Japan surrendered in August, ending
        World War II. Eleanor lived at Val Kill and in New York
        City, became a delegate to the United Nations.

1946   Eleanor headed UN's Committee III, negotiated
        resolution of the European refugee problem.

1947–1948 Eleanor chaired the UN Commission for Human Rights
        and directed the commission in drawing up the Universal
        Declaration of Human Rights.

1948   UN General Assembly adopted the Universal
        Declaration of Human Rights on December 10.

1949   Eleanor's second biographical book, *This I Remember*,
        published.

1952   Eleanor visited Arab countries, Israel, and India.
        Eisenhower elected president.

1953   Eleanor resigned from the United Nations, volunteered
        for the American Association for the United Nations,
        and visited Japan and Yugoslavia.

1956   Eleanor campaigned for Adlai Stevenson for president.
        Eisenhower reelected.

1957   Eleanor visited the Soviet Union as a journalist and
        interviewed Khrushchev.

1958   Eleanor's third biographical book, *On My Own*,
        published.

1960   Eleanor supported John F. Kennedy for president. Her
        health began to fail.

1962   Eleanor died November 7.

ACRONYMS

AAA	Agricultural Adjustment Act
AAUN	American Association for the United Nations
ADA	Americans for Democratic Action
AP	Associated Press
AYC	American Youth Congress
CCC	Civilian Conservation Corps
CORE	Congress of Racial Equality
CIC	Counter-Intelligence Corps
CWA	Civil Works Administration
DAR	Daughters of the American Revolution
FERA	Federal Emergency Relief Administration
HUAC	House Un-American Activities Committee
NAACP	National Association for the Advancement of Colored People
NDAC	National Defense Advisory Commission
NIRA	National Industrial Recovery Act
NRA	National Recovery Administration

NYA	National Youth Administration
OCD	Office of Civilian Defense
PCA	Progressive Citizens of America
PWA	Public Works Administration
SCHW	Southern Conference for Human Welfare
UNRRA	United Nations Relief and Rehabilitation Administration
WRA	War Relocation Authority
WPA	Works Progress Administration
WTUL	Women's Trade Union League

Chapter 1

GROWING UP

In the 1930s, millions of Americans—farmers, clerical workers, respected members of the new middle class—lost their money, their work, their homes, and joined a multitude of unemployed "bums," camping in primitive tent cities, struggling to find work, to feed their children, to survive. Many others labored long hours for pitiful wages in coal mines, factories, or mills. The country was in the depths of the worst depression in its history.

In the midst of this despair, a political cartoon showing two astonished coal miners poked fun at the first lady of the United States, Eleanor Roosevelt. Deep in the bowels of the mine, the two men looked in surprise as one exclaimed, "For gosh sakes. Here comes Mrs. Roosevelt!"[1] Although probably fictitious, the cartoon epitomizes the type of thing Mrs. Roosevelt, a unique first lady, was likely to do. She had, in fact, visited coal miners in West Virginia to see firsthand their horrendous living conditions, and she would fight to improve those conditions. With genuine compassion for those less fortunate, Eleanor Roosevelt had become known as a champion of the disadvantaged, the poor, the victims of discrimination and prejudice.

Yet Eleanor had been born into a very different kind of world, a world far removed from ordinary workers, from the plight of newly arrived immigrants, from the struggles of blacks freed just two decades earlier from slavery. In the 1880s, an era referred to as the Gilded Age, Eleanor Roosevelt was born into the New York aristocracy.

The Roosevelts, the Livingstons, the Halls, all part of Eleanor's family, belonged to that select group of families known as New York Society (spelled with a capital S to indicate its official status). Members of that society had elegant, finely furnished townhouses in Manhattan, complete with staffs of maids, kitchen help, and children's nurses, where they lived during the official social season. During the season they entertained elaborately, giving dinners for all "the right people," and went to gala balls, the most famous being those given by Mrs. Mary Astor. They could be seen riding up Fifth Avenue in magnificent horse-drawn carriages. They also had large country estates on Long Island or in the Hudson River valley, where they might spend the summer unless they decided to tour Europe or vacation in some fashionable spot like Newport, Rhode Island. Their extravagant lifestyles, gala balls, and ornate gilded furniture inspired the era's name, the Gilded Age.

THE FAMILY PEDIGREE

Eleanor's Mother

Eleanor's mother, Anna Livingston Ludlow Hall, was a popular member of society. Widely admired for her grace and beauty, she was the belle of any ball, as her mother, Mary Livingston Hall, had been before her. The Livingstons had been the most important family in the Hudson River valley since the seventeenth century, and Anna's ancestors had signed the Declaration of Independence and presided over George Washington's inauguration. Anna's father, Valentine Hall, was extremely rich, having inherited a fortune from Anna's grandfather, and he never felt the need to work. Also extremely religious, he had his own personal theologian. Life in the Hall household was religious and somber. The Halls saw to it, however, that Anna, the oldest of six children, was well prepared for society. As a child, she had to walk each day while holding a stick locked through her arms behind her back. That, her father believed, would ensure that she had the necessary grace as a young lady. "My mother," the adult Eleanor wrote, "belonged to that New York City Society which thought itself all-important."[2]

Eleanor's Father

Eleanor's father, Elliott Roosevelt, was a great charmer. He had a twinkle in his eye and a spontaneous, easy way with people. He was well liked, although he sometimes had trouble finding direction in his life, and he came from a well-established society family. He was a member of the Republican Roosevelt clan known as the Oyster Bay Roosevelts.

In the 1640s, a common ancestor for all Roosevelts arrived in New Amsterdam (later to become New York), where subsequent generations of Roosevelts were successful merchants. In the early 1800s, when more than 50 Roosevelt families lived in the city, one adventurous Roosevelt, Isaac, moved upstate to become a gentleman farmer, and his descendants became the Hyde Park Roosevelts. The future Oyster Bay Roosevelts stayed in the city, where Elliott's grandfather, with an importing business, real estate, and a career in banking, became one of the richest men in New York. Outside the city, he had a country estate in Oyster Bay, overlooking Long Island Sound, and his family became the Oyster Bay Roosevelts. His youngest son, Theodore Roosevelt Sr., was Elliott's father.

Nicknamed "Greatheart," Theodore Sr. was a philanthropist. As an Oyster Bay Roosevelt, his wealth and his place in society were well established, and he became involved in many charitable causes. He would spend his time doing such things as visiting orphaned children. He founded the New York Orthopedic Hospital and played a role in the creation of the Metropolitan Museum of Art and the Museum of Natural History. Elliott's mother, Martha ("Mittie") Bulloch, was not a New Yorker. A descendant of the first Revolutionary-era governor of Georgia, she came from an old Georgia family. Although the family's wealth was declining, her family owned nineteen slaves, and loyalties were divided in the Roosevelt home during the Civil War. Mittie loved the South, and her two brothers fought for the Confederacy. As a child Elliott and his siblings heard many stories of the Old South. Theodore and Mittie had five children, including Elliott and his older brother Teddy, who would become president of the United States.

When the Roosevelt men were in Oyster Bay, life centered around their hunt club, where well-heeled men spent their time playing polo, riding, and hunting. The Roosevelts were accomplished, competitive sportsmen. Elliott and his brother Teddy were competitive from childhood. As a teenager, however, Elliott became more introspective and less athletic than his older brother, and he developed a strange, undiagnosed malady, which caused him to have seizures. When he was 15, his parents sent him to Texas, thinking the frontier would toughen him up. He spent a year hunting buffalo while Teddy was at Harvard laying the foundations for his future career. Upon returning home, Elliott and his two sisters nursed their father, who had intestinal cancer, and after his father's death, he became despondent. At the age of 20, Elliott decided to take a hunting trip around the world, a great adventure that would keep him away from home for a couple of years. He visited such faraway places as the British colony of India, where he hunted, went on shopping sprees, and enjoyed

the company of rugged hard-drinking sportsmen. He returned home with
another strange malady, Indian fever, which caused him to have sporadic
fevers. He also had a problem that had probably begun in adolescence, an
overfondness for alcohol.

Shortly after Elliott returned from India, he met the lovely, ever-
popular Anna Hall. She was his idea of perfection, and he idolized her.
Although he had yet to focus on a career, Elliott was one of the more eli-
gible bachelors in society. Spontaneous, good-looking, and congenial, he
was from one of the original society families. Although Anna found him
a bit too unpredictable at first, she came to love him. They were married
on December 2, 1883, in a ceremony described by the *New York Times* as
"one of the most brilliant weddings of the season."[3] He was 23, and she
was 19.

ELEANOR'S CHILDHOOD
Bittersweet Early Years

Anna Eleanor Roosevelt, known as Eleanor, was born on October 11,
1884. The days before her birth had been anxious ones, for childbirth was
dangerous in the 1880s, and Teddy's wife had recently died after giving
birth to Eleanor's cousin Alice. Once Elliott knew his wife and baby were
fine, he was delighted with Eleanor. She was "a miracle from heaven,"
and he would always dote on his little girl, although they were frequently
separated as she grew up. Eleanor would come to idolize him, never acknowledging that he had serious weaknesses. Her early memories included
being dressed up, dancing, and his picking her up and holding her high
in the air. She wrote as an adult that "he dominated my life as long as he
lived. . . . With my father I was perfectly happy."[4]

Anna, however, did not show the same delight as Elliott. She did
not find this wrinkled little baby a thing of beauty, and even as Eleanor
became a little girl, her mother found her wanting. A society belle from
a family of women celebrated for their looks, Anna had expected any
daughter of hers to have the renowned Livingston beauty. Although
Eleanor was cute enough as a little girl, she did not look like a Livingston. She had the less glamorous looks of a Roosevelt. Nor did she have
a lively personality that would make her popular in society. A shy, serious child who rarely smiled, Eleanor was acutely aware of her mother's
feelings toward her. "My mother was troubled by my lack of beauty,"
the adult Eleanor wrote, "and I knew it as a child senses these things.
She tried . . . to bring me up so . . . my manners would compensate for my

looks, but her efforts only made me more keenly conscious of my short-comings."[5]

Anna was not able to show Eleanor the spontaneous affection that Elliott did. Although she read to Eleanor and spent extra time with her after her younger brothers went to bed, Eleanor always felt the boys were closer to their mother than she was. She could remember "standing in the door, very often with my finger in my mouth," watching her mother with the boys. And Eleanor could remember "the look in her eyes and . . . the tone of her voice" as her mother would say, "Come in, Granny." If other adults were present, Anna would explain that Eleanor "is such a funny child, so-fashioned that we always call her 'Granny.'" Eleanor "wanted to sink through the floor in shame."[6]

Perhaps Anna was naturally more aloof than Elliott. Perhaps she was too preoccupied with the growing problems in her marriage to give Eleanor much attention. Although early in their marriage Anna and Elliott were still popular and active in society, their marital problems began almost immediately. Just two months after the wedding, Elliott's mother, Mittie, died, and Elliott was devastated, as he had been when his father died. He began drinking heavily.

While his brother Teddy was in the New York state legislature, Elliott worked nominally in his uncle's banking business. He devoted more time to partying, drinking, and nursing his amorphous illnesses than he did to business. For most of Eleanor's early years, her parents—as well as her uncle and godfather, Teddy—were focused on finding a cure for Elliott. Eleanor spent a lot of time with relatives and servants. She learned French from a French-speaking nurse before she learned English. In the Roosevelts' aristocratic world, it was not unusual for children to spend time with hired help. Anna, as the lady of the household, was not expected to attend to the day-to-day details of caring for her children. Her role, as defined by society, was to direct the household staff, provide an enriched cultural and spiritual environment in the home, and oversee the care of her children. However, Eleanor's separations from her parents were also driven by Elliott's illnesses.

When she was two and a half years old, her parents thought Elliott would benefit from a European trip, and they started to take Eleanor on an ill-fated ocean voyage. Shortly after leaving port, the boat collided with a steamer, and they had to abandon ship. Terrified, Eleanor clung to the deck rail, refusing to move. Elliott got into a lifeboat, and the petrified Eleanor was tossed from the deck into her father's arms below. Too traumatized to get on another boat, Eleanor was left behind with her Oyster Bay relatives while her parents went off to Europe for six months. From that time on, Eleanor was generally fearful, a feeling that lasted through-out her childhood.

Upon her parents' return, Elliott built a house on ten acres of land in Hempstead, Long Island, close to the Meadowbrook Hunt Club, where he spent time with his hunting buddies, and he returned to his uncle's bank-ing business. Although Elliott was not completely cured, life appeared to go smoothly for a while, and Eleanor was content with her father present. Her younger brother, Elliott Jr., nicknamed Ellie, was born in 1889. Their life was about to undergo another upheaval, however.

Competitive polo players, Elliott and Eleanor's Uncle Teddy had be-come bitter rivals. Neither would give way to the other when competing in polo matches, and on one occasion their behavior resulted in an ac-cident that knocked Teddy unconscious. A short time later Elliott had another accident, causing him to break a leg, which did not heal properly. His leg had to be broken again and reset. Eleanor had vivid memories of her father's accident and his severe pain. The pain lingered, and Elliott spent most of the summer and fall of 1889 lying in bed. Eleanor was sent to stay at her Grandmother Hall's estate near the Hudson River. To ease the pain, doctors gave Elliott morphine and laudanum, drugs that would be regulated today but were given freely in the 1880s, and Elliott was soon addicted.

In December, he decided, rather suddenly, to take a trip, and Elea-nor, little Ellie, and Anna celebrated Christmas alone that year. When he returned, Elliott was still drinking. His behavior became erratic and abusive, and he was not wanted at dinner parties. Teddy did not want to be associated with him. Unwilling to share her unhappiness with anyone, Anna withdrew emotionally.

With their life deteriorating, Anna and Elliott took their two children on an extended trip to Europe, hoping Elliott would get better abroad. They visited Germany, Italy, France, and Austria. Eleanor had some lovely times with her father in Italy. Taking her for a gondola ride in Ven-ice, he acted as a gondolier, "singing with the other boatmen." "I loved his voice," she later wrote, "and, above all, I loved the way he treated me. . . . I never doubted that I stood first in his heart."[7] However, he could also be abrupt with her, shouting that she lacked "grit" when she was too afraid to ride a donkey downhill after him. He rode off, leaving her and her nurse to ride home alone. Eleanor scolded herself for being afraid, never, even as an adult, thinking that her father might have expected too much of a five-year-old. From Italy they went to Austria, where Elliott sought a cure, and to France, where he thought a spa would help. Anna was pregnant with their third child.

Meanwhile, in New York, Kathy Mann, one of their servants, claimed she was pregnant with Elliott's child and demanded child support. Elliott denied having sex with her, but the baby looked too much like a Roosevelt for Elliott to be believed. Eventually Teddy made financial arrangements with Kathy, preventing a public scandal, and began urging Anna to leave her husband. Anna still believed Elliott would get better. Sending Eleanor to a French convent school, she stayed in France, where Elliott's sister Bye joined them. Eleanor was miserable. The French girls ignored her, and she felt her mother had abandoned her. Elliott became more unpredictable, disappearing for days. He was having an affair with an American woman who lived in Paris. In June 1891, Eleanor's youngest brother, Hall, was born.

While Elliott was writing upbeat letters to his family at home and Anna's letters put up a good front, Bye was sending candid reports to her brother. To Teddy, the situation seemed dire. Not only did he want Anna to leave Elliott, but he believed Elliott belonged in an institution. Finally he convinced Anna to leave Elliott in Paris, and she returned home with Bye, Eleanor, and the two little boys. Although Elliott was not committed to an institution, he was banished from the family. Teddy insisted he had to stay sober for an extended period before he could see his family again. In 1892, after being treated for alcoholism in France and at a facility in Illinois, Elliott moved to Abingdon, Virginia, where he worked for his brother-in-law and began a probationary period of sobriety.

Elliott wanted to see Anna before moving to Virginia, but she refused. Outwardly Anna pretended life was fine, despite newspaper headlines describing Elliott's "excesses," but she was now plagued with depression and headaches, causing her to spend hours in bed. Trying to keep life normal, she arranged for Eleanor to be schooled at home with some other society children. She gave her children religious instruction and read to them in the evenings. Eleanor had a nurse, Madeleine, whom she hated, but she also had some nice memories of those days. She liked watching her beautiful mother get dressed to go out. When her mother suffered from headaches, Eleanor would stroke her mother's hair, making Eleanor feel briefly that she was a comfort to her mother.

She enjoyed summers at her Grandmother Hall's country estate at Tivoli, where she liked walking through the woods. In New York, they lived two blocks from Aunt Bye, who frequently cared for Uncle Teddy's daughter Alice, and Eleanor began to play with her cousin. However, Eleanor was living in the midst of turmoil. She would overhear her mother and aunts talking about Elliott. "Something was wrong with my father," she later wrote, "and from my point of view nothing could be wrong with him."[8] No one explained the true nature of the situation to Eleanor. She just knew she couldn't see her father, and she blamed her mother. She was often difficult, disobeying her mother and defying her teachers. She had crying fits in public and didn't want to go to children's parties. Her life, however, was soon to change yet again, more dramatically than it had ever changed before.

Diphtheria, More Drink, and Death

In November 1892, after having surgery, Anna became seriously ill with diphtheria. She quickly became comatose. Eleanor was sent to stay with her godmother, Cousin Susie Parish, while Grandmother Hall nursed Anna. Her brothers were sent to stay with their mother's aunt. Elliott was sent for, but he did not see Anna. In an era when antibiotics had not yet been discovered, diphtheria killed, and Anna died on December 7. Eleanor was eight, too young to fully understand. To her, "death meant nothing. . . . One fact wiped out everything else. My father was back and I would see him soon."[9]

Although Elliott had remained sober and wanted to take his children to Virginia, Grandmother Hall became the children's guardian, as stipulated in Anna's will. Eleanor and her brothers moved into Grandmother Hall's rather gloomy New York brownstone. Eleanor did see her father that December, and he promised that someday the two of them would live together again. Eleanor began to daydream about the life she would live with her father, although she couldn't quite fit her brothers into her daydreams. Elliott wrote regularly to her, and she cherished his letters. Occasionally he visited, appearing unannounced at the front door. They would walk along Fifth Avenue or take a carriage ride, sometimes a reckless carriage ride with a "spirited" horse, which both excited and terrified Eleanor. Elliott gave her pretty things—hair ribbons, a fancy handkerchief, a gold pin—and sent her flowers. He gave her a puppy and a pony.

However, he was not handling Anna's death well. Compounding the tragedy of her death, Eleanor's brother Ellie came down with scarlet fever, followed by diphtheria, and died in May 1893. Elliott had started drinking again and was in the midst of drinking bouts and depression. Grandmother Hall was afraid to entrust Eleanor to his care and tried to keep them apart. Once when he took Eleanor for a walk, he left her standing on the sidewalk with the doorman while he went into the Knickerbocker Club for a quick drink. She waited patiently until he was carried out unconscious. In July 1894 Elliott wrote his last letter to Eleanor, telling her to remember that he loved her. The day he wrote that letter he died suddenly of alcohol-related problems. When Eleanor was told of his death, she said only, "I did want to see father once more."[10]

Life with Grandmother Hall

A widow for many years, Eleanor's grandmother, Mary Hall, was a somber, religious woman in her early fifties. Eleanor thought she was very old. Grandmother Hall's life centered on her religious faith and her children. In their twenties and late teens, Val, Eddie, Maude, and Pussie, Eleanor's uncles and aunts, lived with their mother in her five-story brownstone. An old-fashioned home with dark furniture and heavy draperies, the house had a gloomy feeling, and as an adult Eleanor would write of the small, cramped quarters for servants. They had one modern invention, however—gas lights. Grandmother Hall welcomed Eleanor and Hall into her home and gave Eleanor a greater sense of belonging than she had had with her own parents.

Religion permeated the house. Twice a day Grandmother Hall held family prayer sessions. After walking home from church on Sundays, Eleanor had to recite biblical passages and sing hymns with the family. She was not to play any games on Sunday. Grandmother Hall was strict with Eleanor, having come to believe that she was too lenient with her own children, and she had some rigid rules. For one, she expected Eleanor to take cold baths, although Eleanor later wrote in her autobiography that she often cheated and added a little hot water. Like her mother, Eleanor was expected to take long walks with a stick locked in her arms behind her back. Good posture was still very important. Eleanor also wore a steel back brace for a while, as it was feared she had a curvature of the spine.

Not wanting Eleanor to grow up too quickly, as she felt her own children had, Grandmother Hall made Eleanor dress like a little girl. As a young teenager, when girls her age were wearing long formal skirts, Eleanor still wore the short frilly skirts of her childhood, thick black stockings, and high-laced shoes. She was a tall girl, and her height accentuated her short skirts. With her basic insecurity about her looks and her odd clothing, she was not comfortable with people her own age. Contact with other young people was rare in her grandmother's house. Although Eleanor played with her brother Hall, she spent most of her time with adults, including the servants. In New York, she liked the butler, who talked with her and let her wipe the dishes. At her grandmother's Tivoli house, near the Hudson River, she enjoyed spending time with the laundress, an upbeat, happy woman who showed Eleanor how to iron. She still hated her nurse, Madeleine, who would make her darn socks and then cut off the toes because Eleanor hadn't done it perfectly.

Eleanor's aunts and uncles also gave her attention, particularly her Uncle Val and Aunt Pussie. At the Tivoli house, Uncle Val took her riding, teaching her to jump the horse, and played tennis with her, while Aunt Pussie took her out on the Hudson in a rowboat. Pussie loved music and the theater, and she shared her interests with Eleanor, taking her to performances in the city. Pussie and Val were not reliable, however. On one occasion, Pussie took Eleanor to Nantucket, then got bored and left Eleanor and her governess without enough money to get home. Pussie had dramatic mood swings. Popular with men, she had many boyfriends, usually for just a short time. When she was in love, she was a joy to be with, but she had dramatic bouts of depression when relationships ended, locking herself in her room and refusing to speak to anyone. Eleanor would then turn to her Aunt Maude. Uncle Val, like Eleanor's father, was an alcoholic. During the years Eleanor lived with Grandmother Hall, his bouts of drunkenness made him increasingly difficult. Grandmother Hall was reluctant to have guests, as Val was both an embarrassment and a danger. She could never be quite sure what he would do. Eleanor, however, was not drawn into the fray as she had been with her parents, and she was able to remain emotionally removed from the turmoil.

Although Eleanor's Uncle Teddy, his family, and Aunt Bye had once been a large part of Eleanor's life, she rarely saw them now. Grandmother Hall did not encourage contact with Elliott's family. She thought Teddy was loud and rambunctious, and she feared his hard-living lifestyle. Nor was Teddy's second wife, Edith, eager to encourage a friendship between Alice and her cousin Eleanor. Ignoring alcoholism in her own family, Edith disapproved of Eleanor's alcoholic relatives. On rare occasions, however, Eleanor was invited to visit Teddy's family in Oyster Bay, where she enjoyed running along the beach and over sand dunes with Teddy and his children. Her cousin Alice was friends with both boys and girls of their age, and Eleanor thought she was very sophisticated. Eleanor was a little afraid of Alice. Eleanor rarely saw boys, and when she did, she felt awkward and self-conscious. Aunt Edith, however, may have recognized Eleanor's potential, for she is quoted as saying, "she is very plain. . . . But the ugly duckling may turn out to be a swan."[11]

Although other people thought Eleanor had a sad, sober life with Mary Hall, Eleanor always appreciated her grandmother's taking in her and Hall. Her life was more stable than it had been, and she was not unhappy. She was quiet and introspective, but she liked to read and spent hours absorbed in a book. She particularly liked to read poetry, literature, and history. At Tivoli, where the rooms were large and the library had walls lined with books, she liked to rummage through those books. She would often take forbidden reading into the woods, where no one could see what she was reading, and sit under a tree, enjoying her book. Although strict and straight-laced, Grandmother Hall was kind to her. After enduring her hated nurse, Madeleine, for years, Eleanor finally complained about her, and Grandmother Hall fired Madeleine, telling Eleanor she should have spoken up.

Eleanor continued to attend school with a group of society girls, and a private teacher gave her lessons in French, German, and music. She liked school and did well, winning medals for her schoolwork. She developed a love for history, literature, and language. Although she may never have felt she truly fit in with the other girls, they did seem to recognize her abilities. She took ballet lessons and enjoyed ballet. She also had lessons in ballroom dancing, a necessity for the social world she was expected to enter, but she hated parties and dances. Towering above the other girls in her short skirts, self-conscious about her looks, she never expected anyone to ask her to dance. At one party, however, her cousin Franklin, one of the Hyde Park Roosevelts and her father's godson, asked her to dance. She had fun. They enjoyed talking with each other. After the dance, he wrote to his mother that "Cousin Eleanor has a very good mind."[12]

ADOLESCENCE AND YOUNG ADULTHOOD
Boarding School

Grandmother Hall had begun to think about Eleanor's future. Eddie, as well as Val, was now an alcoholic, compounding Mary Hall's problems, and Anna had always wanted Eleanor to attend school in Europe. In 1899, the year she would turn 15, Eleanor sailed to England with her grandmother's married daughter, Aunt Tissie, and began school at Allenswood, a small boarding school outside of London.

To Eleanor, Allenswood was an exciting place, and she was at home almost immediately. Here she was truly happy. Unlike the typical finishing school for wealthy girls expected only to have social grace and a superficial knowledge of the arts, Allenswood aimed to truly educate the daughters of European aristocracy and wealthy Americans. The headmistress, Marie Souvestre, was the daughter of a famous French philosopher and an intellectual in her own right. An early feminist, she did not believe in the traditional roles expected of women. She encouraged her students to think for themselves, to argue for their beliefs, and to become politically aware. She expected them to work to their full potential and had no patience for lazy students. She might, in a fit of temper, tear up a sloppy paper in front of the class, terrifying the poorer students, but the brighter girls adored her. When Marie Souvestre found her students intelligent and eager to learn, she gave them extra attention and stimulated their interests with challenging questions. Eleanor thrived under her influence.

A short woman with pure white hair pulled back in a bun, Marie Souvestre was in her late sixties when Eleanor went to Allenswood. She already knew the Roosevelts, for Eleanor's Aunt Bye, Elliott's sister, had gone to a boarding school in France, where Mlle. Souvestre was then headmistress, and Anna and Elliott had spent time with her in Paris. Although most of the students at Allenswood were British, classes were taught in French, giving Eleanor, who had learned French as a child, an advantage over the other girls. Mlle. Souvestre liked Eleanor and recognized her potential. Eleanor was soon one of her favorites. For the first time in her life, Eleanor was among the leaders in her class, and she formed a group of friends who were also leaders and the brightest girls in the school.

The girls wore uniforms to class and during the day, but they were expected to dress for dinner and on Sundays. Eleanor's clothes were still outlandish. Many were hand-me-downs from her aunts. Mlle. Souvestre saw the need for Eleanor to have a new outfit, and eventually she insisted that Eleanor use part of her allowance to buy a new dress. Finally Eleanor had something fashionable to wear, a long red dress, which she loved and wore to parties and on Sundays. She was now six feet tall, the tallest girl in the school.

Eleanor excelled in her classes, took up sports, and made the first team in hockey. She loved the classes Mlle. Souvestre taught herself and took all of them—history, literature, and languages. She did especially well in Italian, German, and literature. Her education did not end when she left the classroom, however. As one of Mlle. Souvestre's favorites, she sat at the headmistress's dinner table, where conversation could range from poetry to politics, and she was among a select group of students frequently invited to spend evenings with Mlle. Souvestre in her study, where they read aloud and talked.

For the first time, Eleanor heard views contrary to beliefs generally held by her Grandmother Hall, her Oyster Bay relatives, and the isolated world of New York society. Mlle. Souvestre had strong political opinions, and she liked to talk politics outside of class. She was an outspoken liberal who championed the underdog, and her views were not popular at the turn of the century. Eleanor was not unaware of the poor and disadvantaged. When she was five or six, her father had taken her to help feed the poor on Thanksgiving. Her Grandfather Roosevelt, Theodore Sr., had devoted his life to philanthropic causes, and Eleanor had been taken to see the Orthopedic Hospital, where she felt sympathy for the children, having had to wear a back brace herself. Her Uncle Teddy, who was elected vice president of the United States in 1900 and succeeded to the presidency in 1901, was known as a progressive Republican who also championed the underdog. But the mindset of Eleanor's family and of the white Protestant elite in general was very different from Mlle. Souvestre's.

Grandmother Hall, like others in her isolated, self-important world, assumed the wealthy were wealthy because they were inherently superior; the poor were poor because they were inferior; and white-skinned people were naturally superior to brown- and black-skinned people. It was, she believed, "the white man's burden" to care for the dark-skinned. Even Eleanor's Uncle Teddy, with his progressive politics, believed in the "white man's burden," for the concept was generally accepted at the time. U.S. policies were based on the premise, and Uncle Teddy was a part of those policies. In 1898 the United States had fought the Spanish-American War to free Cuba from Spanish rule, and Teddy, as commander of the Rough Riders in Cuba, had helped to ensure an American victory. Not only did the war free the oppressed Cubans, but it gave the United States new international power. Mlle. Souvestre did not believe in the "white man's burden." She did not believe any powerful nation had a mandate to interfere in the course of events in less powerful nations.

She did not accept the views of the British elite. When Eleanor was going to school in England, the British Empire included much of Africa and the Indian subcontinent. The British were at war with the Boers, who had descended from the original Dutch settlers, in southern Africa, and all of London was wrapped up in the progress of the war. The British girls naturally expected Great Britain to win, as it did in 1902. Mlle. Souvestre did not side with the British. Although she held her tongue with the British girls, she had long discussions with Eleanor and other "foreign" girls about the rights of the Boers. She did not believe, as the "white man's burden" doctrine proclaimed, that Britain needed to colonize poorer nations in order to take care of them. That idea, she believed, was an excuse to justify greed. She believed in the rights of small, undeveloped nations.

Mlle. Souvestre's views were not limited to colonialism or the military feats of powerful nations. In France, the Dreyfus Affair was dividing the nation. Alfred Dreyfus, a Jewish army officer, was falsely accused of spying, and many assumed he was guilty. Mlle. Souvestre defended his innocence and discussed anti-Semitism with her students. She also supported trade unions. To the elite, trade unions were a subversive idea that would empower working people. Mlle. Souvestre also told her students she was an atheist. Remembering her headmistress years later, Eleanor wrote, "Mlle. Souvestre shocked me into thinking."[13]

After initially spending her school vacations traveling with Aunt Tissie and her husband, Stanley Mortimer, Eleanor was invited to be Mlle. Souvestre's travel companion, and she took several vacation trips with her. They visited Paris and southern France. They went to Italy, spending time in Pisa, Florence, and Rome, and on their last trip, they visited France, Belgium, and Germany. These trips were the high point of Eleanor's years at Allenswood. Traveling with Mlle. Souvestre was very different from traveling with her family. Avoiding large, expensive hotels frequented by rich Americans, they stayed at smaller hotels favored by Europeans. They visited Mlle. Souvestre's friends in Florence, staying in a villa overlooking the city. They ate local dishes and drank local wines. Eleanor handled the details of their travel, checking train schedules, purchasing tickets, and taking care of packing. In the process she became independent and self-confident. When Mlle. Souvestre did not feel like going out, Eleanor saw the sights on her own and became very comfortable looking around shops unaccompanied. At home she had always been chaperoned by a relative or a servant, as was expected for girls her age. In 1901, when Eleanor was alone in Paris, she met some neighbors from Tivoli, and they wrote to Grandmother Hall, telling her they had seen Eleanor "unchaperoned in Paris!"[14]

Shocked, Grandmother Hall insisted Eleanor leave Allenswood. At the end of the school year, she sailed home with Aunt Pussie, who was despondent over one of her failed romances. She spent much of the trip sobbing while Eleanor tried to console her. That summer, Aunt Pussie turned on Eleanor, telling her she was the "ugly duckling" and would never have any boyfriends. She went on to tell Eleanor the truth about her father's alcoholism, his life, and his extended absences. Idealizing her father, Eleanor did not believe it and turned to Grandmother Hall for the truth, but Mary Hall could not tell her anything different. For the first time, Eleanor realized what was "wrong with her father," but she never stopped idealizing him. After a miserable summer, she convinced her grandmother to let her return to London, and she spent one more year at Allenswood.

In 1902, however, she had to return home for good. She was about to turn 18, and she had to make her formal debut into society. Eleanor left London with sadness, for she had become very fond of Mlle. Souvestre. No one, aside from her father, had treated her as well as Mlle. Souvestre. For the next three years they wrote regularly to each other, but they never saw each other again. Mlle. Souvestre died of cancer in 1905, just two weeks before Eleanor arrived in London on her honeymoon.

Making a Debut, Working with the Poor

In stark contrast to her happy, carefree life in England, Eleanor returned to a disintegrating world at Tivoli. Her Aunt Maude was in a debt-ridden, troubled marriage, and Uncle Eddie, also married, was frequently drunk. Uncle Val's alcoholism had totally consumed him, and his behavior was especially destructive. Still living at Tivoli and rarely sober, he antagonized anyone who came to the house. He had even been known to shoot at guests approaching the house from his bedroom window. Grandmother Hall stayed year-round at Tivoli, where she was completely isolated. Afraid of what Val might do, she never invited people to visit, and she no longer had the energy to give attention to Eleanor's brother Hall. Although both Eleanor and her grandmother took Hall to Groton, a prep school outside of Boston, in the fall, Eleanor became responsible for his welfare. She began visiting him at school and wrote to him every day, as she wanted him to "feel he belongs to somebody."[15] After a summer at Tivoli, Eleanor moved to New York, where she stayed with Aunt Pussie in Mary Hall's brownstone for a while. Eventually she moved in with her Cousin Susie. Susie and her family lived in one of two attached brownstones on 76th Street. Her widowed mother lived in the second brownstone.

The official social season began that fall. Pointing to the brilliant debut made by Eleanor's mother, the glamorous Anna Hall, the society pages announced that Eleanor Roosevelt, the niece of President Teddy Roosevelt, was to make her debut. The Assembly Ball, the major event of the season, was held in December. For Eleanor, it was pure agony. At six feet, she was taller than most of the boys. She no longer knew the girls she had been schooled with in New York, and she didn't know any of the boys. Her Aunt Pussie, who was 14 years older and no longer a debutante, had more dance partners than she did. Although Mlle. Souvestre had written to her "that there are more . . . enviable joys than to be among the most sought-after women at a ball,"[16] Eleanor could not shake the ingrained feeling that being the belle of the ball was all-important. Years later, she wrote, "I knew I was the first girl in my mother's family who was not a belle and . . . I was deeply ashamed."[17]

Eleanor did have a few dance partners. A longtime family friend, Bob Ferguson, who had served with Uncle Teddy's Rough Riders and had once been an admirer of Aunt Bye's, asked her to dance and introduced her to his friends. Years later, when the first volume of her autobiography was published, one of those friends told Eleanor that her account of the ball was wrong, that he and his friends had truly wanted to dance with her. Eleanor's cousin Alice also disagreed with her account, claiming that the image of Eleanor as a shy, unattractive girl was one she herself had created. "She was always making herself out to be an ugly duckling," Alice wrote, "but she was really rather attractive . . . It's true . . . her chin went in a bit . . . if only her hateful grandmother had fixed her teeth."[18] At the time, however, Eleanor clearly believed she had failed as a debutante.

At the same time, she was beginning to find social situations where she was comfortable. She would never, even when she was older, like dances or parties with a lot of liquor and silly conversation. These she found boring, and she would always detest and fear alcohol. However, she was now meeting interesting people. Bob Ferguson was introducing her to his wide-ranging friends, including well-known artists living in Greenwich Village, and she enjoyed spending time with them. She was particularly comfortable with people older than she was, and she enjoyed dinners with serious conversation. She became known for her sophisticated conversation, and hostesses needing someone to enliven the conversation frequently invited Eleanor to dinner. She was more like a young woman in her mid-twenties than an 18-year-old.

She did not, however, find a whirl of social activities satisfying. She needed something more to hold her attention. By the winter of 1903 her interests had turned to poor immigrant children on New York's Lower East Side. Here newly arrived immigrants were living in overcrowded tenements. Both adults and children worked up to 12 hours a day in sweatshop conditions. They had few opportunities. A small group of young society women, including some of the girls Eleanor had studied with in New York, had formed the Junior League to promote settlement houses and set up a settlement house on Rivington Street, located on the Lower East Side. The settlement house movement had started in London, founded in part by a friend of Mlle. Souvestre's, and moved to Chicago and then to New York. Run by volunteers, who in theory "settled" in low-income areas to help the poor, the settlement houses provided classes in music and the arts for children and gave practical assistance to immigrant families.

Joining the Junior League, Eleanor gave dancing lessons and taught calisthenics at the Rivington Street Settlement House. Although some debutantes may have volunteered simply to impress society with their concern for the poor, Eleanor truly enjoyed working with the children. Unlike her friends who arrived and left in their private carriages, Eleanor took the Fourth Avenue streetcar and walked to the settlement house. While terrifying at times, when she encountered ragged, "foreign-looking" men outside of bars, the walk gave her a vivid picture of the immigrants' living conditions. Eleanor also joined the Consumer's League, a group that sought to improve working conditions for poor women and children. With an older, experienced social worker, she went into the sweatshops and saw the deplorable working conditions. Although each day Eleanor took the streetcar back to the safety of her own affluent world, the experience of volunteering on the Lower East Side may have been the beginning of her lifelong concern for the disadvantaged.

Although Eleanor's family did not approve of her volunteer work, she found it rewarding. She was now happy with her life in New York. She had friends who shared her interests. She was doing something she considered important. Most of all, she was now seeing her cousin, Franklin Delano Roosevelt.

NOTES

1. Robert Day, *New Yorker*, June 3, 1933.

2. Eleanor Roosevelt, *This Is My Story* (New York: Harper & Brothers, 1937), p. 3.

3. Quoted in Blanche Wiesen Cook, *Eleanor Roosevelt*, vol., *1884–1933* (New York: Viking Penguin, 1992), p. 44.

4. Roosevelt, *This Is My Story*, p. 6.

5. Ibid., p. 11.

6. Ibid., pp. 17–18.

7. Ibid., pp. 8–9.

8. Ibid., p. 16.

9. Ibid., p. 19.

10. Quoted in Joseph P. Lash, *Eleanor and Franklin: The Story of Their Relationship Based on Eleanor Roosevelt's Private Papers* (New York: W. W. Norton, 1971), p. 98.

11. Ibid., p. 114.

12. Ibid., p. 150.

13. Roosevelt, *This Is My Story*, p. 71.

14. Ibid., p. 88.

15. Quoted in J. William T. Youngs, *Eleanor Roosevelt: A Personal and Public Life* (New York: Longman, 2000), p. 64.

16. Quoted in Cook, *Eleanor Roosevelt*, vol. I, p. 121.

17. Eleanor Roosevelt, *The Autobiography of Eleanor Roosevelt* (New York: Harper & Brothers, 1961; repr., Da Capo Press, 1992), p. 37.

18. Quoted in Cook, *Eleanor Roosevelt*, vol. I, pp. 128–29.

Chapter 2

FDR, MARRIAGE, AND FAMILY LIFE

On a summer day in 1902, Eleanor was on the train from New York to Tivoli, absorbed in a book, when Franklin Roosevelt, traveling with his mother to Hyde Park, walked to the dining car and spotted her. He was now a student at Harvard. She was soon to be a debutante. Although she had not seen Franklin since she was 14, she was at ease talking with him, and they were soon deep in conversation. They talked for some time before Franklin suggested they walk back to the car where his mother, Sara Delano Roosevelt, was sitting. A close friend of Eleanor's Aunt Bye, Sara greeted Eleanor warmly, taking her hand as the two women talked. Sara was wearing the long black veil of a Victorian widow. Unlike the party years earlier, when Eleanor had danced with Franklin, this meeting was not an isolated incident. As Eleanor made her debut, she and Franklin ran into each other at various social events, and they were soon anticipating parties and family get-togethers where they could meet. Their courtship had begun.

COURTSHIP, LOVE, AND MARRIAGE
Franklin Delano Roosevelt

The grandson of Isaac Roosevelt, who had settled in the Hudson River valley early in the 1800s, Franklin was Eleanor's fifth cousin. His parents, James and Sara Delano Roosevelt, had an elegant, spacious estate in Hyde Park, overlooking the Hudson River. A well-established member of the Hudson River aristocracy, James had been a lawyer and had invested profitably in coal, railroads, and real estate. He lived the life of a country gentleman, breeding horses and deciding who belonged in society. He was a widower in his early fifties when he met his second wife, the 26-year-old Sara Delano.

The Delanos were a prominent Hudson River family with an American ancestor who had arrived at Plymouth in 1621, a lineage that could be traced back to William the Conqueror, and a fortune acquired by Sara's father, Warren Delano. Although she was one of nine children, Sara eventually inherited over a million dollars, a huge sum at the turn of the century. Heading the Chinese office of a Boston company officially trading tea but also, like many British companies, shipping opium to China, Warren Delano made his fortune in the opium trade. As a child Sara lived in China for three years and found it a great adventure. The family also lived in Europe for a while, and Sara was popular in New York, Boston, and European society. Considered a beauty, she was widely sought after, but she was in no hurry to marry. Supremely self-confident, she did not find her early suitors desirable. She was drawn to James Roosevelt, however. A widower who had also pursued Eleanor's Aunt Bye, James was a lot like Sara's father. She and James had similar views and shared a love of the quiet lifestyle in the Hudson River valley. Although Sara's father raised an eyebrow at their age difference, as did society, he respected James Roosevelt, and James and Sara were married in 1880.

Franklin was a happy, spoiled child. Born at Hyde Park on January 30, 1882, he was James and Sara's only child, as Sara's pregnancy was a difficult one. His half brother, Rosy Roosevelt, was an adult and already married when Franklin was born. Franklin's parents doted on him, giving him whatever he wanted, as did Sara's large, loving family. Sara adored her cute little boy with his curly blond hair. Not wanting him to grow up too fast, she clothed him in dresses—common attire for young boys in the 1880s—until he was five. When she began dressing him in Scottish kilts, his Oyster Bay cousins made fun of them, saying they looked like skirts, and at eight he cajoled his mother into letting him wear sailor suits. He learned as a child to get what he wanted with charm. Although he spent much of his time with his parents, Franklin was schooled with the boys from a neighboring estate, and he also played with Rosy's children and his Delano cousins. His father taught him to swim, ride, sail, and play tennis.

When he was 14, Franklin went to Groton. Although boys generally left for prep school when they were 12, James kept Franklin home for two extra years, just as he had with Rosy. Having begun school two years earlier, the Groton boys had already made friends and formed cliques when Franklin arrived, and he did not make friends at Groton. He "felt hopelessly out of things,"[1] an experience not altogether different from Eleanor's early school years in Paris and New York. He got along well with the school's headmaster, Endicott Peabody, however. Peabody believed the wealthy had a responsibility to help the poor and underprivileged, as did Franklin's parents, and he tried to instill a sense of social responsibility in Groton boys. Peabody had a lasting impact on Franklin's thinking. His influence, however, was significantly different from Mlle. Souvestre's influence on Eleanor. Mlle. Souvestre taught her girls to identify with the underdog, to consider events from the point of view of the disadvantaged. Groton was a school for the elite, and its students viewed the world through the eyes of the elite.

Franklin went to Harvard in 1900. He finished his college courses in three years, and after being elected editor-in-chief of the *Harvard Crimson*, he spent his senior year editing the *Crimson*. His one great disappointment at Harvard was not being chosen to join the prestigious Porcellian Club. Both his father and Teddy Roosevelt had been members of Porcellian, and he was devastated at being rejected. However, he made some good, long-lasting friendships at Harvard, and he began to take an interest in several girls, including Eleanor's cousin Alice, who considered him a mama's boy. The Oyster Bay girls used to laugh at Franklin, claiming FD stood for "feather duster," but other women found him charming and attractive. When he was a freshman, Franklin's father died, and Sara, not wanting to spend winters alone in Hyde Park, rented an apartment in Boston, where she lived during the school year.

Falling in Love

Soon after Eleanor and Franklin met on the train, New York's social season began with a horse show in Madison Square Garden, where Alice Roosevelt, looking glamorous in a white dress and a large feather-plumed hat, drew the attention of society. Her father, Teddy Roosevelt, was now president of the United States, and she was generally known as Princess Alice. Franklin had come down from Boston, and, less conspicuously, he and Eleanor shared Rosy Roosevelt's box at the Garden. During the season, he came to New York for parties, and he was soon meeting Eleanor for lunch or tea. Although Eleanor had other suitors, she apparently never recognized them as such, assuming they saw her only as someone to discuss books with. She could hardly believe the handsome Franklin Roosevelt, who was as tall as she was, could be interested in her.

She was busy with her own social life, her Greenwich Village friends, and her work at the Rivington Street Settlement House. Her Grandmother Hall and Cousin Susie strongly disapproved of Eleanor's settlement house work, fearing she would bring home an "immigrants' disease," but Franklin was impressed by her work on the Lower East Side. She took him to visit the settlement house and introduced him to a side of life he hadn't seen before. "My God," he told her, "I didn't know anyone lived like that."[2] She had initially seen Franklin as a charming, handsome man, much like her father, but she was also seeing his more serious side. She would always believe this first encounter with immigrants on the Lower East Side helped to shape Franklin's later attitudes.

With her Uncle Teddy in the White House, Eleanor also spent time in Washington, where her Aunt Bye rented a house. Bye was an intelligent, politically minded woman, and Eleanor would eventually come to emulate her. Teddy frequently consulted Bye, and her Washington house, where Eleanor stayed, came to be known as the "little White House." Before the era of telephones, society women were expected to call on each other, and Eleanor got her first taste of life in Washington as she joined Bye on her calls, stopping at the homes of all the important women in Washington, leaving Bye's card when they were not at home. Eleanor found Washington a pleasant change from New York, for unlike New York society, which frequently scorned her work at Rivington Street, Washingtonians were more attuned to public service. In December Franklin joined her in Washington for New Year's Eve, and they brought in the year 1903 at an elegant White House party.

During the summer, when society moved to the country and held weekend house parties, Franklin made sure his family's guest lists included Eleanor. She visited Hyde Park, where Sara aroused her basic insecurity by reminiscing about Eleanor as a little girl whose mother called her Granny. Feeling more secure about Franklin's affection, Eleanor confided in him about her own family, telling him about life at Tivoli and her Uncle Val's alcoholism. Gaining confidence that Val would not frighten him away, she invited Franklin to Tivoli, the only man she ever invited to Tivoli. In an age when men rarely courted seriously before their late twenties, Sara was oblivious to the possibility that Franklin might have a serious girlfriend, much less that he might be interested in Eleanor. Franklin kept his thoughts to himself, as he would throughout his life, and he never suggested to his mother that Eleanor was more than a distant cousin, although Eleanor encouraged him to tell her.

In November 1903, the weekend before Thanksgiving, Eleanor went to Cambridge for the Harvard-Yale football game, leaving after the game to visit her brother Hall at Groton. On Sunday, Franklin joined her at Groton and asked her to marry him. Very much in love, she, of course, said yes. "I have never known before what it was to be absolutely happy," she wrote to Franklin,[3] but she was both happy and scared. "I shall never be able to hold him," she told Cousin Susie. "He is so attractive."[4]

Although Franklin did not want to tell Sara, Eleanor thought they should, and over the Thanksgiving holidays, he told his mother they were engaged. Sara was not happy. Some biographers believe she disliked the idea of Eleanor as Franklin's wife, but historian Jan Pottker does not agree. The niece of Sara's closest friend, Eleanor was an intelligent member of an old society family. Her father was Franklin's godfather. She was a fine match for Franklin, but they were too young to get married. That, Pottker claims, was Sara's sole objection. Franklin was only 21 and still a student. Eleanor had just turned 19.

A Secret Engagement, a Stolen Show

Dismayed at their plans, Sara told Eleanor and Franklin to keep their engagement secret for a year, and Franklin agreed, as he knew Sara would have to subsidize them. Attempting to placate his mother, he wrote her, "I know what pain I must have caused you," but "I know my mind, have known it for a long time . . . I am the happiest man just now in the world; likewise the luckiest. . . . Eleanor . . . will always be a daughter to you." Eleanor found Sara's objections hard to handle, as they sparked her basic insecurities. She wrote to Sara, "I know just how you feel and how hard it must be, but I do so want you to learn to love me a little."[5] Eleanor told only her Cousin Susie and Grandmother Hall of her engagement.

At heart, Sara wanted Franklin's happiness. When he returned to college, she wrote, "I am feeling pretty blue. You are gone . . . but I must try to be unselfish & of course dear child I *do* rejoice in your happiness, & shall not put any stones . . . in the way of it."[6] While keeping his engagement a secret, Franklin made weekend trips to New York, staying with an Oyster Bay cousin or Delano relative and spending the day with Eleanor. When Eleanor wanted to attend church with Franklin, the secrecy posed a problem, however, as Sara feared someone would see them and suspect they were courting, leading Eleanor and Franklin to seek out a tiny church in an unfamiliar neighborhood, where no one knew them. Eleanor would frequently suggest to Franklin that they do this or that as his mother wanted.

Sara was quick to modify her initial objections, writing to Franklin, "in the future I shall be glad & shall love Eleanor & adopt her *fully* when the

time comes right."[7] Although Sara made every effort to be kind to Eleanor, calling her "the dear child," Eleanor's self-doubts were returning. She
wrote to Franklin, "I hope . . . she really will love me and I would be very
glad if I thought she was even the least bit reconciled to me now."[8] Eleanor was quick to respond to Sara's overtures of friendship, and they began
to spend time together in New York, meeting for tea, taking walks in the
park, or going shopping and attending the theater. Sara took Eleanor to
meet her large extended family living on the Hudson and in Massachusetts. They "were so kind and warm in their welcome, that I began to feel
that I was part of the clan," Eleanor later wrote.[9]

By the summer Eleanor and Franklin were openly seeing each other,
and in August Eleanor traveled to Campobello Island, off the coast of
northern Maine. Campobello was a lush island of evergreens and rocky
shoreline. Franklin had spent childhood summers on Campobello, where
his parents had a spacious summer cottage, and he loved the island almost
as much as he loved the Hudson. He would sail on the Bay of Fundy,
which separated the island from the Canadian coast, and swim in the icy
ocean water. He and Eleanor spent a couple of weeks exploring the woods,
boating, picnicking, and enjoying the little beach. In the fall, Franklin
moved to Manhattan, where he lived with Sara in a rented house, and
began Columbia Law School.

Eleanor and Franklin announced their engagement in December. Their
wedding was set for March 17, 1905, Saint Patrick's Day, a day chosen
because Uncle Teddy would be in New York for the parade. They were
to be married at Cousin Susie's 76th Street house, where Eleanor had
been living, and Teddy would give the bride away. Uncle Teddy had taken
the country by storm, declaring, when he first became president, that the
twentieth century would be the American century. Inspiring the nation
with the slogan "A Square Deal for Every Man," he had been reelected by
a landside, and Eleanor and Franklin attended the inaugural festivities in
early March. Franklin, like all of the Hyde Park Roosevelts, was a Democrat, but he later said that "in 1904 when I cast my first vote for President,
I voted for the Republican candidate, Theodore Roosevelt, because I felt
he was a better Democrat than the Democratic candidates."[10]

Eleanor and Franklin's wedding attracted a flurry of attention in the
society pages and was anticipated excitedly by the Halls, Roosevelts, and
Delanos. The public, however, anticipated the president's arrival and
crowded the streets on March 17, watching the parade and hoping to
see TR. Both the New York Police Department and the Secret Service
blocked the roads, and not all guests could get to the house in time to see
Eleanor walk down the aisle. Rushing to the wedding between speeches,

Teddy gave Eleanor away with a boisterous "I do." Once the ceremony was over, he went into another room, where refreshments were being served, and entertained the guests, who had followed him, leaving Eleanor and Franklin waiting to greet people in an empty room. They eventually joined Teddy's audience.

MARRIED LIFE

The Early Years

After living in a hotel while Franklin finished the school year, Eleanor and Franklin honeymooned in Europe. They explored out-of-the-way shops, poked around Franklin's favorite bookstores, and visited friends and relatives. Sharing childhood memories, Eleanor talked of being in Venice with her father and traveling to Paris with Mlle. Souvestre. She had one embarrassing moment when visiting friends in Scotland. She was asked the difference between America's federal and state governments, and Franklin had to come to her rescue, as she had not learned that at Allenswood. Eleanor swore to herself she would study U.S. politics and never again be so ignorant.

Differences in their personalities began to emerge as they met an attractive, independent woman, Kitty Gandy, in Italy. In his casual easy way, Franklin learned that Kitty, unlike Eleanor, enjoyed hiking, and he decided to climb a peak with her. Jealous and insecure, Eleanor had a miserable day while Franklin went hiking, although he had no idea he had caused her pain. He could make her happy, however, with a simple gesture. When he saw wildflowers growing in Switzerland, he stopped their carriage and enthusiastically picked a bouquet for her. When they set sail for home, Eleanor was pregnant.

While Eleanor and Franklin were in Europe, Sara rented a townhouse for them on 36th Street, just three blocks from her own house, and she took care of furnishing and decorating it as well as hiring the servants, leaving little for Eleanor to do. Although Franklin had a trust fund from his father and Eleanor had a small trust of her own, the couple was dependent on Sara for luxuries, and Sara was providing for Eleanor and Franklin just as she and James had always provided for Franklin. Having moved as a bride into her husband's home, a home decorated by his late wife, Sara may have assumed she was saving Eleanor the trouble of decorating.

Perhaps Eleanor would have liked to decorate her own house, as some biographers suggest, but she was also insecure about her ability to manage a household. She was, in part, relieved. "I did not have to display the depths of my ignorance as a housewife," she later admitted. Unwittingly, however, Eleanor and Sara were setting the beginnings of a pattern. Unsure of herself, Eleanor hesitated to tell her mother-in-law what she wanted, and in the face of Eleanor's insecurity, Sara, who had always been self-assured, made the decisions Eleanor hesitated to make. Taking the course of least resistance, Eleanor slipped into letting Sara handle everything, becoming, as she later wrote, "an entirely dependent person."[11] Franklin, who was continuing with law school, did not concern himself with the house.

Early in the twentieth century pregnant women did not go out in public, pregnancy being considered a private matter, and soon after her honeymoon Eleanor had to remain at home, missing her cousin Alice's wedding. Eleanor and Franklin's first child and only daughter, Anna, was born on May 3, 1906. Unsure of how to care for a baby, Eleanor was intimidated not only by the baby but also by the baby's nurses, who, sensing her insecurity, told her what to do. Years later she would write, "I know now . . . what we should have done was to have no servants those first few years. . . . Had I done this, . . . my children would have had far happier childhoods."[12] At the time, however, Eleanor would never have considered raising her own children, and she was ill equipped to do so.

She was drawn to and loved Anna, as she did all of her children, but she did not know how to be a relaxed, loving mother. Although she tried to provide Anna with special benefits, her efforts sometimes had odd results. Having read that fresh air was good for babies, she got a boxlike contraption "with wire on the sides and top" and hung it from the window, placing Anna in the box to get some air while she napped. Anna must not have been happy, for she cried with some urgency until a neighbor threatened to alert the Society for the Prevention of Cruelty to Children. At times Eleanor felt overwhelmed, and Sara would take care of the baby. Unlike Eleanor, Sara found it easy to shower love on Anna, and she doted on her granddaughter, just as she had on Franklin.

On December 23, 1907, Eleanor and Franklin's first son, James, was born. Franklin had finished law school that year and begun working for a Wall Street law firm. Hall was living with them when he was not away at school. With the house getting crowded, Sara gave them a new one. Buying two lots on 65th Street, she had twin houses built, one for herself and one for Franklin's family. Although the houses had separate front doors, they had connecting inside doors on the first and fourth floors, making it easy for Sara, Franklin, and Eleanor to go from one house to the other. Similar to the houses that Cousin Susie's family shared with Susie's mother, the arrangement was not unusual for the era. Eleanor said little during construction, leaving all decisions to Franklin and his mother, and she appeared to look forward to the move. Like the rest of the family, she found the 36th Street house crowded.

Once she was in the new house, however, Eleanor was not happy. She had come to resent Sara's role in their lives and disliked the fact that Sara could appear in the doorway at any moment. Sara was genuinely perplexed at Eleanor's unhappiness, as Eleanor did not tell her mother-in-law how she felt. Unwittingly, Sara compounded the situation by showering her love on Anna and James. Watching the children smile up at their grandmother, Eleanor felt Sara was trying to usurp her role as mother. Sensing Eleanor's tenseness, the children were not as relaxed with her as they were with their grandmother. At one point Franklin found Eleanor sitting at her dressing table, sobbing. She told him she "did not like to live in a house which was not in any way [hers], one that . . . did not represent the way [she] wanted to live."[13] A befuddled Franklin told her she would feel better later and left her alone to calm down.

Trying to keep her spirits up, Eleanor attended art and literature classes, took French and Italian lessons, and read extensively. While serving on the boards of several charity organizations, she thought of her days at Rivington House and considered returning to settlement house work. Although Sara believed in helping the poor and was active in several charities in New York and Hyde Park, she balked at that idea, as did Eleanor's Cousin Susie. They were living in an era when children often died in childhood, and both women were afraid Eleanor could bring a deadly virus home from the slums.

Finding her life unfulfilling, Eleanor kept her emotions pent up and let them tear at her insides. Like Griselda, a long-suffering character in Chaucer's *Canterbury Tales*, she developed dark, depressed moods—her Griselda moods. Acting hurt, she would sink into cold, stony silences, a trait she would never completely lose, and when Franklin asked why she was upset, she would not tell him. Perhaps she did not know herself. Franklin could not understand. With a light, casual side that Eleanor did not possess, he did not dwell on matters he considered unpleasant and preferred not to see the growing tension between Eleanor and Sara. Unable to see what was upsetting Eleanor, he avoided her when she was in one of her moods.

Although Franklin wanted his children to experience life on the Hudson River, he did not have the funds to buy his own country estate, and he adopted Sara's home as his country residence, taking his family to Hyde Park on weekends. Sometimes, when he and Eleanor returned to the city, they would leave the children in Sara's care for a week or two. Summers the entire family stayed in Hyde Park before and after their vacation on Campobello Island, and the children came to love Sara's house overlooking the Hudson River. Sara's estate was not home to Eleanor, however, and she was not happy or comfortable in Hyde Park. She did not love the Hudson River sports of tennis, golf, and boating as Franklin did, and she would complain in later years that she never had a comfortable place to sit in Sara's house. Learning to drive the family's exciting new vehicle, an early Ford with a hand-cranked engine, she drove it into a post, an experience that did nothing to endear her to Hyde Park.

Late in 1908, Sara bought a neighbor's cottage on Campobello for Eleanor and Franklin. Staying in that cottage, Eleanor enjoyed the following summer on Campobello. She loved the quiet, secluded island with its foggy days and spectacular sunsets. Although the cottage was only a short walk from Sara's, Eleanor felt removed from Sara. For the first time Eleanor felt free to arrange the furniture as she pleased. She hired her own servants and entertained her own guests. Her brother Hall stayed with her and Franklin on the island, and Eleanor invited a former baby nurse, Miss Spring, to visit. Although Sara may have thought Miss Spring an odd companion, she wouldn't have been bothered by the visit. As Jan Pottker points out, Sara was not the snob some biographers claim she was.

Eleanor and Franklin's third child, a son, was born in March 1909, and he was with them that summer. Named Franklin Jr., he was a sickly baby and died in the fall. Eleanor feared she had done something wrong. Perhaps if she had let a wet nurse breastfeed him, the baby would have been less sickly. Her Griselda moods came back in full force. She was pregnant and depressed for much of 1910. "For ten years," she later wrote, "I was always just getting over having a baby or about to have one."[14] Increasingly, Franklin sought companionship with his male friends, often staying at the Knickerbocker Club until three or four in the morning. Another son, Elliott, was born on September 23, 1910.

Becoming a Political Wife

Unlike the Oyster Bay Roosevelts, the Hyde Park Roosevelts were Democrats, and Franklin, like his father, belonged to the local Dutchess County Democratic Committee. In 1910, when he was becoming bored with law, the committee was looking for a Democratic candidate to run for the state senate and offered Franklin the task. Until then, Franklin had not been especially political, and the county was overwhelmingly Republican. It was assumed he would lose, but the idea appealed to

Franklin, as it did to Eleanor. He agreed to run. Although Sara might not have chosen politics for her son, she expected him to win once he decided to run and told him she would make up any difference in salary. Charming, friendly, and upbeat, Franklin gave speeches, met the people, and rode around the county in a red touring car, traveling on rough dirt roads at the amazing speed of 20 miles an hour. The Democrats swept the state, and at the age of 28 Franklin won the district, the first time a Democrat had won it in 32 years.

The Roosevelts moved to Albany, and Eleanor, leaving her depression behind, began a flurry of activity, setting up their house, hiring servants, arranging furniture, and preparing for a Democratic open house within a couple of days. Sara continued to live in New York. With neither Sara nor Cousin Susie telling her what to do, Eleanor felt free. She took to the role of political wife with enthusiasm. As she had with Aunt Bye in Washington, she made calls, visiting important politicians and political wives, and she held parties and dinners for both politicians and Albany society. She attended state senate sessions, identifying key issues and key politicians as she listened from the gallery. She was popular with the Albany politicians. Even those who disliked her husband liked Eleanor, and she became a bridge between them.

In 1911 Tammany Hall, the frequently corrupt political machine dominating New York Democratic politics, was being challenged. Identifying himself with progressive Democrats, Franklin joined the anti-Tammany insurgents and became their leader, thereby catching the eye of the nation. He invited the group to meet at his home, and Eleanor sat in on the meetings, considering them an opportunity to learn the inner workings of politics. Eleanor had the respect of both the insurgents and Tammany members. Her interest in social causes—decent wages for the poor, better working conditions, improved education—was reawakened, and the Tammany reformers were, in fact, more attuned to these issues than Franklin was. Al Smith, a member of Tammany who sought to reform the machine, liked Eleanor, although he disliked FDR, and Eleanor was able to bring Franklin and Smith together. In time, their political careers would become closely entwined.

Eleanor started to talk with Franklin about her ideas, as she had earlier in their relationship, and their marriage came back to life. Franklin recognized her talents and began seeking her advice, always listening to and considering her opinions. Although Eleanor was interested in social reform, she was not yet a feminist. Women had not yet won the right to vote, and Franklin surprised her by supporting women's suffrage. She was "shocked," having always taken "it for granted that men were superior creatures and . . . knew more about politics than women."[15] Although later in life she would join former suffragettes in other causes, she supported women's suffrage only because her husband did. Considering politics a man's business, she did not see a role for herself as a political player, although she had acquired the knowledge of a political insider. She was content to be a political wife.

Afternoon teatime she devoted to her three children, frequently reading to them as her mother had read to her. Anna, James, and Elliott spent most of their time with nurses, however. Eleanor worried about her brother Hall, who, like their father, had an overfondness for drink. Still preferring serious conversation to lively, lighthearted parties involving drinks, she abhorred alcohol. Franklin, who enjoyed a drink as well as parties, frequently stayed at a party after Eleanor had left. She encouraged him to enjoy himself even if she could not.

In 1912, when Franklin was seeking reelection, he as well as Eleanor came down with typhoid fever. He was in no condition to campaign. A scrawny little newspaper man, whom Eleanor disliked, came to the rescue. Louis Howe, a political reporter covering Albany, saw FDR's potential and allied himself with Franklin's career. At Franklin's request, he took over the campaign. He was an unhealthy, unkempt man, whose ill-fitting suits were always covered with cigarette ashes. Although he would eventually become one of Eleanor's closest allies, she found him repulsive and resented his presence. He was a brilliant political strategist, however, and thanks to his efforts, Franklin was reelected.

When Woodrow Wilson made a bid for the presidential nomination in 1912, Franklin supported him, and Eleanor and Franklin went to the Democratic National Convention in Baltimore. Expecting serious discussions of vital issues, Eleanor was disillusioned by the noise and party-like atmosphere, and she left early to take her children to Campobello. Wilson was nominated, and a wedge began to appear between the two branches of the Roosevelt family. The Republican Party had split, and Eleanor's Uncle Teddy was also running for president on the new Progressive Party ticket. Franklin was to play a prominent role in Wilson's campaign, and Eleanor had to choose sides. Raised in a Republican family, she was loyal to her Uncle Teddy, and had Franklin not gone into politics, she would have supported him. Teddy's Bull Moose platform included many of the reforms she would come to fight for—laws prohibiting child labor and protecting women workers, old age pensions, and unemployment insurance. Ultimately, however, her loyalty belonged to her husband, and she joined Franklin in supporting Wilson. With the split in the Republican

Party, Wilson easily won the election, and in 1913 he appointed FDR assistant secretary of the navy.

Life in Washington, D.C.

When they moved to Washington, Eleanor and Franklin were both in good spirits. Franklin was following in Teddy's footsteps, first as a member of the New York state legislature and now as assistant secretary of the navy. He hoped to follow Teddy's route to the White House. Louis Howe, as Franklin's assistant in the Navy Department, would keep an eye on his political future. Their life in Albany had rejuvenated their marriage, and Eleanor and Franklin had come to understand each other. Aunt Bye, who was now living in Connecticut, sublet her Washington house to them, and although Sara helped them settle in, she then returned to New York. Uncle Teddy, unruffled by their support of Wilson, made sure his friends welcomed them to Washington.

They quickly became friends with foreign dignitaries, officials in Wilson's administration, and influential Washingtonians, and Eleanor's time was taken up with entertaining, planning formal dinners, and considering menus. Adopting the Gibson girl look, an S-shaped profile created with a tightly corseted waist and padded bust and behind, Eleanor was a tall, slender, attractive figure. When she and Franklin were not entertaining, they attended political dinners, society parties, or White House receptions. Eleanor's knowledge of French, German, and Italian frequently gave her an advantage at diplomatic events, as she could easily switch from one language to another. On Sunday evenings she and Franklin dined informally with his political intimates, the men he, and on occasion Eleanor, turned to for help on political issues. Eleanor served them scrambled eggs, which she cooked herself, and cold cuts.

Eleanor spent her afternoons making calls and was quite methodical about them, calling, for instance, on the wives of Supreme Court justices on Mondays and the wives of Congressmen on Tuesdays. Believing her calls were important, she was shocked when her cousin, Alice Longworth, once the president's daughter, stopped making calls, saying they were a boring waste of time. Eleanor took her duties very seriously. Her social schedule quickly became more than Eleanor could keep track of, and in 1914 she hired a social secretary, the lovely Lucy Mercer. Lucy came from an aristocratic family in dire financial straits, and she needed some income. She was pretty, poised, and socially adept, and she was an efficient secretary. Eleanor came to rely on her and felt they were good friends.

Although Anna, James, and Elliott were being raised primarily by governesses, Eleanor believed her first responsibility was to her children. Making sure to give them the proper amount of attention, she ate breakfast with them, read to them, and heard their bedtime prayers. She worried about their education and sent them to the right schools. She could be strict, however, having heard the word *no* a lot as a child, and she could be aloof if they bothered her when she was focusing on her social responsibilities. She had two more babies during these Washington years. Franklin Jr. was born on August 17, 1914, and the youngest, John, was born on March 17, 1916. Eleanor was more relaxed with Franklin Jr. and John than she had been with the older three, but she could not enjoy her children as Franklin did. No one had played with her as a child, and she did not know how to play with her own children. As Anna later said, "She felt a tremendous sense of duty to us . . . but she did not understand or satisfy the need of a child for a primary closeness to a parent."[16]

Franklin, on the other hand, enjoyed his children, telling Eleanor at Hyde Park, "Let the chicks run wild. . . . It won't hurt them."[17] He laughed and roughhoused with them and taught them the sports he had learned as a child. He did not like to say no to them and left that to Eleanor. When Eleanor or Franklin needed help with the children, they turned to Sara, and she became an anchor. Staying in Hyde Park for weeks at a time when their parents' schedules took them elsewhere, all of the children felt Hyde Park was home. Sara comforted them when they were upset and took care of them when they were sick. Generous to a fault, she spoiled them with gifts, and they learned early to turn to Granny when their parents said no. "I was your real mother," Sara would tell them, "Eleanor merely bore you."[18]

Politics, War, and Red Cross Canteens

Early in 1913 political crusaders were marching for reform, and the mood in Washington was one of excitement, for Wilson, like Eleanor's Uncle Teddy, believed in reform. Opposing the power of big business, he supported working people and was committed to improving their lot in life, a goal Eleanor had long been committed to. His mindset, however, was tainted by racism. Wilson was from the South, where segregation was prevalent, and he introduced segregation into governmental offices, even having partitions built to separate black and white employees. Segregation was new in Washington, D.C. In time Eleanor would be among the first white Americans to publicly support African American civil rights, but in 1913 she was not yet attuned to the needs of blacks. She, like FDR, embraced Wilson's support of struggling, working-class, white Americans.

Soon, however, the reform movement dwindled, as Washington and the nation watched events unfold in Europe.

With European nations building up their militaries and making alliances, Europe was a tinderbox waiting for a spark to ignite war. The spark came in 1914, when Archduke Franz Ferdinand of Austro-Hungary was assassinated, and World War I broke out. Hoping to keep the United States out of the war, Wilson and his administration called for neutrality. FDR's immediate impulse was to build up the navy, to prepare for the possibility of war. Josephus Daniels, secretary of the navy and Franklin's superior, supported Wilson's stance. He did not agree with FDR until 1916. Teddy Roosevelt, unlike Wilson, wanted to rush into the fray, to build up the military and get into the war. He got a cold reception from Wilson. Political crusaders began to march for peace. Although Eleanor did not join the crusaders, she sympathized with Wilson's peace efforts. Like Wilson, she prayed for peace, but she supported Franklin's crusade to build up the navy. In April 1917, after Germany sank American ships, Wilson told Congress, "The world must be made safe for democracy," and the United States declared war on Germany.

Societal standards changed as the world began to crumble. Once war was declared, the nation was swept up in a spirit of patriotism. Young and not-so-young men joined the military, as did Eleanor's brother. Grandmother Hall wondered why he did not "buy a substitute," as gentlemen had during the Civil War. Horrified at the idea, Eleanor told her that "a gentleman was no different from any other . . . citizen. . . . It would be a disgrace to pay anyone to risk his life . . . Hall could leave his wife and children with . . . enough money to live on." It was, she later wrote, her "first really outspoken declaration" against her family's standards.[19]

Anticipating shortages, Wilson asked the nation to conserve food, and Eleanor took an unfortunate stab at conservation. Giving her servants austerity guidelines—serve meat only once a day, cut the number of dinner courses down to three—she, rather naively, told a *New York Times* reporter of her austerity program, and the *Times* ran an article making her a laughingstock. Treating it as a joke, Franklin wrote the paper, "I am proud to be the husband of the Originator, Discoverer, and Inventor of the New Household Economy for Millionaires!" but Eleanor was mortified. "I will never be caught again that's sure," she vowed. She learned not to discuss household affairs with the press.[20]

Although Eleanor continued to entertain European delegations arriving in Washington, she stopped making calls on Washington notables and, like millions of other women, became a Red Cross volunteer. Throughout the nation, soldiers by the hundreds were passing through train stations, stopping at Red Cross canteens for food, coffee, newspapers, or postcards. Working at the canteen in Washington's Union Station, Eleanor did whatever needed to be done—mopped the floor, filled baskets with sandwiches, made coffee, served bowls of soup from steaming pots, and said a few kind words to energized, frightened soldiers. She sold cigarettes and chewing tobacco at cost.

Eventually she helped to organize the canteen and streamline its accounting system, bringing out her latent administrative ability. Extending her efforts beyond the canteen, she spoke, somewhat nervously, at Red Cross rallies and, approaching other organizations, raised money to help the wounded. Learning to drive, she delivered supplies for the Red Cross. As women began knitting sweaters and socks for soldiers, Eleanor joined the Navy League's Comfort Committee and was put in charge of coordinating volunteers. She gave them wool and knitting instructions and then collected and distributed the finished clothing. She also started to knit herself, and for the rest of her life, she would be seen knitting as she traveled, attended meetings, or took up a new venture.

Eleanor also visited naval hospitals, bringing the wounded men newspapers and flowers. She saw shell-shocked patients suffering, in today's terminology, from post-traumatic stress disorder and was touched particularly by a young blond boy. Staring with vacant eyes, he was meaninglessly repeating orders he had heard as planes bombed Dunkirk. The hospital, St. Elizabeth's, was a federal hospital under the Department of the Interior, and it was understaffed. The patients got little attention. Eleanor knew the secretary of the interior, Franklin Lane, from her Sunday evening suppers, when she scrambled eggs for Franklin's inner circle, and she went to him about the hospital, telling him of the overcrowding, the lack of staff, and the neglected patients. Appointing a committee to investigate, Lane found her report accurate and located the funds necessary to make St. Elizabeth's a model hospital. In her first experience using political connections, Eleanor was a success. Through her war work, she came to know the satisfaction of a job well done and to recognize her own abilities.

Her Worst Fear

During the war Eleanor worked long hours at the canteen, leaving at 5 in the morning and frequently staying until 9 or 10 at night. Her children were often in Hyde Park with Sara. Franklin's position as assistant secretary of the navy kept him at the Navy Department. They saw little of each other. Even as early as 1916, they began seeing less of each other. Eleanor still took the children to Campobello, staying until the end of September in 1916 because of a polio scare along the East Coast. Franklin remained in Washington, leaving only for Navy Department business. Resuming friendships with his party-loving friends from Harvard, Franklin spent increasing amounts of time with them, while Eleanor became less and less interested in parties. She did not want to waste her time with frivolity, while Franklin needed time to relax. Increasingly he went to parties without her. When Eleanor was too busy to entertain, her secretary, Lucy Mercer, would fill in as hostess.

In July 1918, Franklin went to Europe, where he inspected the American fleet. That year America experienced the worst flu epidemic in its history. Millions died. Many of the soldiers on Franklin's ship were buried at sea. In September, when Eleanor was at Hyde Park with Sara and the children, the Navy Department notified her that Franklin's ship was due in New York and he had pneumonia and influenza. She met the ship with an ambulance and a doctor. She took his suitcase home and unpacked it, finding a bundle of letters. The handwriting was familiar, and she opened the letters. They were not, as she hoped, business letters. They were love letters. Her worst fear—"I shall never be able to hold him"—had been realized. Franklin was having an affair with Lucy Mercer.

Most of Washington—Eleanor's friends, her family—already knew. Franklin had been seeing Lucy for some time, and he had made no effort to hide his affection for her. The couple ate at popular restaurants, and they could be seen driving in Franklin's car. They went to Alice Longworth's parties together and frequently had dinner at her home. Actively encouraging the romance, Alice would quip that Franklin "deserved a good time. He was married to Eleanor."[21] Eleanor's immediate reaction was to offer Franklin a divorce, a scandalous idea in 1918. Divorce would have put an immediate end to Franklin's political career. Louis Howe made sure he realized that. Sara was disappointed in her son and sympathized with Eleanor, but she discouraged divorce, telling Franklin she would cut him off financially if he left Eleanor. Eleanor agreed to stay with Franklin on one condition—that he would never see Lucy again. Franklin agreed, and for many years he kept that promise.

Outwardly Eleanor and Franklin tried to repair their damaged marriage. Franklin gave up his Sunday morning golf games and went to church with Eleanor, something she had wanted him to do for years, and she became more willing to go to parties. They were attentive to each other, and Franklin would not allow anyone to criticize Eleanor. There was tension, however. The nature of their marriage had changed forever. With time they would form a strong partnership, but they would never resume a traditional marriage. Years later, Eleanor would say, "I can forgive, but I cannot forget."[22]

In January 1919 they went to Europe. The war had ended in November, and Franklin was to oversee the demobilization of naval facilities. Eleanor had not been in Europe since their honeymoon 14 years earlier. Although not exactly a second honeymoon, the trip did help. It also further sensitized Eleanor to the horrors of war. Visiting the front with Franklin, she saw the trenches and barbed wire fences, heard stories of the fighting, and was moved particularly by the many young widows dressed in black. She visited hospitals and saw the war-wounded with Mrs. Woodrow Wilson, whose husband was at the Paris Peace Conference. Eleanor and Franklin returned home on the same ship as the Wilsons. Although Eleanor considered Wilson a poor politician, she supported his ill-fated vision for a League of Nations.

Her Life Revisited

Back in Washington, Eleanor began a year of introspection, a reconsideration of her life. For 14 years she had devoted herself to her husband, to his career, and to her family. She had been the perfect Washington wife, and her world had collapsed. Her self-esteem, always fragile, was gone. She entered another period of depression, the worst she would ever experience. With her stomach in knots, she had trouble eating and couldn't keep her food down. One historian, Blanche Wiesen Cook, believes she became anorexic, for she had the classic symptoms. She began to look emaciated, and as she lost weight, her teeth loosened and became more pronounced.

At the age of 35, Eleanor still had five children at home. Anna was 13, John only 3. Like her mother, Eleanor became self-absorbed. Much as she wanted to give her children attention, they experienced the same aloofness Eleanor had felt, and resented, in her own mother. Seeking peace in solitude, Eleanor started taking walks in Rock Creek Cemetery, where she was drawn to the statue of a solemn, solitary figure. Seated, robed, and pensive, the figure had eyes that Eleanor found haunting. She would sit for hours in front of the statue, finding it strangely soothing. She called the statue "Grief."

Eleanor's Uncle Teddy had died while she and Franklin were in Europe. Eleanor mourned for the country as much as she did for herself. In August her Grandmother Hall died, and Eleanor began to think about her grandmother's life, a life sacrificed to the needs of her family. She was not convinced her grandmother's sacrifice had, in fact, helped her alcoholic uncles. Eleanor considered Sara's and Cousin Susie's lives. Neither Sara nor Susie had a life outside of their family. Eleanor's thoughts turned also to her

Aunt Bye and to Mlle. Souvestre. Both were strong independent women whose lives had been <u>stimulated by their beliefs</u>, their interests, their passions. They were women who had lived their own lives. Eleanor came to believe she, too, had to live her own life. Continuing her work with the Red Cross and at St. Elizabeth's Hospital, she began to regain her sense of self-worth. For the rest of her life, Eleanor would find salvation from unhappiness in work. Slowly Eleanor emerged from her depression a changed woman, a woman who would not only serve as Franklin's partner but would also pursue her own interests, her own goals, and her own ideals.

The Beginnings of a New Life

With the end of World War I, the world changed dramatically. Abroad, Germany was stripped of its strength, and Russia was in the midst of a revolution. At home, Woodrow Wilson, still envisioning a world of peace, suffered a severe stroke. His fight for U.S. support of a League of Nations was defeated by an unsympathetic Congress. The prewar spirit of reform had disappeared. Although American women won the right to vote, laborers resuming their fight for decent working conditions met with resistance. As they joined unions and went on strike, the U.S. attorney general, A. Mitchell Palmer, afraid of events in Russia, initiated surveillance of activists, protestors, and labor organizers, anyone who by virtue of their views could be considered a "Red." Undaunted, activist women took up the cause of working women. Eleanor met these activists in 1919, when she attended an International Congress of Working Women, and she was inspired by their ideas and their dedication. Although she didn't act immediately, her interest in the labor movement was sparked.

In an odd move for a member of the New York aristocracy, Eleanor suddenly replaced all but two of her white servants with African Americans, a move that would have been less startling in the Deep South, where the wealthy often hired black servants. Perhaps she was challenging aristocratic views or even the bigotry of the Wilson administration, but she may simply have wanted new servants. Some writers speculate that she was defying Sara, but Sara was more attuned to the needs of African Americans than Eleanor was. Sara's charity work included a campaign for African American education, and she had met with black activist and educator Booker T. Washington. Although Eleanor liked her new servants, finding them easier to work with than her white servants, she was not yet an advocate of African American rights. While she was in Hyde Park that summer, the bigotry simmering in Washington erupted into violence, creating a race riot. Blacks rioted in the streets, and whites lynched blacks. Although Eleanor would eventually fight to outlaw lynching, that summer she was primarily worried about Franklin's safety.

In 1920 Franklin caught the attention of the Democratic Party. Wilson's campaign for a League of Nations had split the party into factions, and the Democratic National Convention was deadlocked. Franklin gave a speech seconding Al Smith's nomination for president, and the party nominated Franklin for vice president after choosing a compromise candidate, James Cox, for president. Franklin was happy to run, as the campaign would improve his prospects for 1924, although the nation was more attuned to the conservative politics of Republican candidates Warren Harding and Calvin Coolidge.

Although Eleanor had never participated in Franklin's campaigns, Louis Howe thought she should join this one, as her presence could help to win the new female vote. She joined Franklin's campaign train, traveling across country, waving at the public, and sitting happily at his side as he gave his speeches. She felt superfluous, however. As the only woman on the train, she had no one to talk to. She was uncomfortable with reporters, and she resented and disliked Louis Howe. Louis, however, liked Eleanor. He saw her potential and sensed her unhappiness. Despite her rebuffs, he set out to befriend her. Respecting her judgment, he began to discuss drafts of speeches and campaign issues with her. As they traveled, he told her about local politics, and she came to recognize the breadth of his knowledge and to see that he had a sharp mind. He encouraged her to be friendly to reporters, and she came to truly enjoy their company. By the end of the trip, Eleanor and Louis had become good friends. As their friendship grew, she came to realize she should not judge people by their surface. Louis Howe would always be Eleanor's strongest ally.

Warren Harding won the election, and Eleanor and Franklin returned to New York, where he returned to practicing law. Since their house was rented out, they moved in with Sara, and Eleanor and Sara began to clash. They sparred over dinner menus and the gifts Sara gave to her grandchildren. Although Eleanor frequently complained about her mother-in-law, Sara's letters consistently refer to Eleanor as "sweet" and "dear," and she appears to have been genuinely fond of Eleanor. Although Sara suggested that she join the board of various charities, Eleanor decided, instead, to join the newly formed League of Women Voters, and she was soon active in the League.

As women began to vote for the first time, leaders of the suffrage movement established the League of Women Voters to help first-time voters educate themselves. The League's leaders also turned to new reforms. Committed to the welfare of working women and children, they sought an eight-hour workday, equal pay for women workers, minimum wage laws, legislation preventing child labor, unemployment insurance, old-age pensions, and a national health program. Also committed to the League of Nations, they sought U.S. membership in a world court for settling international disputes. These were all causes Eleanor embraced, and she, along with the women who were to become her close friends, would fight for them for decades to come. In the 1920s, however, these ideas were controversial. A. Mitchell Palmer as well as members of the Harding administration thought the League of Women Voters might be a Bolshevik organization. At the very least, they believed, the League sought to destroy the American family.

Working with Elizabeth Read, an attorney and scholar, Eleanor became codirector of a committee charged with alerting the League to any national legislation affecting its agenda. Elizabeth, using her legal expertise, skimmed the *Congressional Record* for pertinent bills, and Eleanor, after discussing the bills with Elizabeth, wrote a monthly report, making recommendations for League members. Franklin found her activities amusing and sometimes joked about his political wife, but he also encouraged her. He, in fact, helped her to become a better politician, teaching her the tricks that worked for him. Both he and Louis Howe shared their professional experience with Eleanor and Elizabeth, meeting with them occasionally to work out League strategies. Louis would help Eleanor with publicity. In return, Eleanor stopped short of making public statements that would hurt Franklin's career.

Elizabeth Read shared an apartment in Greenwich Village with her friend and life partner, Esther Lape. Elizabeth and Esther were part of a group of women devoted to the reform movement, women who were very different from the New York socialites Eleanor had always known. Eleanor became good friends with the two women, often spending evenings at their apartment instead of going uptown to Sara's house. She would soon become an integral part of their circle of feminist reformers. She found their conversation stimulating, their ideas exciting, and she began to regain the sense of purpose she had felt at Allenswood.

Her Family in Crisis

In June 1921 Eleanor went to Campobello with Anna and the boys. Franklin had to spend some time in Washington but was to join them in August. Eager to get back into politics, he wanted to map out a strategy for seeking the governorship of New York, and Louis Howe, along with his wife and son, was also to join them on Campobello. Sara spent the summer in Europe. Anna was 15, and Eleanor, not realizing Anna was unhappy, found her difficult. After living in Washington, Anna felt like an outsider in New York. She did poorly in school and found her mother unapproachable. The boys looked forward to Franklin's arrival, for he spent much of his time at Campobello swimming, sailing, and playing ball games with them.

That year Franklin felt sluggish when he arrived, but he entertained the boys with his usual enthusiasm. On August 10, after sailing on the Bay of Fundy, they went swimming in an inland lake, and Franklin jogged two miles back to their cottage. There he went for another quick dip in the cold bay water. He was exhausted when he got home. Feeling chilled, he went to bed without supper, and he did not feel better in the morning. His legs began to hurt, and soon he could not move them. His temperature shot up. Their local doctor thought he had a cold. Another claimed it was a blood clot. For two weeks, as Franklin deteriorated, they did not know the cause. He became delirious and lost the use of his arms. Eleanor nursed him, sleeping on a couch in his room, getting Louis's help in lifting her paralyzed husband. Finally, a specialist made the diagnosis. Franklin had polio, a deadly viral disease that often swept the East Coast during summer months, killing many, leaving others severely paralyzed. Doctors could not predict Franklin's fate.

Both Franklin and Eleanor tried to be optimistic. They did not want the public to know, however, and Franklin was moved secretly to New York in a private railroad car. Louis kept the press in the dark. Entering New York Presbyterian Hospital, Franklin had weeks of tortuous physical therapy, and he regained the use of his arms. His legs remained paralyzed, however. By December there was little the doctors could do, and Franklin left the hospital. He and Eleanor returned to their twin house next to Sara's. Louis Howe moved in also, living with them during the week and traveling to Poughkeepsie to see his family on weekends. He kept Franklin informed of Democratic politics and attended to Franklin's business affairs. Eleanor devoted all her energy to Franklin. Sleeping on a nearby cot, she nursed and encouraged him. She applauded his every effort to move a limb.

Sara did not learn of Franklin's condition until she returned from Europe. She wanted him to recuperate in Hyde Park. Although she has been portrayed as wanting Franklin to quit politics and become a gentleman of leisure living in Hyde Park, Jan Pottker believes Sara was thinking only of the present. She was unhappy with Louis Howe's presence and wanted Franklin in the country, where she could take care of him. As Eleanor and

Louis kept Franklin in the city, the atmosphere became tense. Frequently in conflict, Eleanor and Sara expressed their feelings in lowered tones, trying to keep Franklin out of the fray.

Although Eleanor focused her attention on Franklin, she tried also to deal with the children. The boys, in a sense, had lost the parent they had fun with. Eleanor tried to fill the void. She made an effort to play with them and took swimming lessons, hoping to swim with the boys despite her fear of the water. As an adult John would claim that he had no parents after his father got sick, that only his grandmother gave him attention. At the time, however, the boys appeared to adjust more quickly than Anna. Anna was unhappy with the entire situation. She felt her mother ignored her and cared more for Louis Howe. She did not see why Louis should have the large bedroom she felt was rightfully hers, and Sara did not disagree with her.

Finding it "the most trying winter of my entire life,"[23] Eleanor tried to keep her emotions under control, having been taught never to cry in front of others. In April, however, she suddenly lost control. Bursting into tears as she read to John and Franklin Jr., she sobbed uncontrollably for hours. Louis tried to console her and could not. The boys were bewildered. Elliott came into the room and fled immediately. It was the only time she ever truly broke down. The meltdown provided a badly needed emotional release. It also awakened Anna to her mother's pain, and finally she and Eleanor began to talk. With time, they would become friends as well as mother and daughter.

Eleanor believed Franklin would only get better if he kept up his interest in politics. She, Franklin, and Louis Howe talked about Franklin's future. The bond between Eleanor and Franklin was as strong as it had ever been. The ordeal had strengthened their partnership. They agreed that Franklin's political career should be kept alive. He still had his eyes on the White House. First, however, he had to get well. He was on a strict exercise regime. If that failed, he would seek the benefits of a warmer climate. Someone had to keep the Roosevelt name in the public eye. The task, with Louis's help, fell to Eleanor.

NOTES

1. Quoted in Jan Pottker, *Sara and Eleanor: The Story of Sara Delano Roosevelt and Her Daughter-in-Law, Eleanor Roosevelt* (New York: St. Martin's Griffin, 2004), p. 83.

2. Quoted in Maurine H. Beasley, Holly C. Shulman, and Henry R. Beasley, eds., *Eleanor Roosevelt Encyclopedia*, (Westport, CT: Greenwood Press, 2001), p. 452.

3. Quoted in Lash, *Eleanor and Franklin*, p. 160.

4. Quoted in Beasley, Shulman, and Beasley, *Eleanor Roosevelt Encyclopedia*, p. 453.
5. Quoted in Pottker, *Sara and Eleanor*, p. 103.
6. Quoted in Lash, *Eleanor and Franklin*, p. 193.
7. Quoted in Pottker, *Sara and Eleanor*, p. 106.
8. Quoted in Lash, *Eleanor and Franklin*, p. 193.
9. Roosevelt, *This Is My Story*, p. 117.
10. Quoted in Lash, Eleanor and Franklin, p. 202.
11. Roosevelt, *This Is My Story*, p. 138.
12. Ibid., p. 145.
13. Ibid., p. 162.
14. Ibid., p. 163.
15. Ibid., pp. 180–81.
16. Quoted in Lash, *Eleanor and Franklin*, p. 274.
17. Ibid., p. 273.
18. Quoted in Cook, *Eleanor Roosevelt*, vol. I, p. 179.
19. Roosevelt, *This Is My Story*, pp. 251–252.
20. Quoted in Lash, *Eleanor and Franklin*, p. 290.
21. Quoted in ibid., p. 309.
22. Quoted in ibid., p. 311.
23. Roosevelt, *Autobiography*, p. 117.

Chapter 3

A NEW ELEANOR ROOSEVELT

In Albany, just 10 years earlier, Eleanor had assumed "men were superior creatures . . . and knew more about politics than women." She had entertained society and politicians, but her role was limited to political wife, society matron, and mother. Although she had sympathy for the poor, she still lived in an isolated upper-class world. While popular in Albany, she had few close friends, the kind of friends she could confide in and share her passions with. By 1922, however, she had begun to form a new life, and it was now about to open up dramatically. Her personal circumstances, her new self-awareness, and her growing self-confidence would propel Eleanor Roosevelt into a world of new activities, new careers, and new friends.

ELEANOR AS ACTIVIST, REFORMER, AND POLITICIAN
Reform and Real Women Workers

As a member of the League of Women Voters, Eleanor supported working women, but she did not actually know or work with any. In 1922, however, when she joined the Women's Trade Union League (WTUL), she met real women workers—women who worked 10 hours a day for three dollars a week and dared not complain, women whose work put them in danger of physical injury with no hope of compensation. The WTUL brought reform-minded upper-class women and working women together, and Eleanor immediately befriended the women workers, particularly Rose Schneiderman, the president of the League's New York chapter. An uneducated Polish immigrant, Rose was an outspoken, red-headed cap maker and a leader in the movement to get women into unions. Undaunted by Eleanor's elite upbringing, Rose educated Eleanor, and later Franklin, about the plight of women workers, giving Eleanor an idea of their dangerous working conditions, of how little three dollars would actually buy, of what a living wage really was. Eventually Rose would serve on an advisory board for FDR's administration.

Inviting Rose for supper at the 65th Street house early in their friendship, Eleanor would eventually invite Rose and her WTUL friends, impoverished women struggling to put food on the table, to both Hyde Park, where Sara acted as hostess, and Campobello. In 1925 Eleanor persuaded Franklin Jr. and John to give a Christmas party for their children. With the two boys acting as Santa's deputies, giving out dolls, roller skates, and clothing purchased by Eleanor and her affluent reformer friends, the party was a great success. Franklin Jr. and John not only met children from the slums but also learned that Christmas parties could be for giving as well as getting presents. The party became an annual event, which Eleanor hosted every year until the 1940s.

Initially formed earlier in the century as part of the trade union movement, the Women's Trade Union League (WTUL) included militant woman who had joined unions and banded together to fight for some basic rights. In 1922, when Eleanor joined the WTUL, the women sought both to strengthen unions and to get some laws on the books that would protect women workers—laws that would guarantee a minimum wage, limit their work week to 48 hours per week, require safe working conditions, provide compensation for work-related injuries, and prohibit child labor. Eleanor embraced these goals. Becoming an active fundraiser, she would raise substantial sums for the WTUL, even donating her own earnings as she began to earn money on her own. Joining a protest march in 1926, she marched with women who made cardboard boxes when they went on strike. The League also provided educational programs for women workers, and Eleanor contributed to those programs, spending time each week introducing the women to American literature.

Eleanor quickly became a recognized leader in the reform movement. Already prominent in the League of Women Voters, she joined the Women's City Club, another organization formed to educate women voters, in 1922, and in 1924 she became a member of the Club's board. She would continue to take an active part in all three reform organizations throughout the 1920s, but Louis Howe wanted her to do more.

Democratic Politics and Democratic Women

Although not objecting to Eleanor's reform activities, Louis wanted her to play a role in the Democratic Party, the kind of role Franklin would have played if he had not become sick. Eleanor was interested in politics, but she was reluctant to enter the political fray. Still harboring some inherent insecurity, she may have had lingering feelings that politics was a man's world, but a few women were entering politics. One of them, Nancy Cook, asked Eleanor to speak at a Democratic fundraiser, and with Louis's encouragement, she accepted the invitation.

She was a nervous wreck, however. The thought of speaking at an official Democratic function terrified her, even though she had spoken at smaller gatherings for the Red Cross and the WTUL. In a huge-looking hall, she spoke at a ladies luncheon. Her knees felt weak. Her voice became high-pitched, and she giggled nervously. Her audience was receptive, however, and the luncheon raised the desired funds. At the back of the hall, Louis Howe slipped into the audience, as he would for many of Eleanor's speeches, and he was not impressed with her delivery. Becoming her speaking coach, he began to give her tips on how to control her voice and look composed. He said her laughter was "inane" and she should "have something . . . to say, say it, and sit down."[1] With Louis's coaching, Eleanor eventually became a comfortable, adept public speaker. Her sincerity, her dedication to reform, and the Roosevelt name all made her an ideal speaker, and before too long she was in great demand.

After this initial foray into politics, Eleanor quickly became active in Dutchess County and New York state politics. Helping Dutchess County Democrats with the 1922 gubernatorial election, she spoke at rallies to get out the women's vote, and, supporting Franklin's choice for governor, she campaigned for Al Smith. She drove local Democrats in need of a ride to the polls, learning, to her horror, that in Dutchess County votes could be bought, and she cemented relationships with Democratic notables, becoming friends with her Hudson River neighbors Elinor and Henry Morgenthau Jr. She kept the Roosevelt name in the public eye and held Franklin's place as a force in the local Democratic Party. He remained focused on his exercises, determined to regain the use of his legs.

Joining the Women's Division of the New York State Democratic Committee, Eleanor became part of a closely knit group of reform-minded women who ran the Women's Division—Nancy Cook, Marion Dickerman, Caroline

O'Day, and Elinor Morgenthau. Increasingly impatient with women who had no political interests, who laughed at their own ignorance, Eleanor was immediately drawn to these women, particularly Nancy Cook and Marion Dickerman, who would become her close friends. A couple since their university days, Nancy and Marion were trained as schoolteachers, although Nancy had left teaching to work full-time for the Democratic Party. Marion taught at a private school in Manhattan. In 1919 she had run for public office in upstate New York with Nancy as her campaign manager. Both women were active in the reform movement as well as politics. While supporting reforms sought by the WTUL, they were also concerned with the need for better sanitation and sewage removal, public parks and playgrounds, school lunch programs, public transportation, and public housing.

Devoting her abundant energy to the Women's Division, Eleanor became a member of its board and was named chair of its finance committee. Working for Caroline O'Day, who headed the Women's Division, Eleanor helped organize the state's Democratic women, setting up local centers where rural women could attend meetings, hold programs, and get information. Continuing to speak throughout the state, Eleanor raised funds and participated in local events. With Marion Dickerman, she began publishing a short, mimeographed newspaper, which eventually grew into the widely circulated *Women's Democratic News*.

Although both Franklin and Louis gave their help and guidance to the Women's Division, Eleanor was forming a role for herself as more than Franklin's stand-in. As she came to realize how closely the principles of the Democratic Party matched her own ideals, how staunchly the Democrats supported the working class rather than big business, she began to bring her own reform agenda to her political activities and to promote that agenda as well as Franklin's political career.

She learned quickly, however, that her agenda could bring a personal backlash. Believing strongly in the peace movement, she agreed in 1923 to serve on an organizing committee for the Bok Peace Prize, a prize of $50,000 for a plan in which the United States could help preserve world peace. Offered by the former publisher of the *Ladies' Home Journal*, Edward Bok, the prize attracted some 22,000 entries, including one from FDR. The winning plan, submitted by a scholar, recommended that the United States participate in a world court and cooperate with the League of Nations. Neither idea was popular. The nation wanted, instead, to isolate itself. The very idea of women organizing such a contest was considered scandalous. Conservatives in Congress thought it was an international plot to influence American foreign policy, and a Senate committee investigated the prize. As the press attacked Eleanor and her colleagues, she

attended a congressional committee on "un-American" activities for the
first time. '

The 1924 Election

Undaunted, Eleanor became thoroughly embroiled in the 1924 election, experiencing both victory and decisive defeat. Attending the New
York state convention prior to the national convention, she found women
cast in a secondary role and became outraged. Although she and Caroline O'Day had organized women throughout the state, the Women's
Division would not be allowed to send their own representatives to the
Democratic National Convention, as Tammany Hall planned to choose
delegates for them. Although Eleanor protested, the Tammany boss was
adamant, but she refused to give up. In a speech that made the front page
of the *New York Times*, she spurred the women on, challenging them to
work *with* the men, not *for* them. Leading a group of women to meet
with Governor Al Smith, also a Tammany politician, she won Smith's
support, and the Tammany boss capitulated. Eleanor became a delegate
to the national convention. With both Eleanor's and Franklin's support,
Smith was seeking the Democratic nomination for president, and Eleanor
was particularly impressed by his efforts to improve working conditions in
New York's sweatshops. She proposed that the New York delegates pledge
themselves to Smith for president, and they agreed. The *Times* applauded
Mrs. Roosevelt's success as a politician.

As a delegate to the national convention, Eleanor chaired a committee
of women who suggested their ideas to the party's official platform committee. They wanted the party to endorse such items as the League of Nations,
enforcement of Prohibition, equal pay for women workers, the creation of
a department of education, a constitutional amendment prohibiting child
labor, a 48-hour work week, a living wage for all workers, and safe working conditions. The Democratic men, however, were not about to accept
suggestions from these female upstarts. The official platform committee,
composed entirely of men, did not, as far as Eleanor could tell, even consider their recommendations. She wrote later that she saw "for the first time
where women stood when it came to a national convention. . . . They stood
outside the door of all important meetings and waited."[2]

Returning briefly to the political arena, Franklin made the nominating speech for Al Smith, eliciting considerable excitement as he stood
propped up by his eldest son, James. Neither Smith nor his opponent,
William McAdoo, won the presidential nomination, however. The party
settled instead for a Wall Street lawyer, John Davis. Seeing the election

as ill fated, Franklin retreated once again and resumed his physical ther-apy. Al Smith ran for another term as governor of New York, opposing Eleanor's cousin, Theodore Roosevelt Jr. Eleanor turned her energies to Smith's gubernatorial campaign. She felt none of the guilt she had in 1912, when she supported Woodrow Wilson over her Uncle Teddy for president. Theodore Jr. had engendered Eleanor's anger four years earlier, when, in a political speech, he had said Franklin "is a maverick. He does not have the brand of our family."[3]

Theodore Jr. had been a member of Harding's administration, a scandal-ridden administration tainted in particular by the Teapot Dome scandal. In return for interest-free loans, Harding's secretary of the interior had leased out oil fields in Teapot Dome, Wyoming, without obtaining competitive bids and had been indicted for taking bribes. Eleanor took full advantage of emotions elicited by the scandal. Egged on by Louis Howe, she rode around the state in an outrageous automobile spouting steam from a gigantic tea-pot on its roof. Although the Republican presidential candidate, Calvin Coolidge, won the national election by a landslide, Smith was reelected governor of New York. Some of the planks Eleanor supported, including the prevention of child labor and minimum wage legislation, were included in the Democratic platform for New York State.

Louis Howe applauded Eleanor's activities. A prominent figure through-out the election, she had kept the Roosevelt name in the public eye, and despite her setback at the national convention, she had proven herself to be a political force in her own right.

NEW HOMES, NEW CAREERS, SEPARATE LIVES
FDR, Florida, and Warm Springs

As Eleanor began to establish a political role for herself, Franklin spent winters living on a houseboat off the coast of Florida, seeking a cure in the warm southern water. Full of hope that with discipline he could regain use of his legs, he swam, did his exercises, took fishing trips, and relaxed. Elea-nor visited him occasionally, but she hated Florida. Never fond of boating, she disliked both the houseboat and the climate. She and Franklin were beginning a pattern of separate but complementary lives. Franklin had his own group of friends who met his need for relaxation and light con-versation. Eleanor was making new friends who would meet her need for approval, purpose, and affection. While remaining committed political allies, Eleanor and Franklin would live separate personal and social lives for the rest of their marriage.

In 1924 Franklin visited an old, rundown health resort in Warm Springs, Georgia, known for its pool of warm spring water once thought to have medicinal value. Finding the warm bubbly water buoyant, Franklin could swim and exercise with ease, and he loved the place immediately, despite its dilapidated appearance. Visiting frequently over the next few years, Franklin bought the resort in 1926, despite Eleanor's objections and advice from business associates not to risk his money. He built a separate cottage to live in and turned the resort into a therapeutic facility for polio victims, putting considerable money into upgrading the neglected buildings. Franklin loved Warm Springs for the rest of his life, making it his retreat and "little White House" when he was president.

Eleanor disliked Warm Springs even more than she disliked Florida. The red Georgia dirt and ramshackle buildings repelled her. The hot, humid climate oppressed her, and the entire area—its poverty, illegal liquor, and segregated racial environment—depressed her. Although she had heard stories of Georgia "darkies" from her grandmother, Mittie Bulloch Roosevelt, the reality of segregation hit Eleanor full force in Warm Springs. No longer hesitant to say what she thought, Eleanor antagonized white residents with her frank opinions, and she was not popular in Warm Springs. She spent as little time there as she could.

In both Florida and Georgia, Franklin's personal needs were well attended to by his private secretary, Missy Le Hand. Franklin had hired Missy in 1920 after she worked on his vice presidential campaign, and she would remain his secretary until 1941. Supervising Franklin's household, paying his bills, and acting as his hostess, Missy was Franklin's friend and companion as well as his secretary. Superficially, at least, Eleanor treated Missy as a friend, never letting on if she was ever jealous. Eleanor had come to recognize Franklin's need for a kind of companionship she could not provide. Missy was content to play cards with Franklin and admire his stamp collection. Her presence seemed to bother Sara more than Eleanor.

The Family in the 1920s

Spending his winters in Florida and Georgia, Franklin was absent from the children's lives as well as from Eleanor's, and she tried, as best she could, to fill Franklin's role with the children. Although they often spent weekends with Sara, Eleanor attempted to play with the boys. James and Elliott both left for Groton when they were 12. Eleanor would have liked them to stay home longer, but Franklin did not want them to have the same lonely experience he had had going to Groton at the age of 14. Following the Roosevelt tradition, James went on to Harvard, while Elliott rebelled, saying he was going to Princeton. In the end, Elliott did not go to college. Both Franklin Jr. and John followed tradition, going first to Groton and then to Harvard. Eleanor took her youngest, John, to Groton in 1928.

Although Eleanor and Anna were getting along better, Anna was still unhappy. Living at home with her two young brothers, she did poorly in school and had an "I don't care" attitude. She had no interest in being a debutante or in going to college. When she turned 18, however, Sara insisted she make a debut, and Eleanor, despite her own unhappy experience, agreed. Although Sara was against Anna's attending college, believing she should make a good marriage instead, she went briefly to Cornell University. In 1926, at the age of 20, she married a New York stockbroker, primarily, she wrote later, to get away from the tensions between her mother and Sara. As a wedding present, Sara bought the couple a Manhattan apartment, asking Anna not to tell her mother. Sara's overly generous gifts were always a source of friction, and the gesture infuriated Eleanor. The couple had two children before separating in the early 1930s.

Val Kill

During the summers both Eleanor and Franklin spent time at Hyde Park, and Eleanor frequently invited her friends, particularly Nancy Cook and Marion Dickerman, to come out from the city. Although Sara was not fond of these two women—single women sharing an apartment in Greenwich Village—Franklin liked them well enough. Realizing they could help him politically, he referred to them, affectionately, as "the girls." Eleanor, Nancy, and Marion liked to picnic on the banks of the Val Kill, a quiet brook running peacefully through the woods two miles east of Sara's house, and at times Franklin joined them. Enjoying the quiet peacefulness, they often daydreamed about living near the Val Kill, and Franklin took the idea seriously. He knew how Eleanor felt about living in Sara's house. She wanted a home she could call her own, and Val Kill was a perfect spot for it. He decided to build a cottage for Eleanor and her friends on a piece of land belonging to him, not to Sara.

Construction began in 1925, and Franklin took full charge of the architecture and building plans. He would not let Eleanor suggest even the placement of a window. Having no say in the construction, Eleanor, showing a bit of pique, took Nancy, Marion, and her two youngest boys on a camping trip, traveling through New Hampshire, Quebec, and Maine to Campobello, a place she had avoided since the summer of 1921. Moving into the Val Kill cottage in 1926, Marion and Nancy made it their primary residence. For Eleanor it became a vacation retreat, a home where she could entertain people as she pleased without having to rely on Sara's hospitality. Living at Val Kill whenever she was in Hyde Park, Eleanor moved to Sara's house for appearances' sake when Franklin had political guests. She felt closer to Nancy and Marion than she did to members of her own family, and the three women lived at Val Kill like a family.

Very quickly, Val Kill became more than their home. A carpenter as well as a political worker, Nancy Cook had an interest in handcrafted furniture, particularly fine reproductions of early American furniture, and her talent was soon put to work. With the idea of creating jobs for local workers, the women set up a furniture factory, Val Kill Industries, in another small building on the property. Eleanor provided most of the capital, although Caroline O'Day, the widow of a Standard Oil millionaire, also provided support. Furnishing their cottage with Val Kill furniture, Nancy supervised the workers and their furniture making, while Eleanor handled promotion, selling the furniture to Vassar College and Sloane's Department Store. One of the factory's first orders came from FDR in Warm Springs. Providing some local work, they kept the factory going until 1936, although it was never profitable.

Eleanor as Teacher, Lecturer, and Journalist

In 1927 Eleanor took on another challenge and began to teach English literature, drama, and American history at the Todhunter School, a private girls' school in Manhattan, where Marion Dickerman had been teaching since 1922. The opportunity came when she and Marion decided to buy the school and Marion became its principal. Teaching the daughters of wealthy New Yorkers, Eleanor tried to model her teaching style after Mlle. Souvestre's, challenging her students to think for themselves, disdaining parents who clung to the idea of preparing their daughters for society. Bringing her own reform agenda to her teaching, she often took history students to see settlement houses or to witness court proceedings. After a while she also taught current events, bringing such issues as child labor, sweatshops, and the League of Nations to her students' attention. Eleanor truly loved teaching.

Throughout the 1920s, however, Eleanor found that she needed money. Buying Todhunter took money, as did her many charitable projects and setting up Val Kill Industries. The income from her small trust fund was not enough to support her projects, and she could not ask Franklin for the money. A good part of his trust fund had been spent on restoring Warm Springs, and Franklin sometimes had to ask Sara for financial help. Although eventually teaching gave Eleanor additional income, it was not enough. She sought a way to finance her own projects, and she found it through writing and public speaking.

With her increasing reputation, Eleanor easily found jobs speaking as a guest lecturer or as a guest on radio talk shows. She also began a long and lucrative career in journalism, writing articles for *Success Magazine*, *Redbook*, and the *Ladies' Home Journal*. While writing and speaking to earn money, she also used these venues to put forth her own ideas, frequently writing about women, politics, or world peace. She wrote feminist articles urging women to get involved in politics as well as an article about her own life in politics, being careful to portray herself as a wife and mother who put her husband's career and her children first, a stance that made her acceptable as a woman in politics. In 1933, believing that only women could bring about world peace, she published her first book, *It's Up to the Women*.

BACK IN ALBANY
The 1928 Election

Although she was now juggling a lot of activities, Eleanor remained a force in the Democratic Party. She edited the *Women's Democratic News*, was active in the Women's Division of the State Democratic Committee, and in 1928 played a role in the presidential campaign. That year, Al Smith was seeking the party's presidential nomination for a second time. Eleanor had always been one of his staunchest supporters, but she had some reservations about his stance on Prohibition. Although the sale of liquor had been illegal since 1919, illegal liquor was widely available, leading many to believe Prohibition had opened the door to corruption and crime. The issue was dividing the nation, and Smith stood on the side of those who would repeal Prohibition, causing Eleanor, who had never lost her abhorrence of alcohol, to pause. After deciding Prohibition was of secondary importance, however, she supported Smith, believing his reform agenda would benefit the nation, and she organized the women working for Smith prior to the Democratic National Convention.

As he had four years earlier, Franklin gave Smith's nominating speech. Eleanor, however, did not attend the national convention, as she had assigned all necessary tasks to others. She listened, instead, on the radio. Using only a cane and his son Elliott's support, Franklin walked across the stage, creating an enthusiastic uproar, and gave a speech that elicited the same kind of excitement he had created four years earlier. Al Smith was nominated on the first ballot. Eleanor ended up feeling sorry she had not gone to the convention.

With Smith running for president, New York State Democrats considered Franklin an ideal candidate for governor, and Smith spearheaded a movement to draft him, although Franklin had not planned to reenter politics so soon. He had anticipated two more years of physical therapy, and Louis Howe did not support the idea. With strong Republican sympathy in the country, Howe felt 1928 would not be a good year for Democrats and wanted Franklin to wait for 1932. Franklin retreated to Warm Springs and avoided Smith's calls. Eleanor was ambivalent about his running. When Democrats urged her to help draft him, she said she would not try to influence him. At Smith's request, however, she did place a call to Franklin from the New York state convention. Once she had reached him, she handed the phone to Smith and left in a hurry. She had no idea what Franklin would say, but she had a class to teach and had to catch a train. The next day she learned from the newspapers that Franklin had accepted the nomination. Already committed to Smith's campaign, she did not campaign for her husband.

With Nellie Ross, the governor of Wyoming, Eleanor cochaired women's activities for Smith's national campaign. While Nellie did most of the campaign traveling, Eleanor hired a young secretary, Malvina Thompson, and directed activities from party headquarters in New York. Although she was often at headquarters from 9 A.M. until late in the evening, Eleanor continued to teach two and a half days a week, frequently grading papers well after midnight. As Louis Howe had anticipated, it was not a good year for Democrats. The country had been prosperous under the Republicans and was not inclined to change. Moreover, Al Smith was Catholic, and anti-Catholicism was rampant in the nation. Many non-Catholics believed a Catholic president would be ruled by the pope. Allying themselves with racist organizations, Southerners supporting Prohibition labeled Smith a "Negro lover." After fighting a losing battle, he was defeated by Herbert Hoover.

Franklin, however, won the governorship of New York by a narrow margin. Eleanor had mixed feelings about his victory. Although happy for her husband, she liked her new life and did not want to give it up. As the governor's wife, she would be expected to fade into the background.

Albany's First Lady

Although Eleanor assumed the role of governor's wife, redecorating the governor's mansion, entertaining political notables, and running the household, she did not give up her own life. Franklin agreed she could continue nonpolitical activities as long as she muted her political voice, and she continued to teach, telling the press, "I teach because I love it, I cannot give it up."[4] Leaving Albany on Sunday evenings, she took the train to New York, taught two and a half days, and returned to Albany on Wednesday, using her time on the train to read political articles, write, prepare lesson plans, and grade papers. Although she avoided political topics, she also continued to write articles, and she still helped Nancy Cook run Val Kill Industries.

Giving up official political roles, Eleanor resigned from the New York State Democratic Committee and removed her name as editor of the *Women's Democratic News*, but she did not refrain from making her voice heard. Working behind the scenes, she advised the Women's Division of the Democratic Committee, and with Caroline O'Day's name on the masthead, she still edited the *Women's Democratic News*, writing unsigned articles and attending to publication details. Although she always respected Franklin's wish that she not make public political statements, she was soon attending political events and telling Franklin about them. With time she became a pathway to Franklin, as individuals hesitant to approach him frequently took their concerns to Eleanor. Making it a part of her routine to receive them, she was always gracious and sympathetic, and she faithfully gave their requests to Franklin.

Nor did Eleanor abandon the women's reform movement. To celebrate the Women's Trade Union League's 25th anniversary, she gave a party at Hyde Park, chartering an excursion boat to bring sweatshop girls and union leaders up the Hudson. Always the charming host, Franklin lent his support, welcoming the girls to his home. Seeking to bring women's issues to Albany, Eleanor invited women lobbyists for dinner or tea at the executive mansion, for despite Al Smith's efforts to improve sweatshops, he had paid little attention to women seeking to abolish child labor or protect women workers. As Franklin moved ahead with legislative reform, Eleanor would not let him forget about the women.

Along with Louis Howe, Eleanor liked working behind the scenes. Urging Franklin to extricate himself from Al Smith's influence, she did not hesitate to voice her opinion, although she would never admit publicly to trying to influence him. Both Eleanor and Louis influenced Franklin's early appointments, as Smith, apparently expecting to retain control of the office, tried to dictate Franklin's appointments, telling him to keep Robert Moses and Belle Moskowitz, two key players in his own administration. Franklin wanted to make a clean break, as Louis and Eleanor thought he should, and he dismissed Robert Moses without hesitation. Belle Moskowitz, however, knew the inner workings of the office, and Franklin was not so sure it was necessary to fire her. A woman a lot like Eleanor, Belle was as loyal to Al Smith as Louis Howe was to FDR, and Eleanor, who liked and admired Belle, felt strongly that Franklin had to fire her if he was to rid himself of Smith's meddling. With Eleanor telling him she "will make good decisions. . . . But they will be her decisions, not yours,"[5] Franklin dismissed Belle. He was never again on good terms with Al Smith, although Eleanor managed to maintain a cool but cordial acquaintance.

Although Franklin had a solid political base in New York City, he did not have the support of rural upstate farmers, and, asking Eleanor to join him, he began taking yearly upstate tours. Stopping in small towns and talking with farming families, he and Eleanor hoped to win their support as well. Eleanor used the skills she had learned in the Women's Division to rally the support of farmers' wives. Franklin and Eleanor also talked with local officials and inspected state prisons, mental institutions, and hospitals. Although Franklin knew what he wanted to see, he could not easily look for himself, as he had never regained use of his legs. Eleanor checked the facilities while Franklin talked with their administration. He gave her detailed instructions and quizzed her afterwards, teaching her to look for cots squeezed together or hidden in closets, telltale signs of overcrowding. When she checked the food by simply looking at a menu, he told her to look inside the pots. She talked with staff and residents, looking for hidden tensions, and learned to read their body language. She became Franklin's "eyes and ears," a role she would also play during his presidency. They were fine-tuning their political alliance.

Eleanor's approach to politics differed from Franklin's, however. She was driven by her ideals—her desire for reform, world peace, better conditions for women and the underprivileged. She believed political women, in general, were motivated by their ideals, whereas men were driven by their political ambitions, as was Franklin. Although Eleanor thought Franklin shared her ideals in his heart—and he did share many of them— he found it easier to compromise for the sake of expediency. Driven by his desire for a political career, he could bend to the mood of the time. Knowing this, however, did not keep Eleanor from offering her opinions. She would urge Franklin, for instance, to include women on his staff or set up programs benefiting women workers. At times she got on his nerves, but Franklin would consider her opinions, sometimes taking her suggestions, sometimes ignoring them.

Causing much speculation about the extent of Eleanor's influence, Franklin apparently shared her view of political women and appointed a young woman, Frances Perkins, to be state industrial commissioner. Perkins would eventually become a member of his presidential cabinet. Although Eleanor arranged for a meeting between Perkins and Franklin prior to the appointment, she would always deny having any role in Perkins's appointment, saying it was entirely Franklin's idea.

Two Separate Camps

Strong as their political alliance was, Eleanor and Franklin still lived separate lives even as they shared the governor's mansion. After meeting each day to discuss political questions, they would go about their own lives, each with their own set of friends. Franklin generally socialized with political colleagues who liked to have a drink and relax, including a young lawyer and speechwriter, Sam Rosenman. Never a great fan of Eleanor's, Rosenman considered her a meddlesome pain and, along with other colleagues, wished Franklin would stop listening to her. Franklin was still friends with his secretary, Missy Le Hand, who had moved from Warm Springs, and he also relaxed in her company. Missy filled in as hostess when Eleanor was in New York, and whatever Eleanor's feelings were, she was always warm with Missy.

Only Louis Howe was truly friends with both Eleanor and Franklin, however. Continuing to be Franklin's political strategist, Louis remained in New York, and Eleanor saw him frequently. After working on some political issue, they would eat in a small neighborhood restaurant or go to the theater. Louis Howe was still Eleanor's strongest ally.

Eleanor's network included her political friends—Nancy Cook, Marion Dickerman, Caroline O'Day, Elinor Morgenthau, Esther Lape, Elizabeth Read—and a newcomer, Malvina Thompson. After Al Smith's campaign, Malvina, an imposing but good-natured woman, became Eleanor's personal secretary and longtime friend. "Tommy," as Anna nicknamed her, was completely devoted to Eleanor, even to the point of putting her job ahead of her marriage, and she worked for Eleanor for the next 30 years, taking care of every little detail for her. The two women were always close friends. However, Eleanor's friendships were never static. Although she traveled to Europe with Nancy, Marion, and her two youngest sons in 1929, she was beginning to drift away from these two women as she formed new friendships and interests.

A Different Kind of Friend

In Albany Eleanor made one friend who was different from the others, Earl Miller. With Earl, Eleanor relaxed, flirted, and had fun. A colorful, athletic man who had had varied careers as circus performer, naval officer, boxer, judo instructor, and state trooper, Earl Miller was Eleanor's bodyguard, and they became fast friends, sharing life stories, swimming and riding together, and enjoying each other's company. Like Eleanor, Earl had been orphaned at an early age. Although several years younger than Eleanor, he gave her the kind of attention Franklin no longer gave her, shocking Marion and Nancy by putting his arm around her waist or touching her hand. Earl protected her from press and family, helping with her Uncle Val when he showed up drunk in Albany or removing her brother Hall, also drunk, from a political function, and he helped her in ways others would not, teaching her to dive or to feel relaxed in front of a camera. Sharing and respecting her political beliefs, he was quick to let others know when an idea had originated with Eleanor.

Earl's displays of affection, his traveling with Eleanor, albeit as her bodyguard, and Eleanor's excitement in his presence led people to specu-late about the nature of their relationship. There were rumors they were lovers. Esther Lape thought so, although she was not as shocked at the idea as Eleanor's other friends. Whether or not there was truth to the gos-sip is not known. Somehow their correspondence disappeared. Although Earl was quick to talk about an affair he had with Missy Le Hand and his three failed marriages, claiming he married his second and third wives to stop rumors about him and Eleanor, he did not discuss his friendship with Eleanor. Whatever the true nature of that friendship, they remained friends for over thirty years, and wherever Eleanor was—Val Kill, Green-wich Village, the White House—Earl was welcome.

FROM GOVERNOR TO PRESIDENT
Prelude to the Presidential Campaign

In 1928 Herbert Hoover had been swept into the presidency on a wave of economic prosperity. The stock market was at an all-time high. Specu-lation was rampant. Business was booming; industry, expanding. The era came to be known as the Roaring Twenties, famous for speakeasies, illegal liquor, and "flappers," girls with short hair, short skirts, and transparent silk stockings, dancing the Charleston.

In October 1929, however, the dancing stopped: The stock market crashed. The economy collapsed. Unwise investors lost their money. Busi-nesses failed. Plants closed. People without worries lost their jobs. Ex-pected to take care of themselves, they had no recourse, no government agencies to provide help, no food stamps, no insurance of any kind. Those in power had always assumed the poor had only themselves to blame. The nation began to sink into despair. While assuring the public the economy would bounce back, Hoover did not know what to do. Eleanor's concerns were now the concerns of the nation. People needed food, shelter, jobs. Appalled at the homeless roaming New York City's streets, Eleanor handed out five-dollar bills and sent the hungry to the 65th Street townhouse, telling the servants to have coffee and sandwiches ready. As Republican opposition waned in the state legislature, Franklin stepped up his reform efforts, setting up relief programs and creating a state agency to provide assistance, ideas that would be precursors to his presidential programs as he came to believe government had to help.

With the nation in a very different mood, Franklin ran for governor again in 1930. With his colleagues, particularly James Farley, recognizing the role of the Women's Division, Eleanor and her cochair, Molly Dewson, brought the women's organization to upstate New York. The women's vote played a major part in the election, as did Eleanor and Franklin's upstate tours and Franklin's relief programs. He won by a landslide, the first Democratic candidate to win upstate New York.

While supporting Franklin, Eleanor worried about her family. Anna's husband had lost everything in the stock market crash, and her marriage was in trouble. Elliott couldn't hold a job. Her sons, used to the advantages that came with the Roosevelt name, didn't know what it meant to work for something. Her children rarely saw their father, but she still maintained the image of a happily married woman, even writing an article "Ten Rules for Success in Marriage."

Presidential Campaign

In 1932, with the nation in despair, Franklin made his bid for the presidency. Eleanor had always known that was his goal. She had helped him achieve it. Now, however, her feelings were mixed. She supported her husband, but a part of her, a part she rarely acknowledged, wished he would not run. She had been a political wife, and she had watched her Aunt Edith assume the role of first lady. She was not looking forward to what the future might bring. She never told Franklin how she felt, however.

With Louis Howe mapping strategy and his protégé James Farley taking charge of the campaign, Franklin quickly became the Democratic frontrunner, but he faced a roadblock. His split in 1929 with Al Smith, also a candidate, had led to a bitter "Stop Roosevelt" movement, and the Democratic convention was badly divided. None of the party's six candidates had enough delegates to get the nomination. Franklin, politician that he was, broke the deadlock, in a deal brokered by James Farley and

Louis Howe, by compromising on the League of Nations. To Eleanor's chagrin, her husband, one of Wilson's earliest supporters, agreed to renounce the League of Nations and the World Court, causing her to stop speaking to him for three days. In exchange, Franklin received the Texas and California delegates initially pledged to Texas favorite son John Garner, his soon-to-be vice-presidential candidate. Once California shifted its support, all but the staunchest Smith supporters switched their allegiance, and Franklin became the party's presidential candidate with an overwhelming victory.

Although James Farley, Louis Howe, and three of the Roosevelt children were at the convention, Eleanor and Franklin were in Albany, listening on the radio. The press corps was in their garage, and Lorena Hickok, an Associated Press (AP) reporter who had covered Eleanor, sought her out after the news arrived. Finding her in the kitchen, scrambling eggs for Franklin, Lorena watched a young reporter ask, "Mrs. Roosevelt, aren't you *thrilled* at the idea of living in the White House?" Eleanor "did not answer. . . . The expression on her face, almost angry, stopped all questions along that line."[6] Although she was gracious, Eleanor "seemed rather withdrawn—shut up inside herself," leading Hickok to note, "That woman is unhappy about something."[7]

Although candidates were not expected at conventions in 1932, Franklin broke with tradition and left in the morning for the convention, taking Eleanor, the two boys, and Sam Rosenman. In an age of air travel, he saw no reason to wait. The convention was alive with excitement and the upbeat sound of "Happy Days Are Here Again," and Franklin got a standing ovation. Formally accepting the nomination, he spoke of the nation's crisis, the millions of citizens who had lost their standards of living, and the political philosophy that precluded governmental help, and he pledged himself "to a new deal for the American people," bringing the hall to cheers. The "New Deal" became the hallmark of his presidency. For Louis Howe, the victory was bittersweet. Although the theme song, "Happy Days Are Here Again," was his choice, the speech was primarily Sam Rosenman's, not his. The reins of power were imperceptibly shifting from Howe to Rosenman and his colleagues, Franklin's "brain trust."

Louis Howe and Jim Farley were still in charge of campaign strategy, however. Although Eleanor was teaching, she campaigned some, traveling primarily in New York State, speaking to small women's groups, and joining Franklin's campaign train when she could. From train windows she and Franklin saw the nation's poverty, the ragged clothing hanging out to dry, the failing crops, the rusting cars. At every train stop there were mobs of people, but they were not cheering. Somber, grim, hungry, they stood silently and listened to what Franklin had to say, giving no indication of what they thought. There were no campaign signs supporting Franklin. Eleanor began to fear he would lose. She also worried about his winning, about his ability to bring the nation out of crisis. Franklin, however, was confident he could pull the country out of poverty.

The evening of Tuesday, November 8, the Roosevelt family went into the city. Eleanor had taught in the morning, having driven into the city the evening before, and then returned to Hyde Park to vote. The family would be hearing election returns in a suite at the Biltmore Hotel. Eleanor, standing erect in a white evening gown, was gracious and smiling. It was clear early on that Franklin would win. He would carry 42 of the nation's 48 states, a landslide victory. Everyone was ecstatic. Celebrations started early, spilling out into the hallways. Sara beamed with pride. Franklin had overcome a devastating blow, moved on, and become president. Eleanor was happy for him. As she answered reporters' questions, however, and stared back at flashing cameras, she reminded one reporter "of a fox, surrounded by a pack of baying hounds."[8] Eleanor had "never wanted to be a President's wife, and [she didn't] want it now."[9]

NOTES

1. Roosevelt, *This Is My Story*, p. 352.

2. Ibid., p. 354.

3. Quoted in Lash, *Eleanor and Franklin*, p. 345.

4. Quoted in ibid., p. 430.

5. Quoted in Cook, *Eleanor Roosevelt*, vol. I, p. 392.

6. Lorena A. Hickok, *Eleanor Roosevelt: Reluctant First Lady* (1962; repr., New York: Dodd, Mead, & Co., 1980), p. xxiii.

7. Ibid., p. 33.

8. Ibid., p. 59.

9. Ibid., p. 2.

Chapter 4

ELEANOR BECOMES FIRST LADY

Franklin was inaugurated president on March 4, 1933. Speaking with strength and confidence, he sought to calm the nation, proclaiming, "This great nation will endure as it has endured. . . . The only thing we have to fear is fear itself." Telling his audience, "This nation asks for action, and action now," he signaled his readiness. "Our greatest primary task is to put people to work." If necessary, "I shall seek power to wage a war against the emergency as great as the power that would be given to me if we were in fact invaded by a foreign foe." The crowd responded enthusiastically. Franklin would act swiftly to stall the nation's downhill spiral, and his presidency would have bold beginnings. His cabinet, already chosen, was sworn into office that very afternoon. While Franklin was swinging into action, however, one Washington reporter wrote of Eleanor's first day as first lady, concluding that "Washington has never seen the likes of Eleanor Roosevelt!"[1]

ELEANOR AS FIRST LADY-ELECT
Initial Impressions

From the moment Franklin won the election, Eleanor astounded reporters, friends, and servants as she broke one precedent after another. Resisting the mandate to assume a more regal lifestyle, she rode in train coaches, refusing to take a private compartment. She walked from her hotel to the White House despite insistence that she take a private limousine. She disregarded her clothing, leading one reporter to write that "her hats looked as though she had rushed in and bought them while her bus waited for the traffic light to change."[2] She decorated the White House lawn with swings, slides, and a sandbox for her grandchildren and, becoming impatient with the movers, moved furniture herself. She upset the White House usher, who had known her as a girl visiting her Uncle Teddy, by operating the White House elevator herself, seeing no reason to wait for him to run the hand-operated device. Telling Franklin, "nobody's going to . . . shoot me. I'm not that important," she refused Secret Service protection.[3] Although once she was in the White House Eleanor hired a Fifth Avenue dress designer and eventually came to accept special travel arrangements, she never accepted Secret Service protection.

Initially telling reporters an Inaugural Ball would be a ridiculous expense with millions of Americans going hungry, she created quite a stir among hotel operators, florists, dressmakers, and caterers who hoped to get extra work from the ball. In the end, she attended the ball while Franklin met with his advisors. After the inauguration ceremony, Eleanor had 3,000 guests for tea, an astounding number causing guests to spill over into rooms never used for tea, and 75 guests for dinner. Breaking with tradition, she did not wait for the servants to announce her dinner guests, but opened the White House's front door and greeted her guests there. Yet, as startling as that may have been, the reporter writing of these activities probably had no idea of the extent to which "Washington [had] never seen the likes of Eleanor Roosevelt!"

All other first ladies, even those who had been outspoken, independent women or had had careers of their own, muted their own voice when becoming first lady and devoted themselves to being mistress of the White House. Not Eleanor Roosevelt. While she would give up teaching and do less for the Women's Division of the Democratic Party, she would not give up everything. Nor would she keep silent. Although she could not always sway Franklin's opinion, he had always welcomed her views on domestic issues, weighing her opinions just as he weighed those of his advisors, and she was not about to mute her voice now. She may not have wanted to be first lady, but she would take full advantage of the role, using it to promote her own causes, expanding her activities to include an ever-widening array of people and causes.

A Sympathetic Friend

Only one person truly realized the reluctance with which Eleanor became first lady—Lorena Hickok, the AP reporter who noticed her mixed emotions on the night of Franklin's election. An overweight, diabetic woman who had trouble keeping up with Eleanor's fast pace, Lorena Hickok, or "Hick" as she was called, was a topnotch reporter. Like Eleanor, she had had a difficult childhood, although one that was very different from Eleanor's. Growing up in the rural Midwest, Hick was poor and started working as hired help at the age of 14. Her mother had died. Her father was abusive and rarely home. Finishing high school while living with a cousin, she attended college briefly before taking a job with a local newspaper. Rising rapidly in the newspaper world, she became an AP reporter in New York when she was 23. When she met Eleanor, Hick was a highly regarded reporter whose articles appeared on the front page, a unique accomplishment for a woman in the early twentieth century.

Hick was assigned to cover Eleanor shortly before the election. Although she had written a couple of articles on Eleanor, she had been covering Franklin and would have preferred to continue covering him, as she had little interest in writing "women's stories." She found Eleanor interesting, though, and suggested to the Associated Press that they assign a reporter to her, ultimately getting the assignment herself. Initially, Eleanor did not make the assignment easy, shutting Hick out in an effort to retain her privacy. Befriending Eleanor's secretary, however, Hick gained Tommy's trust, and eventually Eleanor became more receptive to her.

When Missy Le Hand's mother died in October, Eleanor, along with Hick, accompanied Missy to the funeral in Potsdam, New York, and on that trip, Eleanor began to confide in Hick. Eleanor was in need of a new confidant, as Franklin had appointed Earl Miller director of personnel for New York State's Department of Correction, forcing him to stay in Albany, and her friendship with Nancy Cook and Marion Dickerman was waning. Driving Hick to see the St. Lawrence Seaway, she shared her feelings about the election, including her worries about the impact on her children if Franklin won and the momentous task he would face. She only hinted at the dread she had of the impact on herself. On the train back, she told Hick of her childhood, of how she was called Granny or the ugly duckling, of her father's death, and of her Grandmother Hall.

As the two women became friends, they began dining together at the 65th Street townhouse or at Hick's apartment. Eleanor shared her dread of being first lady, her fear of being a prisoner in the White House, her certainty that she would be criticized. By Inauguration Day, Lorena Hickok had become Eleanor's closest friend. Sharing the statue of "Grief" with Hick, Eleanor took her to Rock Creek Cemetery early on the morning of March 3 and told her of Franklin's affair with Lucy Mercer and the hours she had spent sitting before the statue.

When they were not together, Eleanor and Hick wrote regularly, and their letters have led some historians to speculate about the exact nature of their relationship. One biographer, Blanche Wiesen Cook, believes strongly that they were more than friends, that they were involved romantically. Hick, admittedly, was not attracted to men. Others, however, are not as quick to draw Cook's conclusion. If the two women's letters were sent today as emails, they would most likely lead to Cook's conclusion, as Eleanor does profess her love for Lorena and even refers to wanting to caress her. Early in the twentieth century, however, women frequently used such endearing terms with each other, and, as some historians and Franklin Jr. have pointed out, Eleanor wrote affectionately to a lot of people, often professing her love. She would even write to her mother-in-law, whom she resented, "I do so want to kiss you."[4] Edna Gurewitsch, who knew Eleanor later in life, believes Cook's conclusion "is a false assumption . . . based on wishful thinking by those who claim it." "Nowhere" in their friendship or in her husband's friendship with Eleanor "was there any indication that Eleanor Roosevelt was ever attracted to same-sex love."[5]

Whatever the nature of Eleanor and Hick's relationship, Lorena Hickok was the person Eleanor confided in during her first two years in the White House. Once they were friends, Eleanor trusted Hick not to reveal her confidences, a trust that Hick honored to the detriment of her own career on the eve of FDR's inauguration. Dining with Eleanor in her sitting room at the Mayflower Hotel, Hick watched as Louis Howe rushed in and out with news. In an adjoining room, Franklin and his entourage were in a state of turmoil, listening to accounts of a worsening banking crisis, putting the final touches on Franklin's inaugural address, eventually sending a copy of the speech to Eleanor. Eleanor read the speech to Hick and proclaimed, "It's a good speech, a courageous speech." As Hick wrote later, she could have taken advantage of the situation: "I could have slipped out to a telephone . . . and given the AP the gist of [the address]. . . . I could have told about the reports coming in from around the country. . . . It would have been . . . the biggest scoop of my career. But scoops . . . did not seem important that night. . . . That night Lorena Hickok ceased to be a newspaper reporter."[6]

In June Hick resigned from the Associated Press and took a job with the Roosevelt administration, working as an investigator for one of the new relief agencies. Eleanor, who was on good terms with Harry Hopkins, director of Franklin's new federal relief program, had recommended Hick for the job. Hick was given a bedroom in the White House, as were Louis Howe, Anna and her two children, and Missy Le Hand, and she lived there when she was in Washington. She and Eleanor remained friends for the rest of their lives, although the intensity of the friendship waned as they each became absorbed in their own schedules. In the early years of FDR's presidency, their daily correspondence gave a detailed account of Eleanor's activities, reactions, and mood swings—mood swings that frequently reflected whether she agreed or disagreed with Franklin's actions.

THE EARLY NEW DEAL

Already desperate when Franklin was elected president, the national crisis had reached new depths by the time he was inaugurated. Some fifteen million people were without work, most with no hope of finding it. People who had never known hunger feared starvation. Millions had lost their homes. Those without shelter had built makeshift tents out of cardboard, tin cans, whatever materials they could find, and tent cities had sprung up throughout the country. In February one crazed laborer tried to shoot FDR and killed the mayor of Chicago instead, increasing Eleanor's concern for Franklin. The mood of the nation was grim. To Eleanor, it was frightening.

Fearing they too would lose everything, people who still had money in the bank were closing their accounts, and on the eve of Franklin's inauguration, one bank after another failed as depositors demanded their money and bankers ran out of cash on hand. With his cabinet and staff already in place, Franklin acted immediately to put a brake on the banking crisis, a crisis that had begun during the preceding week, when Hoover was still president. Hoover, like Roosevelt, believed the banks needed a holiday, time to regroup, but he would not close banks as his last act in office. Sunday evening, the day after his inauguration, Franklin declared a bank holiday, telling bankers not to open on Monday and giving the first of his famous fireside chats. Speaking with complete calm, he reassured radio listeners that the nation's banks were sound, urging them not to withdraw their funds and appealing to their sense of patriotism.

On Monday, after the fact, he sent his Emergency Banking Act to Congress, and Congress, responding to the national panic, passed it within the week. When the banks reopened, the panic had passed, and people left their money in the bank. The act was a temporary fix, however, and the administration went on to set up the Federal Deposit Insurance Corporation (FDIC), which provided insurance for depositors' accounts. Ultimately, Franklin took the country off the Gold Standard, as Great Britain had done several years earlier. No longer backed by gold held by the government, the dollar decreased in value, while prices increased slightly.

Banking reform was but a beginning. Franklin's presidency began with a flurry of legislation to create jobs, provide relief, reform industry, and save farmers. Although he and his advisors had anticipated resistance from conservative Republican holdovers in Congress, Franklin was able to move a great deal of legislation through Congress in the early months. Those months, known as "the Hundred Days," marked the beginning of the New Deal.

By the end of March, Franklin had created the Civilian Conservation Corps (CCC) and by May the Federal Emergency Relief Administration (FERA). Using federal projects to create jobs, the CCC put young men to work building roads, planting trees, or creating hiking trails. Living in work camps, CCC workers received free board and room and $30 a month, a typical wage in 1933. The CCC was a start, providing jobs for some 225,000 men, but FERA was larger in scope. Under the direction of Harry Hopkins, a social worker greatly admired by Eleanor and the head of Franklin's relief efforts in New York, FERA filtered federal funds, allocated by Congress, to local relief agencies. Those funds provided direct financial assistance to the impoverished. Expanding on the CCC concept, Hopkins also created the Civil Works Administration (CWA) under FERA, putting some four million men to work. Eleanor embraced these programs but found them wanting, for they excluded women. Her voice would be heard on that subject.

For the first time the federal government began to regulate private industry. In May Congress passed the National Industrial Recovery Act (NIRA), establishing the National Recovery Administration (NRA) to regulate business. Working with industry leaders, the NRA created employment standards for industry and encouraged negotiations with unions. Reminiscent of the reforms sought by early women reformers, the standards included an eight-hour workday and decent wages. The textile industry even prohibited child labor—a cause dear to Eleanor's heart—although other industries did not follow suit. The NRA promoted accuracy in advertising, also advocated by early women reformers. It also set guidelines for pricing and production levels and sought to control toxic waste. Although compliance with NRA standards was not mandatory, businesses that complied could display a "Blue Eagle" placard in their windows, encouraging those who believed in the program to do business with them—another concept initiated by early female reformers, although Franklin's advisors were too young to have had contact with those reformers.

The NIRA also established the Public Works Administration (PWA). Like the CCC, the PWA put young men to work on public projects. Headed by Franklin's secretary of the interior, Harold Ickes, the PWA often encompassed larger projects, such as hospitals, highways, bridges, and dams, than either the CCC or Hopkins's Civil Works Administration. Eleanor welcomed yet another effort to create jobs, but Harold Ickes did not appreciate her input. She and Ickes would often clash.

Although Eleanor was fully behind Franklin's efforts to create jobs and the NRA's employment standards, she was not so happy with his farm policy. America's farmers were in dire straits even before the stock market crash in 1929. Since the end of World War I, they had not been able to get a decent price for their crops, and they could not, therefore, get ahead even when crops were plentiful, as extra produce simply pushed prices down further, making crops unprofitable. Unable to pay their mortgages, farmers were losing their land. Many migrated to the city, often to live in tent cities. Introducing the Agricultural Adjustment Act (AAA) in May, Franklin believed the key to solving the farmers' plight was to reduce supply and thus to increase farm prices. Under the AAA, the federal government subsidized farmers who agreed to reduce the size of their crops, paying them to leave fields unattended. In some instances farmers were paid to slaughter cattle, discard milk, or burn crops rather than take them to market. The idea of destroying food when so many were hungry horrified and depressed Eleanor. The program also elicited criticism from those who opposed the New Deal.

Nor was Eleanor sympathetic with an act Franklin initiated after closing the banks, the Economy in Government Act. A politically conservative piece of legislation welcomed by Republicans, the Economy in Government Act, unlike other New Deal legislation, cut federal spending. It cut the salary of all federal employees by 15 percent, closed some government agencies, causing both men and women to lose their jobs, and fired any woman whose husband also worked for the government. The latter clause, in particular, disturbed Eleanor.

ELEANOR AS FIRST LADY
Finding a Useful Role

Attending to the first lady's official duties as quickly as possible, Eleanor hired a social secretary, Edith Helm, to help with the details of official entertaining and kept Tommy as her personal secretary. Firing the existing White House staff, she brought her African American servants, many of whom had been with her for years, to Washington, and she declared an eight-hour workday, bringing workers' rights to the White House. To supervise the kitchen staff and handle housekeeping, she hired a housewife from Hyde Park, Henrietta Nesbitt, a woman Blanche Wiesen Cook has dubbed "ER's Revenge." Henrietta was struggling to feed her family, selling baked goods from her farmhouse kitchen as her husband sought work, when Eleanor met her at the League of Women Voters. She was a rude, bigoted woman, and her presence at the White House created tension among the staff. Taking over the kitchen, she doggedly served plain, overcooked food that Franklin disliked, telling him it was good for him. Even as the White House became famous for its unappealing meals, Eleanor was loyal to Henrietta, leading many to believe Eleanor had no interest in food. Cook is not so sure, given her interest in the cuisine at fine restaurants.

Eleanor sought a role as more than a social hostess, however. Just two days after the inauguration, she departed dramatically from the first lady's traditional role. On March 6, she held a press conference for female reporters, an idea that Hick, as a female reporter, suggested and Louis Howe thought was a good one. Initially ridiculed by male reporters, who predicted her press conferences would not last more than six months, Eleanor continued to hold her own press conferences until she left the White House in 1945. Although her first conference was not particularly newsworthy, male reporters took notice on April 3, when Franklin left it to Eleanor to announce that beer, no longer illegal, would be served in the White House, although she personally would not drink it. Even as male reporters began to seek admittance, Eleanor retained the women-only policy, forcing a press that dared not ignore her to hire female reporters.

Initially Eleanor did not answer political questions at her press conferences, as some of Franklin's advisors worried that she would say something to embarrass him, a possibility that did not concern Franklin or Louis Howe. Eleanor submitted her agenda to Louis and Hick as well as to Franklin's press secretary, Steve Early. She also asked Tommy to take notes, hoping to avoid being misquoted. With time Eleanor ceased to avoid political controversy and came to use her press conferences to promote her own take on New Deal programs.

An essentially male establishment, the Washington press corps held an annual Gridiron Dinner shortly after the inauguration, inviting the new president and his cabinet, but excluding women, even the new secretary of labor, Frances Perkins. Considering it an insult to Frances, women reporters, and herself, Eleanor held her own party, a Gridiron Widows' Party, inviting Perkins, female reporters, cabinet wives, and women from both the government and the arts. The Gridiron Widows' Party became an annual gala event as well. As a journalist Eleanor sympathized with the female reporters, many of whom owed their jobs to her, and she had a warm relationship with them.

Eleanor would not give up her own writing and editing. When Franklin was inaugurated, she had published three books—*It's Up to the Women*, *When You Grow Up to Vote*, which she wrote for children, and *Hunting Big Game in the Eighties*, a collection of letters her father had written. She had also signed a contract to edit a new monthly magazine, *Babies—Just Babies*, an illustrated glossy magazine featuring pictures of cute babies and advice to parents. Hiring her daughter, Anna, as her assistant, she edited the magazine for six months, receiving $500 per issue, and was widely criticized. Many considered it unseemly for her to edit a slick, glossy publication, and both she and the magazine were ridiculed. She resigned in May, and the magazine ceased publication.

More successfully, she began writing a monthly column for the *Woman's Home Companion*, a vehicle that enabled her to reach women beyond the Democratic Party. Using the column to express her ideas, Eleanor encouraged readers to write to her and then responded to their concerns, receiving $1,000 a month for the column. In addition, she continued to edit the *Women's Democratic News*. While keeping her name off the masthead, she still wrote an unsigned editorial, and in February she started writing a signed column, "Passing Thoughts of Mrs. Franklin D. Roosevelt." In her very first column, written before Franklin's inauguration, she inadvertently criticized his initial efforts, writing that she disapproved of cutting taxes and reducing government spending. The government should, she wrote, increase spending to provide relief, jobs, and job training. Although Franklin never expected Eleanor to remain silent, he did not let that go unnoticed. Requesting space in the March issue, he wrote a rebuttal, defending his Economy in Government Act. In future issues, Eleanor avoided writing columns that would elicit further rebuttals.

She still had a drive for reform, however. By the end of March, she had toured Washington's alley slums—narrow alleys, hidden between buildings, where destitute, often black, residents lived in squalor, without running water or garbage removal, sharing outhouses, often sleeping 14 or 15 people to a room. Eleanor walked the alleys, guided by a longtime Washington activist, and talked with the residents, listening to tales of death and tuberculosis. Immediately, she began to agitate for slum cleanup, insisting that no one should live with water pumps next to outdoor toilets. Although work crews were dispatched to clean up the worst health threats, Eleanor and other reformers envisioned more. She sought to replace the slums with better buildings, upsetting Washingtonians who would maintain the status quo.

In May, the Second Bonus Army—war veterans harboring a long-standing grievance against the government—descended on Washington, and Eleanor would help to defuse a potentially volatile situation. These veterans had fought in World War I. Many were war heroes. Yet they were receiving only a meager pension and could not find work. They had been promised a bonus—a bonus they hoped would bring them out of poverty—but had not yet received it. A year earlier, some 20,000 of them, along with their families, had marched on Washington, hoping to lobby Congress and win their bonus. Creating a massive, dilapidated tent city, they camped for weeks across the river from the nation's capitol. To President Hoover, they were alarming, an unruly mob, probably led by communists, likely to erupt in violence. He offered to pay their train fare home. When they did not move, he ordered the military to remove them. Under the command of General Douglas MacArthur, the military came in with tear gas, tanks, and bayonets, slashing and killing many, driving them out, and burning their campground. Eleanor, along with much of the nation, was horrified.

In May 1933, the Bonus Marchers returned, their pensions slashed by the Economy in Government Act, their bonus still unpaid, and again they camped across the river from the capitol. Although money for their bonus was nowhere to be found, Roosevelt tried to placate them, sending Louis Howe to the camps to appease them. On one trip Eleanor also went to the camps, mingling with the veterans while Louis waited in the car. She asked how they were doing, sympathized with their woes, talked of soldiers she had met at World War I canteens, and sang World War I songs with them. While she could not get their bonus, the veterans left feeling they had a champion in the first lady. They also felt better about Roosevelt. As one veteran is reputed to have said, "Hoover sent the army. Roosevelt sent his wife."[7]

Quickly acquiring a reputation for being accessible, Eleanor was flooded with mail. By the end of a year, she had received more than 300,000 letters, several hundred a day. She received letters from children, telling of how hard their parents worked, how sick their mother was, how little money they had, asking for her old clothes, saying "I don't have no shoes to wear to school," or asking "for $8.00 to get me a winter coat."[8] She got letters from people writing of injustices, of how New Deal programs had not reached them, asking if she would tell Mr. Roosevelt, who they knew was very busy. If she could, Eleanor would try to help, sometimes bringing an issue to Franklin's attention or forwarding a request to Harry Hopkins or Harold Ickes. On rare occasions she would send money from her earnings, although Earl Miller warned her that she could be duped. She would try to reply even if she could not help, sometimes writing a note herself, more often dictating a letter to Tommy or asking her to reply, eventually hiring Anna to help as well. Seen as a sympathetic ear, a potential champion, a pathway to the president, Eleanor became an unofficial ombudsman for the nation.

She had perhaps found her niche, the same niche she had had in Albany, as Franklin's bridge to the underprivileged, as his eyes and ears. Whenever she traveled, and she would travel a lot, Eleanor would report back to Franklin, giving him every detail of how people lived, of conditions wherever she went. As Franklin once told a colleague, referring to Eleanor, "There goes the opinion of the average man in the streets."[9] He encouraged her to give voice to the people's needs and to speak her mind, telling her once, "Say what you think. If you get me in Dutch, I'll manage to get myself out. Anyway, the whole world knows I can't control you."[10] He often used her outspokenness to his own advantage, letting her test the waters, encouraging her to speak out on an issue just to see how Congress would react. If she got a negative outcry, he remained silent and acted accordingly.

Although she did not seek credit, Eleanor actively sought to influence policy. Louis Howe was still her strongest ally, but his power was waning, as Franklin now turned to his brain trust, young university men whom Howe neither liked nor respected. Both Eleanor and Howe were outside Franklin's inner circle, but Eleanor still had Franklin's ear. Although she was more idealistic and less willing to compromise than Franklin, he respected her integrity, and he would consider her opinions, sometimes adopting her view, sometimes rejecting it. Together Eleanor and Louis Howe were a force to be reckoned with. They had more influence than the brain trust would have liked.

Looking Out for the Women

Since her earliest ventures into politics, Eleanor had sought to bring women into the political arena, and she now wanted to ensure that women would have a role in Franklin's administration. Working with Molly Dewson, a key figure in the Women's Division, she made up a list of some 60 qualified women, and with Eleanor's support Molly played a critical role in bringing women into the administration. Having first met Molly at the New York Women's City Club, Eleanor brought her into politics in 1928, persuading her to join Al Smith's campaign. Molly worked with Eleanor on Franklin's 1930 gubernatorial campaign and then took charge of women's activities for his presidential campaign. Becoming head of

the Women's Division in 1933, she shared political patronage with James
Farley, now the official party leader as well as postmaster general. Taking charge of patronage for women, Molly submitted women's names to
Farley, and if he hesitated for any reason, perhaps preferring to appoint a
man, Eleanor stepped in and approached Farley, Louis Howe, or Frances
Perkins. She was on good terms with all three, and her recommendations
held some sway. Under Molly and Eleanor's surveillance, more women
were appointed to positions in Franklin's administration than in any pre-
vious administration.

When Franklin appointed Frances Perkins secretary of labor, she became the first woman to hold a cabinet position. Some historians claim
Eleanor influenced his decision. Others claim she did not. Either way,
both Eleanor and Molly were pleased with her appointment. Although Eleanor and Perkins worked well together, Perkins did not share her private
life, and neither Molly nor Eleanor felt close to her. Many of the women
appointed to government positions were Eleanor's friends and colleagues,
however. The guiding spirit behind her activities at the Rivington Street
Settlement House, Mary Harriman Rumsey, was appointed head of the
NRA's Consumer Advisory Board, and WTUL's red-headed cap maker,
Rose Schneiderman, served on the NRA board. Eleanor's cochair for Al
Smith's presidential campaign, Nellie Ross, became director of the U.S.
Mint. By 1935 the administration had appointed more than 50 women to
federal positions. Many more were appointed to local positions.

Despite these victories, however, Eleanor was appalled at the treatment women received at the hands of New Dealers. While New Deal
programs mimicked the goals of early female reformers, women received
few benefits from them. NRA codes mandated lower wages for women
than for men and did not even cover domestic workers, primarily women.
CCC camps excluded women in the belief that they were too weak to do
physical work. FERA and PWA excluded them as well. In the 1930s, men
were expected to support their families. Women were not. With jobs in
short supply, legislators believed, women should not be taking work away
from men. The Economy in Government Act even went so far as to fire
women who were fortunate enough to have both a federal job and a federally employed husband. All women, it was assumed, would be supported
by their husbands. Legislators did not even consider the needs of single
women, widows with young children, or women whose husbands were
sick, disabled, or unable to find work.

These women had needs as great as those of any man, and Eleanor
sought to include them in New Deal relief programs. Hoping to bring
attention to their plight, she wrote of them in her columns and talked of

them at her press conferences. Approaching Franklin, Louis Howe, and officials in the administration, she had little success with PWA, succeeding primarily in irritating Harold Ickes. Living apart from his own outspoken wife, Ickes disliked outspoken women, and he resented Eleanor's interference. She should, he believed, stick to her knitting.

Harry Hopkins, however, was receptive to her ideas. He added a Women's Division to FERA, appointing a young Mississippi widow, Ellen Woodward, to head the new division. Ellen had finished her husband's term as state legislator and become active in politics, working to bring relief programs to Mississippi. She and Eleanor began working together almost immediately. Initially putting several hundred women to work, Ellen found "women's work" for them—knitting and sewing clothes for the needy, canning food, tending to orphaned children. To support Ellen's efforts, Eleanor held a White House Conference on the Emergency Needs of Women, giving congressional women and leaders in women's organizations an opportunity to discuss the needs of impoverished women. With Ellen and Harry leading the discussions, the women talked of health care, the need for food, shelter, and education, and ways to employ women beyond the confines of women's work. Hopkins promised to give 300,000 women work assignments by the end of the year.

In April 1934 Eleanor held a second White House conference to help FERA's education specialist, Hilda Smith, bring educational programs to women. A former dean at Bryn Mawr College, Hilda had directed summer school programs for women workers and wanted to set up educational camps for women, a concept Eleanor endorsed. Calling a White House Conference on Camps for Unemployed Women, Eleanor provided the impetus Hilda needed, and FERA set up several "She She She Camps," as they were called, where jobless women lived free of charge, took courses, and received vocational training. Providing both educational and moral support, the camps helped women face their circumstances, but they did not provide work, as the CCC camps did. Eleanor wanted a series of women's work camps as well, and with Frances Perkins's help, she was able to initiate one, but only one, such camp—Camp Tera at Bear Mountain, New York. The idea ran too much against the grain of popular thought.

Despite a dearth of jobs, Eleanor believed women had as much right to work as men, and she abhorred NRA guidelines recommending lower wages for women. She did not agree, however, with the radical feminists who had formed a National Women's Party. Eleanor wanted laws to protect women from dangerous, unhealthy working conditions, while the National Women's Party believed the very laws Eleanor wanted would hold women back. The radical feminists believed women should have

the same opportunities as men, and they sought a constitutional amendment guaranteeing that. Eleanor, however, had fought to get women out
of sweatshops. Without protective laws, she believed, they could easily be
forced back into sweatshops, and she never supported the Equal Rights
Amendment.

She was, however, the force behind women's progress in the New Deal
era. Most successfully, she supported the women appointed to government
positions, facilitating their access to the White House, inviting them to
discuss their initiatives at her press conferences, writing about their programs in her columns. Although she met with opposition, Eleanor did not
let Washington forget the needs of women in distress.

PRIVATE LIVES

Family

As they had in Albany, Eleanor and Franklin lived separate private
lives. Eleanor got up around 7:00 A.M., did some exercises, and went
horseback riding in Rock Creek Park before breakfast. Franklin generally
ate breakfast in bed, reading newspapers and any reports awaiting his attention, before getting up around 10:00. Eleanor would say good morning
after his breakfast tray had been delivered. Frequently, she would have
left requests, notes, or newspaper articles in his bedside basket the night
before. During the day, they would go their separate ways, although they
often swam together in the afternoon, a pool having been built in the
White House with funds raised by the New York *Daily News.*

In her official role as first lady, Eleanor would hold teas in the late
afternoon. Franklin liked to serve drinks before dinner, inviting family,
friends, and guests. Rarely attending happy hour, Eleanor would join them
for dinner, where she and Franklin generally argued about politics. Guests
would find dinner with the Roosevelts lively and exciting. Franklin liked
to bait Eleanor, and she would dig in her heels to take a stand. One guest
wrote later that "no one who ever saw Eleanor . . . facing her husband and
holding his eye firmly, say to him, 'Franklin, I think you should . . .' Or
'Franklin surely you will not . . .' will ever forget the experience."[11] On
occasion, Eleanor found he had adopted her stand the next day.

As she had for years, Eleanor scrambled eggs for Franklin and his advisors on Sunday evenings. After dinner Eleanor and Franklin frequently
discussed political issues before parting for the evening. Franklin would
spend his evenings with friends and colleagues, sometimes working, often
relaxing or having a drink with Missy and her guests. Eleanor would

typically answer letters, write a column, or do paperwork until late into the evening, slipping into Franklin's room to fill his bedside basket with memos. She rarely slept more than four or five hours.

Although the press respected Eleanor and Franklin's privacy in a way that would not be true today, never, for instance, revealing the extent of FDR's disability, Eleanor worried about her children's lack of privacy. While Franklin Jr. and John were at school, away from the limelight, and James was settled in business, she worried about Anna and Elliott. Anna was in the midst of a nasty divorce, living at the White House with her two children, and having an affair with John Boettiger, a reporter she had met on Franklin's campaign train. Although Eleanor liked John and eventually Anna would marry him, the press took notice, and that distressed Eleanor. Eleanor felt closer to Anna than she did to any of her boys. Elliott, who had left school and married impulsively, also gave the press much to write about, as he was leaving his wife and baby for another impulsive marriage. Moving to rural Texas, where he hoped to "find himself," he had no job and did not want Eleanor's advice. Their relationship was tense.

Her brother Hall was still a heavy drinker, and she had few other relatives left. Aunt Bye, always one of Eleanor's strongest supporters, had died in 1931, and her Aunt Corinne died shortly before Franklin's inauguration. Aunt Edith, Teddy's widow, had never forgiven Eleanor for the nasty Teapot Dome campaign against Theodore Jr. Although Eleanor tried to be gracious to her cousin Alice, she was one of Eleanor's nastiest critics. Quick-witted and cruel, Alice was famous for her "Eleanor imitations." No one could hurt Eleanor quite the same way Alice did.

Friends

Eleanor, of course, had a separate set of friends from Franklin. Although Hick was her closest friend, she remained good friends with Esther Lape and Elizabeth Read, Tommy Thompson, Louis Howe, and Earl Miller. She also included Molly Dewson and Elinor Morgenthau among her friends. Although she still saw Nancy Cook and Marion Dickerman, their friendship was strained, as Nancy and Marion considered Hick too crude and unrefined for their taste. Sensing that they disliked her, Hick did not like to go to Val Kill, and Eleanor also began spending less time there. She still desired a retreat from the White House, however, and in 1935 she rented a third-floor walk-up apartment in Esther and Elizabeth's Greenwich Village brownstone. Although the White House was not as much of a prison as she had feared, she found the apartment a welcome relief, a place where she could spend time alone or entertain friends in private.

Tommy and Louis were a part of Eleanor's daily life. Sacrificing her marriage, Tommy had left her husband in New York and moved to Washington when Eleanor became first lady. She devoted most of her time to Eleanor, traveling with her, often working late into the evening, and acting as gatekeeper to those who sought access to the first lady. Both Eleanor and Franklin treated Tommy like a member of the family, and she frequently joined Eleanor in Greenwich Village. Louis Howe lived at the White House. Years of smoking had taken their toll on his health, and he rarely ventured beyond Washington. Increasingly, he would have to take to his bed.

Eleanor's friendship with Elinor Morgenthau had grown slowly over the years. She first met Elinor, a Hyde Park neighbor, when Franklin entered politics and met Elinor's husband, Henry. An active member of the Democratic Party, Henry Morgenthau was one of Franklin's earliest supporters, and he was now secretary of the treasury. Early in the twentieth century, however, anti-Semitism was rampant in New York society, and the Morgenthaus were the Roosevelts' first Jewish friends. Privately, Eleanor and Sara would exchange anti-Semitic remarks, perhaps speaking without even thinking. Their behavior was typical of the world they lived in. When Eleanor moved beyond New York society, however, she rejected society's anti-Semitic opinions just as she rejected their other self-important ideas. She and Elinor became friends as Elinor became active in the Women's Division of the Democratic Party, and they remained friends when Elinor left the Women's Division to become a traditional political wife. The two women frequently rode together in Rock Creek Park, and Elinor would visit Eleanor in New York, where they ate out and went to the theater.

Although Earl Miller was stuck in Albany, he remained a good friend. Visiting Eleanor at both the White House and her Greenwich Village apartment, he still looked out for her. When she refused Secret Service protection, he gave her a couple of guard dogs and taught her to shoot a gun. Although she adored the dogs, she kept the gun locked and unloaded in her glove compartment. The horse she rode in Rock Creek Park was also a gift from Earl. Over the years she often spent time with Earl and his ever-changing female companions, and occasionally they spent a weekend vacationing in upstate New York

In July, after four months in the White House, Eleanor took a vacation with Hick. Perhaps a bit naively, she hoped she could avoid reporters and travel as an ordinary tourist. Driving alone, they did travel unnoticed for much of the trip. In upstate New York, farmers happily showed Eleanor their farms. Although one farmer suggested she not identify herself in this politically conservative countryside, they did not receive any undue attention. After driving through Vermont and New Hampshire, they crossed the border into Canada, where they visited Quebec and drove around the Gaspé Peninsula. Taken with French-speaking Canada, Eleanor explored each of the small fishing villages on the Gaspé. One local priest asked if she was related to Teddy Roosevelt, but he seemed oblivious to the fact that her husband was president of the United States.

When they crossed the border into Maine, however, they found that word had gotten out. A parade of cheering residents and reporters greeted them. Neither Eleanor nor Hick was particularly happy with the attention, and they did their best to dodge the reporters. It was the first of several trips where Eleanor would find she could no longer travel in private. Leaving the reporters behind, Eleanor bought a local newspaper and read of potato prices and this year's potato crop, a technique she would use frequently to educate herself about local conditions. Driving through Aroostook County, where Maine's potato farmers lived, she stopped to discuss potato prices and local problems with the farmers, impressing both the local population and Hick. From Maine they went to Campobello.

Upon their return, Franklin drilled Eleanor about the conditions in Maine, on the Gaspé, and in upstate New York. Even on vacation, she served as his eyes and ears. She told him of the Gaspé fishermen, the kind of fish they caught, how they lived. She told him of Maine's potato farmers, what they wore, what they ate, what they charged for potatoes. Throughout his presidency Franklin would drill Eleanor on conditions wherever she traveled. With each trip she improved her ability to tune in on the items that would interest the president.

By the end of 1933 Eleanor had made her mark. Many applauded her efforts. People in distress adored her. Affluent conservatives detested her. Many, including some in Franklin's brain trust, thought she was a royal pain, a busybody who should mind her own business. She would not, however, stick to her knitting. She was about to become the most powerful woman in the United States.

NOTES

1. Quoted in Hickok, *Eleanor Roosevelt*, p. 107.
2. Hickok, Eleanor Roosevelt, p. 62.
3. Quoted in ibid., p. 83.
4. Quoted in Pottker, *Sara and Eleanor*, p. 122.
5. Edna P. Gurewitsch, *Kindred Souls: The Devoted Friendship of Eleanor Roosevelt and Dr. David Gurewitsch* (New York: A Plume Book, 2002), p. 170.
6. Hickok, *Eleanor Roosevelt*, pp. 95, 96.

7. Quoted in Beasley, Shulman, and Beasley, *Eleanor Roosevelt Encyclopedia*, p. 255.

8. Robert Cohen, *Dear Mrs. Roosevelt: Letters from Children of the Great Depression* (Chapel Hill: University of North Carolina Press, 2002), pp. 48, 47.

9. Quoted in Youngs, *Eleanor Roosevelt*, p. 190.

10. Quoted in Blanche Wiesen Cook, *Eleanor Roosevelt*, vol. II, *The Defining Years, 1933–1938* (New York: Viking Penguin, 1999), p. 37.

11. Quoted in Beasley, Shulman, and Beasley, *Eleanor Roosevelt Encyclopedia*, p. 529.

"For gosh sakes, here comes Mrs. Roosevelt!"

Cartoon appearing in The New Yorker *after Eleanor visited coal mines in West Virginia and Ohio. © The New Yorker Collection 1933 Robert Day from cartoonbank.com. All Rights Reserved.*

Eleanor Roosevelt at 14. She is about to leave for Allenswood. Courtesy of Franklin D. Roosevelt Library.

Eleanor, Franklin, and their family in Campobello in 1919. Back row: Franklin, Sara (his mother), and Eleanor. Front row: Elliott, Franklin Jr., John, Anna, and James. Courtesy of The Art Archive/Culver Pictures.

Eleanor on horseback in Yosemite National Park. When she was in the White House, Eleanor went riding each morning before breakfast. Courtesy of Franklin D. Roosevelt Library.

Eleanor and Franklin on the campaign train in 1936. Courtesy of the Denver Public Library, Western History Collection, Photo by Harry M. Rhoads, call number Rh-125.

Arthurdale residents show Eleanor the calf of a prizewinning cow during one of her many visits to the homestead. Courtesy of the Franklin D. Roosevelt Library.

Newspaper photo of Howard University students escorting Eleanor to the school's faculty club. Segregationists used this 1936 photograph to attack both Eleanor and Franklin's politics. Courtesy of the Library of Congress.

Eleanor talks with GIs on Bora-Bora Island during her South Pacific Tour. Courtesy of Franklin D. Roosevelt Library.

Eleanor tours the Japanese internment camp in Gila River, Arizona. Courtesy of Franklin D. Roosevelt Library.

Eleanor Roosevelt at the United Nations. Courtesy of the Franklin D. Roosevelt Library.

Chapter 5

ELEANOR'S POWER PEAKS
AND BEGINS TO WANE

From coal miners in Appalachia to migrant workers in the South-
west, from disabled veterans to discouraged youth, from marginalized
African Americans to women displaced from the workforce, Eleanor
believed every American should have a decent quality of life, including
not only a job but also health care, adequate housing, cultural opportunities, and education. She considered early New Deal programs a start, but
only a start, and she would work tirelessly to expand their coverage, using
whatever opportunities she could. The pathway to success, however, was
trickier than she cared to admit. Although the New Deal had gotten
off to a rapid start, the momentum of the first one hundred days would
not last.

Franklin did not have a sympathetic Congress. Conservative Republicans had held the reins of power in Washington for over a decade,
and the country had experienced unprecedented prosperity under their
reign. Throughout the 1920s the mood of the country was politically conservative. Those who did not benefit from the nation's prosperity were
hidden. Although the Depression changed the nation's mood dramatically, leading to Franklin's landslide election, conservative Republicans
still dominated Congress, and by 1934 he felt their opposition. Franklin
could not afford Eleanor's idealism. He would have to compromise, to
concentrate on what he could get through Congress. Eleanor, however,
remained firmly focused on what she believed the New Deal had yet to
accomplish. She would not be daunted by conservatives who criticized
her every move.

COAL MINERS, QUAKERS, AND ELEANOR ROOSEVELT
Scott's Run, West Virginia

Under the direction of Harry Hopkins, Hick was now investigating living conditions nationwide, traveling from one impoverished community to another, and she found Morgantown, West Virginia, to be "the worst place I'd ever seen." Miners, she wrote, were living in conditions most people would not consider fit for a pig.[1] Traveling to West Virginia in August 1933, Eleanor saw the conditions herself and found them heartbreaking. Hidden away in West Virginia's mountains, jobless coal miners and their families lived in some of the nation's most appalling communities. Many miners had not worked for years. Those who had gone on strike years earlier were banned as communists and had no hope of ever working again. Others worked only two or three days a week, as depleted mines ceased to be fully operational. Most owed their pay to the company store. Many were starving.

Close to town, a small polluted stream called Scott's Run trickled downhill beside a solitary dirt road. Families living in makeshift one-room shanties planted pitiful gardens in rocky, infertile soil and used the stream for drinking, washing, cooking, and waste removal. Coal dust was everywhere, blackening the landscape. Typhoid fever was ever reoccurring. As she visited the families, Eleanor was moved particularly by a small boy who clung dearly to his pet rabbit as his sister told her, "He thinks we are not going to eat it, but we are."[2] Eleanor would change Scott's Run forever.

Quaker relief workers, led by Clarence Pickett of the American Friends Service Committee, had been helping the miners for a while, providing soap, food, and other supplies. They sought to find new ways to employ the miners, an approach that Eleanor liked, and she joined forces with the Quakers, forming an alliance with Pickett that would last for years. She was soon contributing the money she earned from writing to the American Friends Service Committee. Returning to Washington, she told anyone who would listen of the shanties in Scott's Run, the lack of sanitation, the disease, and the young boy whose pet rabbit was to be eaten for supper, moving many of her White House guests to donate to the American Friends Service Committee. Relief workers, responding to the publicity, built outhouses for the miners, even as they risked being jailed for trespassing.

Eleanor, however, was not satisfied with makeshift remedies. She envisioned a new community with decent housing, health care, a school for the children, and jobs for the adults. When she told Franklin of the miners' living conditions, he, too, was moved and told her to get the families out of there by Christmas. Sharing Eleanor's belief in helping people to help themselves, Franklin supported her vision. With his approval, she found a way to build a new community under the homestead provision of the National Industrial Recovery Act (NIRA).

Arthurdale

When NIRA was in Congress, advocates for a back-to-the-land movement slipped a Subsistence Homestead Division into the bill, providing funds for resettlement communities under Harold Ickes's Department of the Interior. Although the funds were just what Eleanor needed, she did not go to Harold Ickes, approaching Harry Hopkins and Louis Howe instead. Louis responded enthusiastically, putting Clarence Pickett in charge of the project and assigning Eleanor to an oversight committee. Working with the American Friends Service Committee and the University of West Virginia, they bought "the old Arthur farm," some 15 miles from Scott's Run, and made plans to resettle 200 mining families. Arthurdale would be the first of several communities built under the Subsistence Homestead Division.

As miners from Scott's Run built foundations for their new homes, Louis Howe, in a burst of enthusiasm, ordered 50 prefabricated houses, hoping to resettle some families by Thanksgiving. The result was a fiasco. Designed for Cape Cod summer residents, the houses were flimsy and did not fit the foundations built for them. As workers refitted houses for their foundations, Eleanor argued that they were too flimsy for West Virginia's cold, rugged winters, and sturdier, insulated houses were built. Eleanor wanted the families to have indoor plumbing, a rarity in rural America, as well as electric lights and a refrigerator, unheard-of commodities in West Virginia's mountains. Transporting clean water became difficult in the rocky terrain. Costs skyrocketed.

Harold Ickes was horrified. Critics in Congress were outraged. Even before the costs were known, critics thought the project was a socialist or communist idea. Now the houses were to cost $10,000 apiece, an outrageous sum in 1933, giving critics ample ammunition. Eleanor, in particular, was singled out for criticism. She had overstepped her bounds as first lady. Ickes complained to Franklin, questioning the need to provide luxuries known only to the affluent, claiming that Arthurdale was becoming a model community for the wealthy, not a subsistence homestead. Although Franklin appeased Ickes, telling him Eleanor had no money sense, he made no effort to put a brake on her, and by June 1934 the houses were completed as she wished. Eleanor considered them a success despite the criticism.

After exhausting federal funding, Eleanor contributed her own earnings, asked her friends to donate, and recruited her most generous contributor, Wall Street financier Bernard Baruch. After visiting Arthurdale at Eleanor's invitation, Baruch would contribute considerable sums to the project. With both her own funds and those provided by Baruch, Eleanor built a school and hired a progressive educator to run it. The school was too progressive for West Virginia, however, and was not accredited initially, forcing a switch to a more traditional curriculum. Eleanor also raised funds to build and staff a small hospital and a clinic, the first medical facilities to be built in West Virginia's mountains.

Arthurdale was planned as a self-supporting community with farming and light industry. As each homesteader found employment, he was to purchase his new home. The University of West Virginia's Agricultural Extension Service set up a community farm, and some of the homesteaders raised chickens, selling the eggs, or harvested and sold potatoes, enabling them to purchase their homes as planned. Bringing industry to the community proved more difficult, however. Hoping to sell Appalachian crafts nationally, Eleanor hired Nancy Cook to set up a crafts center, also funded by Bernard Baruch, but like Val Kill, it was never profitable. Eleanor also tried to bring a company that manufactured postal equipment to Arthurdale, but as part of the U.S. Post Office, the move had to be approved by Congress and was defeated by those who opposed Arthurdale. Baruch helped to bring a subsidiary of General Electric to the community, but it was not profitable. Although the homesteaders found defense-related work during World War II, Arthurdale was never fully self-supporting.

Eleanor, however, would always consider Arthurdale a success. The miners were considerably better off, and that, she believed, was more significant than any cost overruns or any criticisms hurled at her or Arthurdale. By 1935, 50 homestead communities had been built throughout the United States. One, also located in West Virginia, was named Eleanor in her honor. Arthurdale, however, was Eleanor's pet project, the first and most luxurious of the homestead communities. She would continue to support Arthurdale, visiting frequently, until 1947, when the government sold it to a private investor.

ELEANOR AND AFRICAN AMERICANS

As pleased as she was with Arthurdale, Eleanor found she could not include all of the miners. Many were immigrants or African Americans, and

Arthurdale admitted only native-born white Americans. She had wanted to include both African American and foreign-born miners, but neither the homesteaders nor the government would accept an integrated community. Segregation was too firmly ingrained in the American psyche.

Hard as the Depression was on white America, it was worse for blacks, who faced virulent racism as well as worsening economic conditions. In the 1930s racism was not only pervasive, it was generally accepted. In the American South, it was set into law. Segregated into their own ghettos, southern blacks were denied basic rights. They could not vote, and their children could not attend school outside of the ghetto. Beyond the ghetto, signs reading "whites only" were ever present. Blacks could not eat in white restaurants or drink from the same water fountains as whites. Holding only menial jobs, they entered back doors as maids, janitors, or delivery "boys." Any show of disrespect to a white, real or imagined, could be punished by lynching. Although not legally segregated in the North, northern blacks could be denied both jobs and housing on the basis of race.

Excluded from relief and work projects, blacks received no help from early New Deal programs. Racism was as accepted in Washington as it was in the rest of the country. Franklin's press secretary, Steve Early, a native of Virginia, was openly racist, as were others in the administration. Politicians who were not racist were silent. Liberal Democrats needed the support of southern colleagues, as did Franklin. As sympathetic as he may have been to the plight of African Americans, Franklin could not afford to offend southern Democrats, and he too was silent. Eleanor, however, did not shy away from racial issues.

Crowded into Washington's alleyways, some 12,000 African Americans lived in squalor in the nation's capitol, and Eleanor had mingled with alley slum residents, primarily black but some white, soon after Franklin's inauguration. Although she had persuaded officials to clean up the worst health threats, she wanted new housing for alley residents, an unpopular twist on slum removal. Denouncing slumlords, she spoke at a National Public Housing Convention in January, and, joining forces with Washington activists, she tried to win Franklin's support for an alley housing bill. Once race entered the picture, however, the issue was too inflammatory, and Franklin remained silent on the bill, allowing Congress to ignore it. Washington's activists did not let it die, however, and in June 1934 Congress passed the Alley Housing Bill, assigning funding to Harold Ickes's Public Works Administration (PWA). Not only was Eleanor delighted, but she found an unexpected ally in Ickes, who supported her on racial issues. He gave her an advisory position overseeing alley housing.

Although Franklin preferred to skirt racial issues, Eleanor did not hesitate to raise them. She encouraged him, for instance, to integrate Warm Springs, asking about physical therapy for African Americans, but Franklin would not antagonize the white residents. Acknowledging local customs, he excluded African Americans from Warm Springs while supporting a polio clinic for African Americans at Tuskegee Institute. When Franklin built a new school for local white children, Eleanor, having long since antagonized Warm Springs's white residents, worked to get one for black children as well, and eventually the Eleanor Roosevelt School was built for blacks. Years after she left the White House, Warm Springs's residents would say that Eleanor ruined every maid in the South. Rumors abounded that she encouraged black maids to form "Eleanor Clubs" and unionize, although no historical evidence suggests that such clubs existed.

In January 1934 Eleanor, along with Clarence Pickett, broke racial taboos, inviting Walter White, director of the National Association for the Advancement of Colored People (NAACP), black businessmen, and leaders from black colleges to meet at the White House. Never before had blacks been invited to the White House. With Eleanor encouraging them to express their opinions, the men talked of black unemployment, the barriers blacks faced, and their exclusion from New Deal programs. Promising to do what she could for African Americans, Eleanor opened the lines of communication, leading Walter White, in particular, to feel he had a friend in the White House. She would work closely with White, making every effort to give him access to Franklin's ear.

Although she could not change policy, Eleanor did what she could to bring blacks into New Deal programs, attacking each problem individually. Eventually, she got a homestead community built for African Americans excluded from Arthurdale. When a young black girl wrote that Camp Tera, the only CCC work camp for women, "didn't want colored girls," Eleanor wrote to the camp's director, asking if he excluded African Americans, and received assurance that Camp Tera now had 10 "colored girls." Women's educational camps, which Eleanor helped to create, also included blacks. One, an Arkansas camp for sharecroppers' daughters, was located on a black college campus. Although Harold Ickes worked with Eleanor on racial issues and his PWA work programs included racial quotas, the programs were administered locally, enabling southerners to disregard the quotas. Working with Harry Hopkins and his assistant, Aubrey Williams, Eleanor tried to bring blacks into federally administered FERA programs. In May 1934 she spoke at a national conference on the education of Negroes sponsored by the U.S. Office of Education and called for equal educational opportunities.

In an effort to get a black woman appointed to a federal position, Eleanor approached Frances Perkins, suggesting she appoint an African American to the Department of Labor's Women's Bureau, but Perkins, like Franklin, preferred to skirt the race issue. Eleanor turned to Harry Hopkins, and that led to the appointment of Mary McLeod Bethune in June 1935 to the newly formed National Youth Administration. Born to former slaves, the 15th of 17 children, Mary McLeod Bethune was a prominent black educator, fiercely proud of her African American heritage and dedicated to the advancement of her race. She and Eleanor first met in 1927, when Mary was president of the National Association of Colored Women. Once Mary joined the administration, she and Eleanor became close allies. Working for the welfare of African Americans, they often appeared together, traveling to black communities and posing for photographs. Eleanor learned more about African American life from Mary than she could have ever learned on her own. Raised as she was by New York's white Protestant elite, Eleanor was painfully aware that she herself had some latent prejudice from her childhood. As her friendship with Mary grew, however, she kissed Mary's check without thinking and realized "she had at last overcome the racial prejudice within herself."[3]

By far the worst offense against African Americans was lynching, a cruel form of mob violence that had been an integral part of southern life since the end of the Civil War. Throughout the South white mobs used lynching—killing without benefit of trial—as a way to keep blacks from asserting themselves. Hangings were public events, sometimes with families bringing their young children to witness the scene. Local and state police looked the other way. Walter White, a light-skinned man with African American ancestors, had infiltrated Ku Klux Klan meetings and knew well that southern officials would not attempt to stop a lynch mob. In 1933, shortly after Franklin's inauguration, White led the NAACP in a campaign for a federal antilynching law. Only if federal officials stepped in, he believed, could lynching be stopped. In January 1934 two Democratic senators, Edward Costigan and Robert Wagner, introduced the NAACP's antilynching bill.

Eleanor, of course, supported the bill, but Franklin feared the political consequences. Southerners still held positions of power in Congress, and they would not take kindly to his supporting an antilynching bill. Although in December Franklin had spoken out against lynching, condemning it as murder, he had done so only after two white convicts, released from prison in southern California, had been lynched. He did not identify lynching as a racial issue.

White believed the Costigan-Wagner bill would pass if only the president would speak in favor of it, but when he tried to see the president, Franklin was always too busy. White did not give up, sending daily requests to Eleanor, and she faithfully passed them along, urging Franklin to meet with Walter. Sara, who supported Eleanor, also urged Franklin to see White. Eventually Eleanor wore him down, and he met with White in May. Although sympathetic, he told White frankly, "Southerners by reason of seniority rule in Congress. . . . If I come out for the anti-lynching bill now, they will block every bill I ask Congress to pass. . . . I just can't take that risk."[4] Continuing to support an antilynching bill, Eleanor asked Franklin, after a particularly brutal lynching, if she could speak at an antilynching rally in Alabama, but he was reluctant even to let her speak out. She did not attend the rally, and the Costigan-Wagner bill never came to a vote in Congress. Two later attempts to introduce an antilynching bill also failed.

Challenging yet another racial taboo, Eleanor agreed in 1938 to speak before the newly formed Southern Conference for Human Welfare (SCHW), a biracial group dedicated to improving economic and racial conditions in the South. The SCHW held its first convention in Alabama, a state with strict segregation laws. Police, having heard of the integrated meetings, surrounded the building and filtered through the hall as thousands of blacks and whites showed up to hear the first lady speak. Arriving late with Mary Bethune, Eleanor slipped into a seat in the black section, immediately catching the eye of the police, and was asked to move. Announcing that she did not want to be segregated, Eleanor picked up her chair, put it in the aisle, and sat midway between the black and white sections, eliciting an enthusiastic round of applause. For four days she carried a small folding chair from meeting to meeting, sitting midway between black and white sections. Police trailed behind her but dared not arrest her. Eleanor would continue to support the SCHW for the rest of its existence.

Chipping away at prejudice, Eleanor desegregated the White House, lunching on the outdoor patio with Walter White and inviting Mary Bethune for dinner. After visiting girls at a Washington reform school, most of whom were black, she held a picnic for them on the White House lawn. She invited black singers, including the Hampton Boys' Choir and the contralto Marian Anderson, to perform at the White House. Most famously, in 1939, when the Daughters of the American Revolution (DAR) denied Marian Anderson permission to sing at Constitution Hall, Eleanor resigned from the DAR, writing of the resignation in her column and, working behind the scenes with Harold Ickes, arranged for Anderson's monumental concert in front of the Lincoln Memorial.

Eleanor won over the black community, and Franklin was happy to let her do it. While gaining African American support through her, he could remain silent and avoid alienating white southerners. She offended many, however, including some in Franklin's administration who feared she would hurt the president. Steve Early, for instance, was outraged at her support of an antilynching bill. Throughout the South people were aghast at photos of Eleanor with African Americans. A woman ahead of her time, Eleanor was one of the nation's earliest civil rights workers.

A SOARING PERSONAL CAREER

Although she was writing for the *Woman's Home Companion* and the *Women's Democratic News*, Eleanor gave up radio talk shows when she moved to the White House. Like her role editing *Babies—Just Babies*, her radio interviews were considered unseemly by some. After being criticized for using her position to earn money, Eleanor announced she would not make any more radio appearances, but that hiatus did not last long. In 1934, when she was asked to do a series of weekly broadcasts, she was quick to sign a contract. Receiving $500 per minute, she did a series of weekly commentaries on the daily news in 1934 and another series on education in 1935, announcing to the public that her salary would be paid directly to the American Friends Service Committee. A good percentage of her radio income went to Arthurdale. Although most of her broadcasts were not controversial, she did not shy away from discussing women's issues, world peace, or problems facing the nation's youth.

While continuing to write articles for popular magazines, Eleanor began one of her most popular ventures, the syndicated column "My Day," in January 1936. After sending daily accounts of her activities to Hick for two years, she began, at Hick's suggestion, to write of her daily life for a newspaper audience. Forever her rival, Cousin Alice also started a daily column in 1936. Witty and cynical, Alice's column was clever but did not have the popular appeal of Eleanor's, and it was short-lived. Taking the approach of a modern-day blog, Eleanor wrote of her grandchildren, birthday parties, travels to New Deal facilities, visits from foreign dignitaries—whatever her day brought. Generally appearing on the women's page, the column appealed to women throughout the nation, and Eleanor immediately received thousands of letters from housewives who could identify with her day, although they lived in an entirely different world.

Critics were not always kind, parodying her writing style, criticizing her taste in theater, or claiming the daily minutia could put one to sleep, but readers liked the column. Increasing newspaper sales, it lasted for 26 years.

While avoiding questionable details, Eleanor used the column to support New Deal programs, tell people what she thought, or respond to criticism of her husband's policies. Although she denied publicly that he ever tried to tell her what to write, she would occasionally raise a topic at Franklin's request, giving him an opportunity to test the public reaction. Whether she was at the White House or traveling, Eleanor wrote the column every day, six days a week, often jotting it down or dictating it while on the train or in a hotel room. With Tommy generally typing the column, she never missed a deadline.

Hiring an agent to handle her bookings, Eleanor also went on paid speaking tours, traveling for two weeks at a time and appearing at colleges and universities, churches, and community centers. In 1937 she published her first autobiographical book, *This Is My Story*, an account of her childhood and youth. She sold serial rights to the *Ladies' Home Journal*, and both the book and the serialization were a great success. With her income from the book as well as her other writing, her radio appearances, and her speaking tours, Eleanor's income soared to over $75,000, a tremendous sum in 1937 and more than the president himself made. Most of it went to charity.

THE SECOND NEW DEAL

Although the New Deal began with a flurry of programs to relieve poverty and put the nation back to work, the initial impact of those programs slowed down in 1934, leaving many still jobless and hungry, untouched by relief or work programs. Neither the National Recovery Administration (NRA) nor the Agricultural Adjustment Act (AAA) lived up to their promise, perhaps helping large enterprises but doing little for local businesses or family farms. Workers and businessmen alike were disillusioned with NRA guidelines, finding them ineffective. Outspoken liberals criticized Roosevelt for not doing enough. Radical conservatives accused him of communism, of creating cooperative programs that could only be communist. In a climate of continuing discontent, Democrats faced midterm elections.

Defending New Deal programs and campaigning for her female friends, Eleanor played an active role in the 1934 elections. Isabella Greenway, a longtime friend and Bob Ferguson's widow, was Arizona's first congresswoman and a staunch supporter of Arthurdale, and Eleanor, quite naturally, campaigned for Isabella, who was reelected. She campaigned particularly, however, for Caroline O'Day, who ran for Congress from New York and won easily. The elections were a Democratic victory, increasing the number of Democrats in Congress and encouraging Franklin to proceed with the

New Deal. In 1935 he initiated another round of legislation, beginning the Second New Deal and greatly expanding his initial efforts.

Works Progress Administration

In May 1935 Franklin established the Works Progress Administration (WPA), an ambitious program to create federally funded work projects building dams, bridges, airports, or electric power plants. The program replaced the Civil Works Administration (CWA) and Federal Emergency Relief Administration (FERA) programs, and Franklin appointed Harry Hopkins director of WPA. As always, Eleanor, who was at the peak of her power, found Hopkins receptive to her suggestions, and her voice was heard as he set up WPA. Eleanor encouraged him to include work for women, young people, and blacks as well as jobs for unemployed artists, writers, and musicians.

Putting Ellen Woodward in charge, Hopkins created a Women's Division within WPA, just as he had for FERA, and Eleanor continued to work with Ellen. As she had for CWA, Ellen put women to work canning, sewing, and caring for children, but Eleanor sought to provide professional and white-collar jobs for women as well. Working with Eleanor, Ellen created library, teaching, and nursing jobs for women. Those in libraries repaired and catalogued books and did research, while public health nurses inoculated children for smallpox and diphtheria, educated the public about tuberculosis, and ran maternity clinics. When WPA was in full swing, the Women's Division employed some 400,000 women, but the division never employed all of the women seeking work. Like other New Deal agencies, WPA gave preference to men.

With their focus on married men, early New Deal programs did little to help the nation's youth, but young people were also suffering. Kids from poverty-stricken families had little hope of either finding a job or getting an education. Afraid an entire generation would be lost to despair, Eleanor worried about young people. She feared their discontent would erupt into violence, and when the National Youth Administration (NYA) was formed as a part of WPA, it became another of Eleanor's pet projects.

With Hopkins's former assistant, Aubrey Williams, as its director, the NYA helped struggling students to stay in school, setting up part-time work in high schools and colleges, and assisted kids who had quit school, providing job training and work programs. Having worked well with Williams at FERA, often turning to him for help in bringing blacks into the New Deal, Eleanor became closely involved with NYA, asking Williams for reports on each of its project, providing him with access to

Franklin's ear, visiting work sites, and offering her advice. After Eleanor sought to include a black woman in the administration, Mary McLeod Bethune joined NYA, and in 1936 Williams put her in charge of African American activities, naming her director of the Division of Negro Affairs in 1939. With Bethune in a key position, the NYA provided more opportunities for African Americans than any other New Deal agency. Although Franklin referred to NYA as "the missus organization,"[5] it was one of the more successful New Deal agencies, providing help to over a million young people, and in 1939 it became an independent agency, separate from WPA.

Putting artists, performers, and writers to work, Hopkins expanded WPA to include the arts, introducing Eleanor to Hallie Flanagan, director of Vassar College's Experimental Theatre. Flanagan was known for cutting-edge, controversial productions, often with an emphasis on social problems, and Eleanor embraced her ideas. With Eleanor's support, Hopkins created the Federal Theatre Project, putting Flanagan in charge, and Flanagan created a wide variety of theater—ethnic theater, revivals, experimental theater, children's theater. The Negro Theatre in Harlem, for instance, produced Countee Cullen and Arna Bontemps's *St. Louis Woman*, while vaudeville companies toured the country. Local theater groups performed outdoors. Other federal projects employed artists and intellectuals. Historians found jobs with the Federal Writers Project, writing local histories or interviewing former slaves, while the Federal Arts Project had artists painting murals on public buildings. Musicians found work with WPA orchestras. Congress, however, found Flanagan's productions too controversial, touching as they often did on Depression-era hardships, and disapproved of government's involvement in the arts. Although Eleanor fought for the program, Congress eliminated the Federal Theatre Project in 1939 and reduced funding for the others.

Social Security

While encompassing many segments of the American population, WPA programs did not help those who could not work—the elderly poor, the disabled, the children of the nation's poor. Often destitute and hungry, they were left to fend for themselves, to seek help from family or church charities. Responding, in part, to the criticisms of a Florida physician, Francis Townsend, who publicized the plight of the impoverished elderly, eliciting considerable sympathy from the public, Franklin submitted the Social Security Act to Congress in January 1935, perhaps the most significant act of the New Deal. With federally funded pensions, Social Security would provide a safety net for the elderly. It would also provide unemployment insurance for those who lost their jobs, disability insurance for those who were injured or handicapped, and aid for dependent children.

Asking Harry Hopkins to study plans in Europe, Franklin had considered social security long before Townsend's publicity campaign, and Eleanor advocated social security in her radio appearances. Eleanor, along with Harry, hoped for a comprehensive plan that would cover all Americans and include medical insurance. Nodding to the medical profession, Franklin omitted medical insurance early on, but he too envisioned social security for everyone, black and white, male and female. Congress resisted vehemently, however, and Secretary of the Treasury Henry Morgenthau did not support coverage of "every transient or casual laborer . . . every domestic servant . . . and the . . . shifting class of agricultural workers."[6] Throughout the spring the bill's passage was in doubt. When it did pass in August, surprising Eleanor and uplifting her spirits, it excluded agricultural and domestic workers, effectively eliminating coverage for southern blacks, migrant workers, and most women. It also excluded people working for nonprofit organizations, such as hospitals and charities, and government workers, including teachers. Although Eleanor welcomed the act's passage as a victory, she was also disappointed. For years she would work with the Social Security board, hoping to bring universal coverage and medical insurance.

Although Social Security would transform American society, creating a safety net where none had existed, and WPA put some eight and a half million people to work, making it extremely popular, not everyone was happy. Conservatives charged Franklin with overstepping his authority. Even as the second wave of New Deal legislation was underway, the New Deal had a major setback. In two separate cases the Supreme Court ruled the National Industrial Recovery Act and the Agricultural Adjustment Act unconstitutional, declaring that they overstepped federal authority. The decisions struck at the very foundations of the New Deal. Although Eleanor had had her reservations about both acts, she knew the Supreme Court now posed a major challenge. It was a challenge Franklin would not handle well.

1936, A PIVOTAL YEAR

Although 1936 began with her first "My Day" column, gave her time to write *This Is My Story*, and ended with Franklin's reelection, it was a difficult year for Eleanor. Her friend, mentor, and strongest ally, Louis Howe, passed away in April. Years of chain-smoking had destroyed his health, and he had been bedridden for much of 1935. Louis had been instrumental in both her life and Franklin's, and Eleanor mourned his passing.

After Louis died, the dynamics of the White House changed entirely. Only Louis had been a friend to both Eleanor and Franklin, and he kept them united. Only Louis and Eleanor dared to tell Franklin exactly what they thought of an idea. Only Louis could hold Eleanor's detractors at bay. With Louis at her side, Eleanor was a formidable force. In his absence those who resented Eleanor's "meddling" saw an opportunity to "get the pants off Eleanor and onto Franklin."[7] As the brain trust took over, she was shut out of discussions. No one sought her opinion. She and Franklin became more distant, unable to bridge the gap when they disagreed. Their political alliance was slipping.

The 1936 campaign was particularly difficult. As early as February 1935, Eleanor and Molly Dewson had considered strategies to help re-elect Franklin, but Franklin's advisors did not want her help. Considering Eleanor a liability, they sought instead to silence her, telling Franklin to keep Eleanor in the background. They did not want her writing on politi-cal topics, talking on the radio, or going on speaking tours. If she rode the campaign train, she was to play the role of adoring wife standing silently by her husband's side, a role she detested. When Molly asked her to speak at the national convention's breakfast for Democratic women, she de-clined because Franklin's advisors did not want her at the convention. She listened at home on the radio.

Although Eleanor's protégé, Molly Dewson, , had been a favorite for vice-chair of the Democratic National Committee, she did not receive the appointment. When the women's committee drew up its platform, they were ignored, just as the women's platform committee had been ig-nored in 1924. Excluding Democratic women from their meetings, the Democratic men paid little attention to the women's committee, a group that considered Eleanor its acknowledged leader. Yet the women were not idle. Capitalizing on the popularity of Social Security and WPA, they designed a series of "rainbow flyers" to promote New Deal programs, using a different color of the rainbow for each program flyer. Distributed largely by a huge grassroots women's organization, the rainbow flyers became the party's primary campaign literature.

Joining the convention at the end, Eleanor heard Franklin's acceptance speech. Attacking the "tyranny" of "economic royalists" at home and al-luding to a growing military crisis abroad, he brought the hall to cheers as he told his audience, "This generation of Americans has a rendezvous with destiny. . . ." Wherever he went, pledging to fulfill the promise of the New Deal, Franklin met with cheering crowds. Although the nation had yet to see economic prosperity, working people believed in the New Deal, and they supported Roosevelt.

Confident he would win, Franklin went to Campobello in August, leaving the campaign trail to take a vacation. Although early polls suggested the Republican candidate, Alf Landon, might be ahead, he did not have Franklin's charisma, and Franklin did not feel threatened. Eleanor, however, was dismayed. She felt the campaign was in disarray. While the women's committee distributed rainbow flyers, the overall campaign seemed to lack coordination and leadership. Had Louis been in charge, Franklin never would have taken a vacation. Becoming agitated and upset, she sent a memo to Franklin's advisors asking about the details Howe would have handled. She wanted to know who was in charge of speakers, publicity, and answering Landon's charges. Although James Farley sent a reassuring reply, her mood was only partially relieved.

With time on her hands, Eleanor began writing *This Is My Story*, devoting much of her energy to the manuscript, but she did not have enough to do. Activity had always been her antidote to depression. In September she became ill, overcome with undefined aches and pains. Feeling too sick to get out of bed, she alarmed both Franklin and her closest friends. Having never known Eleanor to be sick, Franklin canceled his plans, including a visit to see Sara on her 83rd birthday, and went to Eleanor. For the moment the gulf between them lessened, and Franklin agreed she should take part in the campaign, albeit in a subdued role. Her spirits lifting a bit, she directed the New York state campaign behind the scenes and joined Franklin on the campaign trail, making speeches at some major events.

With Eleanor's advocacy of African American rights, race became a major factor in the election. As anticipated by Franklin's brain trust, southern racists found Eleanor an easy target. Using newspaper photos of Eleanor accepting flowers from a five-year-old black girl or being escorted by two black students at Howard University, critics claimed the Roosevelt administration was devoted to a "mulatto America." Offending Democrats and Republicans alike, their attacks had little impact. With Eleanor having won the favor of black America, Democrats courted the African American vote, asking a black Congressman to speak at the convention, seating a black woman as a delegate, and including black reporters in the press box. Black voters responded and in 1936 switched their allegiance from the party of Abraham Lincoln to the Democratic Party, voting for Franklin Delano Roosevelt.

With the largest margin in American history, Franklin won the election, carrying every state except two, Vermont and Maine. Nationwide, Democrats were elected to Congress, creating a 75 percent majority.

Eleanor believed Franklin could now fulfill the promise of the New Deal. Once she was free to resume her schedule, she booked a four-week speaking tour and, with renewed energy, began touring the Midwest, promoting an expanded Social Security program.

PERSONAL UPHEAVALS

When away from the White House, Eleanor would escape to her Greenwich Village apartment or Val Kill. A pool had been built at Val Kill, and she liked to gather her family, especially the grandchildren, around the pool, sometimes inviting Earl and his current girlfriend. When Franklin was in town, she entertained visiting dignitaries at outdoor barbecues, famously serving hotdogs to British royalty. Believing the yard was as much theirs as Eleanor's, Marion and Nancy did not appreciate the constant traffic. They felt their space was being encroached on, and in 1936 Eleanor and Nancy decided to close Val Kill Industries, a venture that had never been profitable, and turn the building into a separate cottage. With Nancy and Marion living in the original cottage, Eleanor had the factory remodeled as a residence for her and Tommy. Increasingly Tommy was her closest companion.

Although Eleanor settled comfortably into the new cottage, the move created tension and hurt feelings. Nancy felt Eleanor had mandated the factory closing. Marion, who kept Eleanor's name on the Todhunter letterhead, claimed the name was a liability, since the school's students came from Republican families. Both women felt they were responsible for Eleanor's rise in the Democratic Party and should have been acknowledged. When they served drinks to Eleanor's alcoholic brother, she became irate. All three quarreled over who had put how much money into Val Kill. The depth of their feelings did not come out, however, until 1938, when Eleanor and Nancy had a fight that severed their friendship forever. Although Marion wasn't there and felt she was not a part of the fight, she too was excluded from Eleanor's friendship. Franklin remained friends with the two women, forcing Eleanor to be civil, but they never again spoke more than civility required.

Excluded in 1936 from Franklin's political life, Eleanor tried turning to Hick but found her distant. Early in their friendship, their careers and personal lives had intertwined as Hick shared her FERA reports with Eleanor, encouraging her to visit Scott's Run. In March 1934 Eleanor had accompanied Hick to Puerto Rico on a FERA trip, discovering vile slums and convincing Franklin to get them cleaned up. That summer she and Hick had vacationed in Yosemite National Park, traveling by horseback to the backcountry, a new and not completely happy experience for Hick. As Eleanor became involved in new activities, however, she had less and less time for Hick, even when Hick was staying at the White House. Hick began to miss her life as a reporter and to resent the fact that she had given it up. Accusations began to slip into their letters, followed by letters of apology. When Hick decided to leave FERA, Eleanor found her a job publicizing the New York World's Fair, but in 1936, when Eleanor had time on her hands, Hick had moved on, forming a new social life with new friends.

Anna was now married to John Boettiger and living in Seattle, where John was publisher of a Hearst publication, the *Seattle Post-Intelligencer*, and Anna was associate editor of the women's section. Initially one of Franklin's supporters, William Randolph Hearst had turned against Roosevelt and actively campaigned against him in 1936. Neither Eleanor nor Franklin were happy about his employing Anna and John, wooing them to move west with promises of high pay. Hearst also hired Elliott to manage his radio stations in Texas, which was equally upsetting. Linking the family to yet another Roosevelt opponent, Franklin Jr. announced his engagement to Ethel du Pont and married her in 1937. Like Hearst, the du Ponts supported Franklin's worst critics.

Louis Howe's death had left a void in Franklin's life as well as Eleanor's, and Franklin considered hiring their son James to replace him, an idea that Eleanor opposed, angering both Franklin and James. Although James had always been an active campaigner, often supporting his father as he walked across a stage, James did not have a political career, and that, Eleanor believed, would make the appointment suspect. She feared charges of nepotism. When Franklin's personal aide died, however, he hired James to be both his secretary and his personal assistant. James moved into the White House with his wife, Betsey. As Eleanor anticipated, both the press and Congress cried foul at the appointment, while James felt his mother doubted his ability. Working closely with his father, James shut Eleanor out of the loop, denying her access to Franklin's bedside basket.

Lively and charming, Betsey immediately took to life in the White House, entertaining Franklin and becoming one of his favorites. Eleanor detested her presence. Assuming the role of hostess, Betsey began to look at dinner menus and rearrange Eleanor's seating arrangements at the dinner table. While courting Franklin's favor, she virtually ignored Eleanor. Tensions arose not only between Eleanor and her daughter-in-law, but also between Betsey and her husband. Three years later, when James divorced, he blamed Eleanor for the rising tension in his marriage. After working for his father for a year, James developed bleeding ulcers in 1938 and resigned to take care of his health.

A NEW TERM, A NEW DIRECTION

Early in 1937 Eleanor looked forward to the months ahead. She had finished *This Is My Story*, and its financial success was assured. In his inaugural address Franklin had described "one-third of a nation ill-housed, ill-clad, and ill-nourished" and pledged to "paint out" that picture. She anticipated an exciting new round of New Deal legislation and began to campaign for expanded Social Security coverage.

Franklin, however, did not move to expand the New Deal. Catching both Eleanor and his advisors off guard, he turned his attention instead to the Supreme Court. Stung by the court's striking down the NIRA and the AAA, he sought a way to change the makeup of the court and make it less conservative. Without a word to his advisors, he and Attorney General Homer Cummings devised a scheme to increase the number of justices on the Supreme Court. Arguing that the constitution did not require a specific number, Cummings believed Franklin could appoint 6 new justices, one for each of the justices over 70 years of age, increasing the total from 9 to 15. Embracing the idea, Franklin introduced the Judicial Reform Act, astounding Congress, the Supreme Court, and his advisors. It was a political blunder Eleanor could not understand.

Democrats and Republicans alike opposed the act. Even Democrats who supported the New Deal recognized it as a power play, an attempt to pack the court with justices more sympathetic to Franklin's policies. Congress dissolved into bitter controversy. The chief justice issued a statement defending the Supreme Court. After weeks of discord, the act was defeated. Distressed by her inability to influence policy, Eleanor firmly believed Louis Howe would never have allowed Franklin to proceed with the Judicial Reform Act. Although eventually Franklin would replace retiring justices, changing the court's political makeup, his court-packing scheme did serious damage to his popularity.

With judicial reform taking the administration's attention, the New Deal began to lose its momentum. The economy began to slow down and slip backwards. A group of conservative Democrats, Republicans, and "Eleanor haters" formed an anti-Roosevelt, anti-New Deal coalition. Despite some vigorous campaigning on Franklin's part, the 1938 midterm elections increased the number of Republicans in Congress, a first since FDR had become president, and the new, more conservative Congress began to cut New Deal funding.

Eleanor, of course, was distressed at the funding cuts, but the New Deal was soon to be eclipsed by international events. Her thoughts extended beyond the nation's shores. Spain was in the midst of a civil war. Italy had invaded Ethiopia. England sought to appease the German chancellor, Adolf Hitler. Increasingly, Franklin's attention would turn abroad. Although Franklin had never sought Eleanor's opinion on foreign policy as he did on domestic issues, she would not remain silent or inactive as the world erupted in turmoil.

NOTES

1. Quoted in Cook, *Eleanor Roosevelt*, vol. II, p. 130.

2. Eleanor Roosevelt, *This I Remember* (New York: Harper & Brothers,1949; repr., Westport, CT: Greenwood Press, 1975), p. 127.

3. Lash, *Eleanor and Franklin*, p. 682.

4. Quoted in ibid., p. 673.

5. Quoted in Beasley, Shulman, and Beasley, *Eleanor Roosevelt Encyclopedia*, p. 584.

6. Quoted in Cook, *Eleanor Roosevelt*, vol. II, p. 248.

7. Quoted in Sarah J. Purcell and L. Edward Purcell, *Eleanor Roosevelt* (Indianapolis, IN: Alpha, a Pearson Education Co., 2002), p. 138.

Chapter 6

THE APPROACHING WAR

In March 1933, the same month Franklin Roosevelt became president of the United States, Adolf Hitler took control in Germany. America was looking inward and took little notice. Hungry, jobless, desperate Americans were struggling to survive. Still reeling from World War I, the nation did not want to become entangled in European affairs. Even as Italy and Germany encroached on other nations and Japan moved into China, threatening U.S. islands in the Pacific, Americans clung to a policy of isolation, a belief that if America could only remain neutral, the oceans would provide natural protection. Although Franklin would face a growing threat from abroad, he would have to tread lightly, as he could not afford to antagonize the nation's isolationists.

Increasingly, as he turned his attention overseas, Franklin would have to turn away from the projects Eleanor loved—the Works Progress Administration (WPA), the National Youth Administration (NYA), the new Social Security program—and her influence with the administration would decline. Even as she was shut out of the decision-making process, however, Eleanor struggled with issues from abroad. As she came to terms with her own feelings—her belief in pacifism, her compassion for victims, her inability to remain neutral—she would at times find herself at odds with Franklin's policies.

ELEANOR AS PEACE WORKER

Along with her other reform activities, Eleanor was an active member of the women's peace movement in the 1920s. Joining the Women's

International League for Peace and Freedom, an organization formed by one of her mentors, Jane Addams, and the National Conference on the Cause and Cure of War, formed by Carrie Chapman Catt, Eleanor spoke at peace rallies, hosted rallies at Hyde Park, and frequently wrote on war and peace. Struggling to find a way to avoid the devastation of war, she was an early supporter of the ill-fated League of Nations and U.S. membership in the World Court. After she and Esther Lape helped to organize the Bok Peace Prize in 1923, they went on to form the American Foundation, an organization dedicated to advocating U.S. membership in the Court. With Esther as its chair and Eleanor as its most prominent spokesperson, the Foundation petitioned Congress to vote for membership in the World Court, although with little success.

Continuing to support the World Court as first lady, Eleanor advocated peace efforts in her press conferences and during her speaking tours. She invited Carrie Chapman Catt, Esther Lape, and other peace advocates to the White House, enabling them to talk with Franklin, and he agreed to her warming up the subject of the World Court, although he had renounced the Court in 1932, a move to get the Democratic nomination. Eleanor promoted World Court membership in press conferences and radio talks, and in 1935, with a nod from Franklin, the issue came to a vote in Congress, eliciting immediate and bitter conflict.

Isolationists hated the idea, believing membership in the World Court would bring America into war, while Eleanor believed it was the only way to avoid war. In a widely publicized speech, "Because the War Idea Is Obsolete," she promoted the World Court as the only way to resolve conflicts abroad. Appealing to the nation's women, she asked them to remember World War I and let Congress know how they felt. Women by the thousands sent telegrams supporting the bill, while Eleanor's most vicious opponents, hating her ideas, attacked Eleanor personally. Staying out of the fray, Franklin watched from the sidelines and did not speak out for the bill. It was defeated by seven votes, prompting Harold Ickes to claim Eleanor should have remained out of the picture. Had she minded "her own business," as he thought she should, the Democrats would never have raised the issue, which could only hurt Franklin in the 1936 election. Eleanor was devastated at the defeat.

As tensions increased abroad, Eleanor's views on pacifism began to change. In 1937 she wrote an essay, *This Troubled World*, which was published as a book early in 1938. A tiny little book, it outlined her beliefs, touching on the need for an organization to resolve conflicts between nations, equating nations with families that inevitably have misunderstandings. Pointing to Spain and China, it questioned a belief in the

Atlantic and Pacific oceans as natural protection, talked of building up the military, and recognized the need for all men to fight in time of war. Somewhat idealistically, it concluded with an appeal to brotherly love. Some part of her must have known that brotherly love would not be able to solve the crises abroad.

ELEANOR AS ANTI-FASCIST

In 1935 Benito Mussolini's forces attacked and overran the African nation of Ethiopia, declaring it a part of Italian East Africa in 1936. Civil war erupted in Spain in 1936, and as early as 1933 Japan threatened Chinese territory. Embracing a policy of neutrality, Congress declared an arms embargo in 1935, prohibiting the sale of military equipment to any nation at war, and Franklin, supporting the Embargo Act, banned the sale of arms to both Italy and Ethiopia. Britain and France, thinking of their imperial interests, quietly sold oil, badly needed for the invasion, to Mussolini. Eleanor said little publicly, even when told of Ethiopian women being molested by Italian soldiers, as Franklin did not appreciate her speaking on foreign affairs, but she sympathized with Ethiopia and believed the Embargo Act helped the fascists.

The Spanish Civil War struck at the heart of her beliefs and emotions. A struggle between Spain's newly elected Popular Front government and a small band of Spanish fascists, led by Francisco Franco and backed by fascist Italy and Nazi Germany, Eleanor saw the war as a fascist threat to democracy. Many did not agree with her. The Popular Front was an alliance of wealthy landowners, intellectuals, liberals, socialists, and a few communists. Its only ally was Soviet Russia. In 1936 Europeans and Americans alike saw communism, not fascism, as the enemy. Russian communists had denounced religion, turning the Catholic Church against communism. Stalin was purging, or killing, enemies of the Communist Party, alienating much of the world. To many, Stalin was a greater threat than Franco, Mussolini, or Hitler. To Eleanor, fascism was the greater threat. Spain had a democratically elected government, and that, she believed, outweighed the presence of a few communists.

The United States was in the midst of a Red Scare. The FBI had stepped up its surveillance of suspected communists. Isolationists wanted nothing to do with the Spanish Civil War. American Catholics, taking their lead from the church, sided with Franco. Franklin, perhaps with an eye on the upcoming election, imposed an embargo on Loyalist Spain, or the Popular Front, and turned a blind eye to U.S. trade with Italy and Germany. American companies were profiting from the sale of steel and copper, ingredients for war equipment, to Germany and Italy. Eleanor was appalled. Never, until the day he died, did Eleanor accept Franklin's turning his back on Loyalist Spain.

Initially Eleanor supported neutrality. In theory, at least, it was consistent with pacifism. She still went on peace-related speaking tours late in 1936, but she was no longer neutral. Still a pacifist, she was also antifascist. Neutrality, she believed, had a devastating impact on Loyalist Spain. She wanted blockades that would hurt the aggressors, not the victims. She wanted aid for the victims. As she came to believe American neutrality helped the fascists, her message began to change. She did not believe in absolute pacifism and would tell audiences that at times even pacifists had to go to war. Telling a group of young pacifists it would be crazy to disarm in today's world, she believed in a strong military and supported Franklin's 1933 decision to rearm the navy while disapproving of his stance on Spain. She wrote anti-fascist articles and spoke of fascism in "My Day." When American radicals left for Spain, joining the International Brigades to fight for democracy, she applauded their efforts. In one odd escapade, she even sent her brother Hall on a secret mission to get planes to the Loyalists, a mission that was halted abruptly when Franklin got wind of it.

In 1937 the Basque region of northern Spain was attacked. Most famously, German planes bombed the small village of Guernica, an event depicted in Pablo Picasso's disturbing painting. Eleanor felt for the innocent victims, particularly the children, and took up the Spanish refugees as a cause, sending money to Quaker relief groups and the Spanish Children's Fund. Speaking often of her support for Spain's refugees, she encouraged others to join her. Although England and France took in orphaned children, America was less welcoming, requiring a $500 admission fee for any child who wanted to enter the country.

Japan invaded northern China in 1937. Franklin saw Japanese aggression as a threat to the Philippines and found the Japanese invasion more alarming than war in Spain. Shying away from a blockade on goods destined for Japan, a clear violation of the Neutrality Act, he circumvented the act by calling for a "quarantine" of Japan, a distinction that was not altogether clear. When the quarantine proved to be ineffective, he moved to strengthen the military. While Spain remained a contentious issue, Eleanor and Franklin agreed on the Japanese threat in Asia.

GERMANY, JEWS, AND ELEANOR

When Adolf Hitler came to power, Germany, like the United States, was in the midst of the worst depression in its history. Igniting German nationalism, Hitler won over the nation by promising a great German empire and building up the country's military. Making Germany's Jews a scapegoat, he implemented a policy of vicious anti-Semitism, declaring a boycott of Jewish businesses in 1933, increasingly attacking Jews verbally, and, in 1935, denying Jews all basic rights.

As outspoken as she was about fascism, Eleanor was uncharacteristically silent on the persecution of Germany's Jews. Early biographers claim she didn't know, but as Blanche Wiesen Cook points out, Eleanor was not unaware of the situation in Germany. As early as 1933, she was clipping the *New York Herald Tribune*'s articles on Nazi Germany and putting them in Franklin's bedside basket. Her friend Alice Hamilton, a member of the International League for Peace and Freedom, traveled to Germany in 1933, telling both Eleanor and Franklin of the horrors she saw and writing of them in the *New York Times*. Clarence Pickett, after visiting Germany with the American Friends Service Committee, also painted a grim picture. Eleanor's silence did not stem from lack of knowledge.

Cook believes Eleanor's silence was a reflection of official policy. Neither the State Department nor Franklin wanted to condemn Hitler's early activities. Hitler was seen as a buffer to Stalin's activities. "Human rights" was not yet an internationally accepted concept, and the State Department did not consider Germany's treatment of Jews any of its business, just as it did not consider America's treatment of African Americans any of Germany's business. Germany's early laws segregating Jews into their own ghettos, forcing Jews into their own schools, and regulating where they could do business were, in fact, similar to laws segregating blacks in the American South. Before 1938, violence against German Jews was no worse than the lynching of American blacks. Criticism of German policies would invite similar criticism of U.S. policies. Nor was America free of anti-Semitism. Anti-Semitism, like racism, was virulent in the 1930s. Just as Franklin skirted racial issues at home, he preferred not to attack anti-Semitism abroad, fearing a backlash at the polls. He followed a policy of neutrality and noninvolvement. Eleanor may very well have bowed to his wishes and not spoken out, just as she did not speak at an antilynching rally in Alabama when Franklin asked her not to.

As she did with race prejudice, however, Eleanor sought to fight anti-Semitism through her personal actions. Taking a special interest in a young Jew, Frank Brodsky, and his sister Bertha, Eleanor responded to his letter, one among hundreds she received daily, with utmost generosity. Suffering from the same crippling disease that had affected Eleanor's Aunt Bye, Bertha needed spinal surgery, an operation her parents could not pay for, and Eleanor arranged for her to have the surgery at the New York Orthopedic

Hospital, the same hospital her grandfather, "Greatheart" Roosevelt, had founded. Finding a job for Frank as well, Eleanor became friends with the two young people, inviting them to the White House and following their well-being for years.

In a decade when private schools frequently excluded Jews, Eleanor wrote letters of recommendation for Jewish students applying to college, and when New York's Colony Club blackballed her friend Elinor Morgenthau from membership, Eleanor withdrew her own membership. She supported Jewish groups, giving money to Jewish charities and speaking at Jewish meetings. Initially avoiding controversial topics, she spoke on the New Deal at a gathering sponsored by the Women's Association of the American Jewish Congress. Addressing the women's Zionist organization Hadassah, she spoke of the need for "American women, Jews and Gentiles," to work together "side by side."[1] Increasingly she began to condemn anti-Semitism in the United States, and, looking beyond the United States, she initiated efforts to build a home in Jerusalem for young Jewish women fleeing persecution.

With Jews fleeing from Germany as early as 1933, Eleanor, along with Carrie Chapman Catt, wanted to provide aid to the refugees, but America, shunning foreigners, had rigid immigration policies in place. As Jewish refugees increasingly sought entrance to America, Eleanor and Frances Perkins approached Franklin in 1936, asking him to issue an executive order lifting restrictions on Jewish immigration, but Franklin, along with the State Department, was committed to staying out of Germany's affairs. Not wanting Jewish refugees in the country, the State Department threatened to deport those who had entered on tourist visas, an action that would surely condemn them to concentration camps. Many had been in the country for two or three years. Often they had children born in America. As the State Department moved into action, Eleanor received pleas for help from terrified refugees. She passed them along to Frances Perkins, who, as secretary of labor, had the authority to extend visas. Together, they saved some from deportation, but they could not change policy.

In March 1938 Nazi forces marched into Austria, receiving a surprisingly warm welcome from their German-speaking neighbors, and within a week Austria was part of the German empire. Moving next into Germanic areas of Czechoslovakia, Hitler assured the rest of Europe he intended only to recover German-speaking peoples. His next move, however, shocked the continent. On November 10, 1938, German Nazis attacked the Jewish community. Leaving ghettos strewn with shattered glass, they vandalized Jewish schools, homes, and businesses, set fire to synagogues, and desecrated cemeteries, stripping Jews of everything they owned. On

Kristallnacht, the "night of broken glass," Nazis began shipping Jews en masse to concentration camps. Those who escaped tried to flee the country, but few nations would take them in. The United States did not welcome them.

After *Kristallnacht*, Eleanor embraced the refugee cause. No longer working behind the scenes, she publicly protested deportation hearings, spoke of the Jewish refugees in her press conferences, and advocated a change in immigration policy. Supporting the idea of refugees settling in Palestine, she spoke to an audience of some 1,500 people, sponsored by a national committee for refugees, asking them to contribute to the Leon Blum Colony for Jewish refugees in Palestine. Writing articles on Jewish refugees and the problem of anti-Semitism, she began to develop her concept of international human rights. Hers was a lonely voice, however.

Key figures in the State Department, most notably Breckinridge Long, were anti-Semitic and unsympathetic to Jewish refugees, as were some American ambassadors abroad and such vocal Americans as Henry Ford and Charles Lindbergh. Congress distanced itself from immigration reform. Although Franklin felt for the refugees, he wasn't ready to confront the nation's xenophobia. Breckinridge Long, who controlled the issuing of visas, did not want any immigrants from Germany, claiming they could be Nazi spies. Even after Germany had invaded Poland, Belgium, and France and Franklin, at Eleanor's urging, had moved to ease restrictions on Jewish immigrants, Long blocked their entrance, issuing an order that visa applications be delayed indefinitely with red tape and requests for additional paperwork.

Although Eleanor pestered Franklin about Long's policies, causing him to snap at her on occasion, she could not influence policy. She did manage, however, to rescue 83 Jewish refugees from a Portuguese freighter. After arriving in New York without papers, they were being sent back to Europe, almost certainly to a concentration camp, when Eleanor persuaded Franklin to help, and at his instruction all 83 were declared political refugees. They got off the ship in Norfolk, Virginia, where it was refueling. Breckinridge Long was furious, and with Long as her opponent, Eleanor was not able to repeat that success. Years later her son James recalled that Eleanor's inability to rescue more Jewish refugees was "her deepest regret at the end of her life."[2]

HELPING BRITISH CHILDREN

Eleanor had better success helping British children. As honorary chair of the U.S. Committee for the Care of European Children, she appealed to the American public, asking families to open their homes to displaced European children, and she garnered sympathy for the English-speaking children of Great Britain. Her appeal elicited offers of homes from thousands of Americans. Getting immigration authorities to admit the children was more difficult, as Breckinridge Long wanted to exclude all foreigners, not just Jewish immigrants. Even Long, however, had trouble arguing that British children could be Nazi spies. Eleanor obtained temporary visas for the children, arguing that they were only visitors, not true immigrants, and after further negotiations, U.S. ships were sent to England for the children. Once they were settled, Eleanor had a picnic for the children on the White House lawn.

THE YOUTH MOVEMENT

Always concerned with the nation's youth, Eleanor became involved with the radical youth movement in the late 1930s. While the NYA, one of her favorite projects, helped many young people, it could not reach everyone, and in 1936 the radical American Youth Congress (AYC) protested against the NYA, demonstrating in Washington and denouncing the NYA as a waste. Eleanor and Aubrey Williams met with the youths. Handling them with patience, although telling them not to lecture her, Eleanor acknowledged NYA's limitations and won them over. Argumentative and at times condescending, the boys reminded Eleanor of her sons. She became their ally, and in 1938, when the AYC sponsored an international conference at Vassar College, she was a keynote speaker.

An umbrella organization embracing a variety of subgroups, the AYC was believed, by many, to be a leftist, communist organization. Its most prominent subgroups included the American Student Union, the Young People's Socialist League, and the Young Communist League, but it also included such groups as the Young Women's Christian Association, the Southern Negro Youth Congress, and the Youth Committee against War. Its members were activists. Many were disillusioned— with the New Deal, with capitalism, with the international scene. Some flirted with communism, others with pacifism. Still others despaired over fascism or the Spanish Civil War. A few joined the International Brigades and went to Spain to fight for freedom. Eleanor sympathized with their conflicting beliefs, although she did not always agree with them. She felt they should be kept within the liberal fold and did not believe the AYC was a communist organization.

Many of the leaders, however, were sympathetic to communism. Although Eleanor did not realize it, some were affiliated with the

Russian Communist Party, and they followed the party line. In 1938, when Russia considered Germany the enemy, that was not obvious, as Russian communists supported the American New Deal, and the AYC followed suit. In 1939, however, Russia and Germany startled the world by signing a Nazi–Soviet Pact, enabling Germany to invade Poland without being threatened by Russia, and, with the shift in Russian policy, the AYC turned against the New Deal, causing Eleanor to pause. Increasingly she developed reservations about the group, but she stood by its leaders.

In November 1939 the House Un-American Activities Committee, a group that Eleanor openly opposed, investigated the AYC. Chaired by Texas Democrat Martin Dies, the committee investigated groups it believed to be subversive, including, for instance, Hallie Flanagan's Federal Theatre Project, well known for drama focusing on social protest. When the Dies Committee called AYC leaders to testify, Eleanor attended the hearings to show her support for the youths. Initially cordial, the hearings became increasingly contentious as committee members accused the youths of communism. Moving from the audience to the press table, Eleanor took out her pad and pen and started taking notes, suggesting that, perhaps, she would write about the questioning. The tone of the hearing improved immediately. After the hearings Eleanor invited some of the AYC leaders, including an interesting young man named Joseph Lash, to the White House for dinner.

The following year Eleanor's relationship with AYC deteriorated. She received cold silence from AYC members when speaking in support of Franklin's military buildup, and when Franklin addressed AYC youth on the White House lawn, she watched them boo her husband. She herself was booed the next day. In 1941, when Germany invaded the Soviet Union, both Russia and the AYC switched back to a pro-Roosevelt stance, and Eleanor, finally accepting the AYC's affiliation with the Soviet Communist Party, severed her connection with AYC.

Joseph Lash, however, would come to take a special place in her heart. Dining with him and his friends at the White House, Eleanor took a liking to Joe and invited him to spend time at Val Kill. To Joe, the son of Jewish immigrants, the first lady's interest in him was rather amazing. He admired her greatly, and they became close friends. Joe had joined the American Student Union, one of AYC's subgroups, at Columbia University and become its leader. After flirting with communism, he had rejected the idea and become the AYC's most prominent noncommunist. When he met Eleanor, he was becoming estranged from his friends. Years later, Lash came to believe it was his difficulty with his friends that attracted

Eleanor. He was someone she could help. Eleanor was impressed with the way he conducted himself at the Dies hearing.

Joe was intelligent, liberal, and shared many of Eleanor's interests and beliefs. She guided him away from AYC activism and moved him solidly into the liberal New Deal camp. Like Eleanor, he severed his connection with AYC in 1941. Eleanor liked to talk politics with Joe, knowing there would be no negative consequences when she said what she thought. As he spent time at Val Kill, she also began to confide in him, telling him of Franklin's affair with Lucy Mercer and her early childhood, just as she had told other friends earlier. Joe was 30 when they met, young enough to be her son, but she could speak more freely with him than she could with her own sons. She cared as much for Joe as she did for her own children and would spend as much time with him as she could in the coming years. Eventually, Joseph Lash, a successful journalist, would become known as Eleanor's prizewinning biographer.

LIFE IN THE WHITE HOUSE

Eleanor's popularity with the public soared in the late 1930s. She was chosen Woman of the Year in 1937, and in 1940 Gallup polls gave her a higher rating than her husband. In the White House, however, she was no more popular than she was in 1936, when Franklin's advisors shut her out of campaign planning. She and Franklin were frequently at odds, their political alliance at risk. As Franklin turned his attention to foreign policy, Eleanor watched the New Deal slip into the background and sought to keep it alive. Traveling as much as ever, she would return from trips eager to tell Franklin of conditions at Arthurdale or California's migrant workers, and he would be too busy, too concerned with Europe, or too tired to listen. He expected her to be silent on foreign policy, and although she usually stopped short of openly criticizing him, she antagonized Franklin when she expressed her feelings about the Spanish Civil War or U.S. policy toward refugees. Their emotions ran high when they talked of the Spanish Civil War. Eleanor could not let a subject drop even at the risk of incurring Franklin's ire, and he often lost patience with her.

Most distressing to her, however, was the waning of her friendship with Harry Hopkins. Hopkins was her protégé, her close friend, and her strong ally on the New Deal, and she was very fond of him. When his wife died in 1937, leaving Hopkins alone with their five-year-old daughter Diana, Eleanor offered to become Diana's guardian if necessary, and he changed his will accordingly. Taking Diana under her wing, Eleanor gave Harry's daughter a room at the White House and cared for her until he remarried in 1942. Yet Harry, like Franklin, began to shift his focus away from America's needy to the conflicts abroad. Late in 1938, Franklin appointed Harry secretary of commerce, after asking him to evaluate the country's aircraft industry, and Hopkins, the dedicated social worker, became a politician, leaving the WPA and its programs behind.

Diagnosed earlier with stomach cancer, Harry's health failed in 1939, and he spent close to a year in hospitals and recuperating at home. Franklin found the best doctors for him, however, and despite predictions that he would live only five or six months, he went on to become Franklin's assistant during the war and outlived the president. Working with Franklin on war strategy, Harry had less contact with Eleanor, and gradually his allegiance shifted from Eleanor's circle to Franklin's. One evening in 1940 he felt ill while at the White House, and Franklin suggested he spend the night. Harry, along with his daughter, stayed for the next three and a half years.

Once he was living in the White House, Harry spent considerable time with Franklin, replacing the void left by Louis Howe's death and even, to some extent, usurping Missy Le Hand's place. In the evening, he and Franklin would relax and have a drink together. Like others before him, Harry could not maintain a friendship with both Franklin and Eleanor. Only Louis Howe had accomplished that. Eleanor felt betrayed. Moreover, she felt Harry's influence on Franklin was not good. Louis, who had helped to shape Franklin's career, would openly question his thinking, while Harry, a younger man, was more in awe of the president and would simply agree with him. Eleanor did not believe Franklin needed another "yes" man. Harry's mindset was more attuned to Franklin's than to Eleanor's, however. As he focused on the war, he became impatient with these "goddam New Dealers,"[3] as did Franklin.

Although she kept up appearances, entertaining visiting dignitaries, most notably, the king and queen of England, Eleanor found herself fighting Griselda moods again and occasionally took to her bed. In 1940 her friend Lorena Hickok moved back to Washington, taking a job with the Women's Division of the Democratic National Committee, and Eleanor invited her to stay in the White House. Hick remained in Washington for the next four years. The two women often chatted briefly in the evenings, but their friendship was no longer as close as it had once been. They generally went their separate ways.

"NO ORDINARY TIME"

In 1940, when Franklin's second term was nearing an end, Europe was undeniably at war. On May 10 Hitler's forces invaded Holland,

Luxembourg, and Belgium, taking the Low Countries in six days, and then moved into France, defeating the French government on June 22. British forces fighting alongside the French were forced to retreat back across the English Channel, leaving the dead, along with tanks, guns, and supplies, on the beaches at Dunkirk. With most of its military equipment lost in battle, England stood alone against Hitler. In desperate need of planes, tanks, and guns, Winston Churchill, England's new prime minister, sought help from FDR. With Hitler's *Blitzkrieg*, the reality of Europe's war penetrated America's consciousness. Franklin, recognizing the threat of war at home if England failed to defeat Hitler abroad, sought a way to circumvent America's neutrality laws and give Churchill the aid he needed.

Meanwhile, the Democratic National Convention was approaching rapidly, and no one knew what Franklin intended to do. Eleanor had no idea. Initially she was looking forward to leaving the White House, a place she was finding increasingly depressing, but even as she told reporters she didn't know if Franklin would run again, she realized she was seeing the master politician at work. Franklin was considering an unprecedented third term, but he would not seek it. In a country where the public had come to expect the president to step down after the second term, his campaigning for a third term would not be received favorably. Franklin wanted to be drafted.

Without his go-ahead, Democrats did not feel free to discuss other candidates, and many were irritated at his silence. Although at one time some Democrats had thought Harry Hopkins would be Franklin's anointed successor, Franklin had not groomed a successor. If he did not run, there was no obvious candidate, although James Farley wanted to run. Losing patience with the situation, Farley told Franklin he thought running for a third term would be a mistake and he was going to put his own name in the running. The discussion led to a breach between Franklin and Farley. Franklin wanted a clear mandate to run.

Shortly before the convention, Franklin let it be known that if he was nominated, he would run for a third term, but, he claimed, he was not seeking a third term. Staying at home, he sent Harry Hopkins to the convention, officially as an interested Democrat, although reporters and delegates assumed he was Franklin's representative. Ignoring James Farley, they crowded around Hopkins, hoping for some word from the president. Franklin, in fact, had sent a statement, which was read after the keynote address. An ambiguous statement indicating only that delegates could vote for whomever they wanted, it left the convention hall in total silence until, from out of nowhere, a voice shouted, "We want Roosevelt!"

and the crowd responded in kind, shouting, "We want Roosevelt. We want Roosevelt."[4] Later the source of the voice was found—a microphone in the basement.

Although Franklin's nomination appeared to be a certainty, the convention fell into disarray the next day, as delegates considered a vice-presidential candidate. No longer on good terms with his current vice president, John Garner, Franklin wanted Secretary of Agriculture Henry Wallace. A good administrator, Wallace was not a particularly good politician, and the Democrats preferred any number of candidates over him. Franklin would not budge. Digging in his heels, he claimed he would not run if he could not have Wallace. Frances Perkins, fearing everything would fall apart, tried to persuade Franklin to come and speak, but he would not. Suggesting instead that they ask Eleanor to speak, he told Perkins, "You know Eleanor always makes people feel right. She has a fine way with her." Eleanor, however, was not receptive to the idea. Never before had a first lady spoken at a national convention, and she did not care to set this particular precedent. When Franklin followed up on Perkins's call, she told him, "No, I wouldn't *like* to go! I'm very busy and I wouldn't like to go at all."[5] He, of course, was able to persuade her.

When Eleanor arrived at the convention, it was in chaos, every mention of Wallace's name bringing boos and catcalls. Squeezing Mrs. Wallace's hand, Eleanor waited while vice-presidential candidates were nominated. When she rose to speak at 10:30, the hall quieted immediately. After thanking James Farley, whom only Eleanor was kind enough to acknowledge, she told her audience that the coming president would face "a heavier responsibility, perhaps, than any man has ever faced before in this country. . . . You cannot treat it as you would an ordinary nomination in an ordinary time. . . . This is no ordinary time, no time for weighing anything except what we can best do for the country. . . . You will have to rise above considerations which are narrow and partisan. This . . . time . . . it is the United States we fight for." Without using Wallace's name, she persuaded her audience to unite behind the man Roosevelt wanted for vice president, and he was nominated on the first ballot.

With great excitement on the part of her friends, her daughter, and the press, Eleanor had, by all accounts, saved the nomination. She, herself, discredited her role. Although Franklin's Republican opponent, Wendell Willkie, was more formidable than Alf Landon, Franklin won the November election with 55 percent of the popular vote. Eleanor resigned herself to another four years in the White House.

NOTES

1. Quoted in Cook, *Eleanor Roosevelt*, vol. II, p. 327.

2. Quoted in Doris Kearns Goodwin, *No Ordinary Time, Franklin and Eleanor Roosevelt: The Home Front in World War II* (New York: Simon & Schuster, 1994), p. 176.

3. Quoted in Lash, *Eleanor and Franklin*, p. 660.

4. Quoted in Goodwin, *No Ordinary Time*, p. 126.

5. Quoted in ibid., p. 127.

Chapter 7

THE NATION AT WAR

With Britain at risk, Germany occupying most of the Continent, and Japan threatening the Pacific, Franklin faced unprecedented challenges. Domestically, his primary focus was on the nation's military buildup. His concerns were abroad. In December 1941, when Japan bombed Pearl Harbor, bringing America into the war, he fired the nation's patriotism, challenging the country to put all of its resources, all of its energy into the war effort. Allying with Winston Churchill and eventually Joseph Stalin, he would devote all of his efforts to winning the war.

Eleanor found his single-minded focus difficult to handle. Seeing World War I as a failure leading inevitably to the current war, she wanted more of a focus on democratic ideals, on an effort to prevent all future wars, and she did not want to see the social gains of the past decade left behind. To the irritation of both her husband and members of his administration, she would continue to focus on social justice—on the rights of African Americans, the role of women, and the injustices dealt to Japanese Americans.

GEARING UP FOR WAR

With the nation still clinging to neutrality, Franklin sought to build up the country's military, bolster its defenses, and ensure Great Britain's survival. When Winston Churchill turned to him for help in May 1940, asking for tanks, guns, and destroyers to replace those lost on the beaches of France, the United States was in no position to help. The nation's own munitions were in short supply. Its troops were poorly trained and out of shape. Its factories were set up to produce cars, refrigerators, frying pans—not war materiel. Franklin's military advisors wanted to rebuild the country's own military supplies, not send them to England. Franklin sought to do both.

Using a "cash and carry" policy to bypass the neutrality laws, Franklin began selling guns and bullets to England, but Churchill needed ships, particularly naval destroyers. England's need was dire. German planes were bombing London and England's military bases. German submarines were mining the Atlantic. If England lost its battle to Germany, Franklin believed, Nazis would be landing on the shores of America. Without waiting for congressional approval, Franklin sent destroyers to Great Britain via Canada, receiving permission to lease British military bases in Canada and the Caribbean in exchange. While Congress was irate, the Destroyers for Bases deal had popular support, and ultimately Congress approved it.

In his State of the Union address, Franklin overcame congressional resistance and won support for military spending. Recognizing a need for industry's cooperation, he turned to his traditional enemy, big business, for help in building up the nation's war arsenal. Although businessmen were generally against the New Deal, they supported Franklin's foreign policy more than New Dealers, many of whom were isolationists. Forming an alliance with business leaders, Franklin appointed the head of General Motors, William Knudsen, and the chairman of U.S. Steel, Edward Stettinius, along with labor representative Sidney Hillman and other loyal New Dealers, to a National Defense Advisory Commission (NDAC). For his war cabinet, he also turned to conservative Republicans, appointing Henry Stimson secretary of war and Colonel Frank Knox secretary of the navy.

Although his advisors suggested he wait until after the election, Franklin also introduced a Selective Service Act in the spring of 1940, and it was signed into law in September. Until then America's troops had consisted entirely of volunteers and reserve units. Along with some 16 million other men, Elliott joined the army and James the marines in 1940. That same year, Franklin Jr.'s Naval Reserve unit was called to service, and in 1941 John enlisted in the navy.

Eleanor had reservations about Franklin's alliance with big business, as she feared his new allies would squash New Deal programs. Although breadlines and tent cities were disappearing, America was not yet out of the Depression. Some 17 percent of the nation's workforce did not have jobs, and people in rural areas still lived in poverty, many without indoor toilets or even running water. The poor, Eleanor believed, still needed the New Deal. She also had reservations about the Selective Service Act. Instead of a limited military draft, Eleanor would have liked a more comprehensive draft, one that would also conscript civilians into public service at home.

Although the coming years would be rife with problems—social upheavals, strikes, racial injustices—Eleanor's concern for the economy was misplaced. Once American industry got into full swing producing guns, bombs, and aircraft carriers, the nation would come out of the Depression. New factories would be built. Existing factories would retool. Where once there had been a dearth of jobs, there would now be labor shortages. Rural workers would move from the hinterlands to new factory towns. African Americans would move in record numbers from the rural South to Chicago and Detroit. As young men joined the military, industry would hire women to do men's work, an idea that would have horrified many in peacetime. Eleanor would turn her attention to workers crowded into insufficient housing, African Americans, and the new workforce of women.

PERSONAL LIFE AND LOSS

With the threat of war ever present, Franklin sought relief in light conversation, and although Missy Le Hand had been the center of his cocktail hour for years, his attention turned to Princess Martha of Norway in 1940. When Hitler invaded Norway, forcing the king and Martha's husband into exile in London, Princess Martha fled to America with her two children, staying at the White House before buying an estate in Maryland. Perky, flirtatious, and charming, Martha entertained Franklin, distracting him from the war, and he began to dine with her and take her on drives. Even after Martha left the White House, he visited her in Maryland. Eleanor, having long ago accepted Franklin's need for frivolous distractions, took their flirtation philosophically, telling a friend, "There always was a Martha" providing "an admiring audience for every breath."[1]

Missy Le Hand, however, appeared to be jealous, and she did not handle the situation well, sometimes snapping at the president or complaining of her workload. As Missy became more irritable, Franklin spent more time with Harry Hopkins or Princess Martha. In Doris Kearns Goodwin's view, Missy was in love with Franklin. She had essentially devoted her life to him, as his secretary, his companion, and, when Eleanor was away, his hostess—roles she had played since the 1920s. She was clearly important to Franklin. Eleanor had long ago come to accept Missy's presence. Eleanor, in fact, found life easier with Missy there, as she could leave the White House at will, knowing Missy would keep things running smoothly.

In June 1941 Missy became ill at a dinner party, collapsing shortly after Franklin left. Although Franklin's physician, Dr. McIntire, diagnosed her collapse as physical exhaustion, she most likely had a small stroke. Her speech was slurred and difficult to understand. Two weeks later she had a massive stroke, one she would never recover from. Paralyzed on one side and unable to care for herself, she could no longer laugh and joke, and her condition was more than Franklin could handle. Unable to watch her helplessness, he found visiting her difficult and soon stopped. Although he took care of Missy's medical bills, Franklin distanced himself from her personal misery, shocking those who knew him. Years later Elliott would say, "The strange thing was that Mother was more protective and upset about Missy's illness than Father."[2] Eleanor sent Missy flowers, wrote to her, and visited. Living with her sister, Missy lingered on until 1944, trying twice to commit suicide. When she died, Eleanor attended her funeral. Franklin was away on war business.

In July, soon after Missy's stroke, Eleanor drove her mother-in-law to Campobello. Sara was in her eighties, frail and in failing health, but she wanted to be on Campobello Island. For Franklin's "peace of mind," she allowed Eleanor to hire a live-in nurse, and with some concern, Eleanor left her on the island for the summer. Sara had had a slight stroke in June. While she was on Campobello, Franklin went to Quebec to meet with Winston Churchill, telling Eleanor only that he was going fishing off Cape Cod, a ruse to keep the meeting secret. Sara returned home at the end of August gaunt and frail. Eleanor feared Franklin would not see her in time, and at his wife's urging, Franklin went to Hyde Park in September. Initially Sara perked up at the sight of her son, but she died the next morning, September 7, just two weeks before her 87th birthday.

Sara's death was, of course, a tremendous loss to Franklin. He had been the apple of her eye since infancy, and much of his self-confidence came from the love she had lavished on him. While Eleanor wrote fondly of Sara in "My Day," she found herself strangely unable to mourn. Perhaps too drained to feel any emotion, she wrote to Joe Lash, "I looked at my mother-in-law's face after she was dead & understood so many things I'd never seen before. It is dreadful to have lived so close to someone for 36 years & feel no deep affection or sense of loss. It is hard on Franklin however."[3]

Before Eleanor and Franklin could arrange for Sara's funeral, Eleanor was called to her brother's bedside. After years of heavy drinking, Hall had collapsed and been rushed to the hospital, his liver shot. For two grueling weeks, Eleanor sat at his bedside, watching him suffer. He died on September 25 at the age of 51. For Eleanor, losing Hall was like losing a child. She had promised their father she would take care of him, and she had tried to be his mother, his father, his family. With his death, she grieved for the "little boy" she had "played with & scolded," for the brother who "could have been so much."[4] Like their father, Hall had been a charming young man, well liked and intelligent, but, also like their father, he had destroyed his life with alcohol. Eleanor felt that she was somehow to blame for Hall's succumbing to drink. Looking through his letters, tears in her eyes, she told her secretary Tommy, "I'm trying to find where I failed him."[5]

THE AFRICAN AMERICAN CAUSE

In 1940 Eleanor wrote that "no one can honestly claim . . . the Negroes of this country are free. . . . We have poverty which enslaves and racial prejudice which does the same."[6] For Eleanor, social justice lay at the heart of what she called "winning the peace." To win the peace, she believed, America had to ensure democracy at home, and America would never be truly democratic until it extended democracy to all ethnic groups. Throughout the war years, she continued to be a visible presence in the black community, visiting black colleges and speaking before the Brotherhood of Sleeping Car Porters. She was attacked by the southern press, even blamed for causing race riots, but her esteem rose in the eyes of African American leaders. Although Franklin's advisors cringed at her outspokenness, Eleanor championed blacks in the workplace, federal housing, and the military.

The Workplace

In 1941, with shipyards revving up production and aircraft plants scrambling to produce fighter planes, workers began to flock to defense plants. For the first time in years jobs were easy to find. White America began to prosper, but blacks still lived in the shadows. Moving to Detroit and Chicago, they gained the freedom to sit in the front of a bus or to use public restrooms, but they still found only menial, low-paying jobs, as they had in the South. Even blacks with technical training or higher education had difficulty finding skilled jobs. Discrimination was rampant in the defense industry. North American Aviation made it official policy to hire blacks only as janitors. Standard Steel never hired blacks. Want ads read "Wanted, White Mechanics." Skilled jobs often required membership in unions excluding blacks. When youths trained by the National Youth Administration applied for jobs at an aircraft plant in upstate New York, only one—the only black in the program—failed to be hired.

Viewed as someone to turn to, Eleanor had the trust of black leaders—Walter White, Mary McLeod Bethune, and a new figure, A. Philip Randolph, black America's most prominent activist in the 1940s. An attractive man who had considered an acting career, Randolph had founded an African American journal, the *Messenger*, and organized railroad car porters into an all-black union, the Brotherhood of Sleeping Car Porters. Eleanor still had Franklin's ear on civil rights issues, and she encouraged him to end discrimination in the defense industry. With Eleanor telling him of educated blacks who could only find work sweeping floors or cleaning restrooms, Franklin asked the NDAC to consider introducing racial quotas in defense plants, but the idea was considered too dramatic, an action that would elicit discontent among white workers

Although Walter White had always acceded to Franklin's concerns, A. Philip Randolph was not as patient with the white establishment. Finding Walter's approach too conservative, he sought in 1941 to mobilize black workers, to act dramatically, and to win their fair share of defense jobs. In a bold, new move, he declared an African American March on Washington. Initially a frightening thought for blacks who were used to "staying in their place," the idea took off rapidly once it took hold. Forming a March on Washington committee, Randolph announced the march in black newspapers, promoted it in black communities, and reserved railroad cars to take marchers to Washington. Some 25,000 blacks planned to march on Washington. Randolph threatened a march of 100,000.

Franklin found the upcoming march alarming. Fearing it would erupt into violence, he asked Eleanor to intercede with Randolph. Eleanor and Franklin both knew the Washington police were racist. The march could end in disaster. Although Eleanor told Randolph she was afraid it could incite a riot, setting back all gains made so far, he was tired of appeasing white concerns. While gracious, he told Eleanor he "could not think of calling [the march] off" unless the president issued an executive order banning discrimination in the defense industry. Well aware that Franklin had been avoiding a meeting with Walter White, Eleanor relayed Randolph's message to Franklin and told him he and his advisors had better meet with Randolph and White. They met in June. Despite resistance on the part of his advisors, Franklin ultimately issued an executive order providing "for full and equitable participation of all workers in defense industries, without discrimination because of race, creed, color or national origin." Thanking Eleanor for her "help in securing this action on the part of the president,"[7] Randolph called off the March on Washington.

While the black press hailed Franklin's order "as the most significant move on the part of the government since the Emancipation

Proclamation,"[8] racial hatreds still prevailed. When skilled African Americans found jobs that only whites had held before, they became objects of verbal and physical attack. In Mobile, Alabama, for instance, when the Addsco Shipyards upgraded black welders, assigning them to work on the same job as white welders, a riot ensued. Feeling their own tenuous hold on economic well-being threatened, white welders attacked the blacks, using rocks, bats, and clubs and yelling racial slurs. Violence spread throughout the shipyard, halting production for seven days. Eleven blacks went to the hospital. Only when black welders were moved to a separate, segregated job did the violence subside. Eleanor, of course, was distressed by the outbreak, but she felt the compromise, moving blacks to a segregated job, was a setback.

Earlier, at Ford Motor Company, Eleanor's input had helped to avert a riot. A nonunionized company, Ford had hired some 2,000 African Americans, and when white laborers, demanding a union shop, went on strike, black workers, grateful for their jobs, sided with management. Taking refuge on the plant's roof, they became caught up in racial tensions and began throwing objects at picketers below. Some fought one-on-one with striking white workers. With Ford producing engines for the aircraft industry, Franklin's primary concern was to end the work stoppage. His initial impulse was to use black workers as strikebreakers, but Eleanor, taking the advice of Mary McLeod Bethune, urged him to reconsider. If black workers were pitted against white workers, Mary warned, the result could be the worst race riot in the nation's history. Heeding Mary's warning, Franklin took no public action and sent Walter White to calm the blacks. Talking black workers into leaving the roof and uniting with white laborers, Walter helped to relieve the racial tension and opened the way for negotiations. The strike was settled without a riot.

Housing

With workers of all races migrating in record numbers, industrial centers became overcrowded, and housing became scarce. Workers with high-paying jobs found themselves sharing apartments with strangers, sometimes even sharing a bed with a stranger who worked a later shift. Some workers found no housing at all and slept in tents or on church pews. While Charles Palmer, the national housing coordinator, moved to provide housing as cheaply and quickly as possible, Eleanor sought to replace slums with new permanent housing. She saw the housing crisis as an opportunity to remove the slums, but neither Franklin nor Palmer wanted to divert funds for slum clearance. Eleanor's wishes prevailed, however, in one instance, when Congress appropriated funds for the Sojourner Truth Project, a federal housing project for African Americans in Detroit.

Once word of the project got out, it caused an uproar in the white community. White workers saw no reason to give desperately needed housing to African Americans. Polish neighbors did not want blacks in their neighborhood. Taking the issue to Washington, Detroit's local congressman got the Sojourner Truth Project, a project named after a famous black slave, changed to housing for whites only. Black leaders became outraged and implored Eleanor to do something. She turned to Franklin, convincing him they could not renege on housing promised to blacks. With pressure from Franklin, Palmer reversed the white-only policy, and in February 1942 24 blacks, accompanied by 300 supporters, tried to move in. A crowd of whites wielding knives and guns forced them back. A cross burned in front of the project. A riot ensued. Some 100 protestors, black and white, were injured.

No further attempts were made for over a year, and the issue seemed to lie dormant. Eleanor, however, continued to agitate, as she believed the government had an obligation to honor its promise to the black families. In April 1943, they moved in while state troopers provided protection. The city remained quiet for a couple of months, but in June racial tensions turned violent. Two racial incidents in a Detroit amusement park turned into a bloody riot as wild rumors of black men murdered and a black baby drowned spread through the city, fueling tempers in black neighborhoods and in the area surrounding the Sojourner Truth Project. Mobs of black and white youths swarmed into the streets, attacking anyone of the wrong color. Innocent victims of both races were beaten to death. Twenty-five blacks and nine whites died. Hundreds were taken to the hospital. After 24 hours of rioting, federal troops quelled the mobs.

The nation was horrified. Some blamed Eleanor, the southern press writing "It is blood on your hands, Mrs. Roosevelt. . . . You have been personally proclaiming and practicing social equality at the White House. . . . What followed is now history."[9] While "sick at heart . . . over race riots,"[10] Eleanor felt the Detroit riot could have been avoided if only her call for better housing had been heeded.

The Military

As early as 1940, African Americans sought to join the military, only to find they were not wanted. The army air corps excluded all blacks, even those with pilot licenses, as did the marines. The navy enlisted blacks only as mess men to clean facilities, serve meals, and act as servants for naval officers. Claiming black and white sailors could not live together, Secretary of the Navy Knox banned blacks from ships, thereby excluding them from combat. Segregating blacks into separate units, the army had four African American units, only one of which was trained for combat. The other three were service units limited to menial tasks. The entire army had three black chaplains and only two black officers. Secretary of War Stimson had no faith in the ability of blacks to lead or to fight, although they were eager to receive the same basic training as whites.

Telling Eleanor how deeply blacks felt, A. Philip Randolph and Walter White tried to take their cause to Franklin, only to be blocked by Franklin's aides until Eleanor urged Franklin to see them. In a meeting with the two black leaders, the secretary of the navy, and the assistant secretary of war, Franklin, with his superb ability to placate his audience, gave the impression he did not object to slowly integrating the army. Randolph and White believed he was sympathetic to their cause, although Secretary Knox was blunt in saying the navy could not accommodate their wishes, as blacks and whites could not live together on a ship. Franklin's military advisors were adamantly opposed to a "social experiment" when war was looming, and Franklin did not pursue the issue further, leaving White and Randolph in limbo.

Expecting a phone call from the White House, Walter turned to Eleanor when one did not arrive, suggesting the White House make a statement about the meeting. When she passed the request along, the War Department issued a statement, but not one either Eleanor or the civil rights leaders anticipated. Presenting a statement that concluded, "The policy of the War Department is not to intermingle colored and white enlisted personnel in the same regimental organizations," Steve Early gave the impression that Walter White and Philip Randolph had agreed to the statement. White and Randolph denounced the statement, calling it "a stab in the back of democracy."[11] With Eleanor imploring him to do something, Franklin offered an apology to the black community, but he could not placate the black press. Perhaps with an eye on the 1940 election, he granted one of Randolph's requests, promoting a black colonel, Benjamin Davis, to brigadier general and appointing the dean of Howard Law School, William Hastie, to the War Department. Considering both appointments a mistake, Secretary of War Stimson blamed them on "Mrs. Roosevelt's intrusive and impulsive folly."[12]

Eleanor felt the two appointments were only a beginning. Voicing her opinion in speeches, columns, and memos, she sought true equality for blacks in the military. Each day she received mail from GIs, including letters from blacks telling of the barriers they faced. Experiencing the insult of segregation for the first time, northern blacks stationed at southern bases would tell of having to wait hours for the bus for blacks, of not being able to eat in restaurants, or of being forced into separate base clubs or movies. Passing their letters along, Eleanor would ask military officials to investigate each insult. Army Chief of Staff George Marshall found her memos so overwhelming he had to assign two staff members just to answer them, but he also took them seriously. Taking an initial step toward desegregation, the War Department issued a directive in March 1943 forbidding the racial designation of recreational facilities on military bases. In July 1944 the department desegregated buses, trucks, and any other transportation provided for military personnel.

Ultimately, the sheer need for manpower loosened the military's policy on sending African Americans into combat. Training for over a year without seeing any combat duty, the all-black Tuskegee Airmen, a unit created after a black pilot sued the army air corps, went into battle in 1943, when Allied forces invaded German-occupied North Africa. In 1944, in a startling reversal of policy, the army asked blacks in service units to volunteer for combat duty. Over 4,000 volunteered immediately. Although separated into black platoons, they fought alongside white platoons, slept in the same facilities as white soldiers, and shared bathrooms with white soldiers, proving both that blacks and whites could serve together and that blacks were equal to whites as soldiers. The navy also lifted its ban on blacks aboard ship, finding that black and white sailors could live and work together in close quarters. Although the move to bring blacks into combat came from the need for replacements, Eleanor's challenge to the military had put a wedge in the long-held belief that black and white soldiers and sailors could not live or fight together.

THE OFFICE OF CIVILIAN DEFENSE

In May 1941 Franklin created the Office of Civilian Defense (OCD), appointing New York City mayor Fiorello La Guardia its director. Charged with preparing the home front for war, the OCD's goals were ill defined. Eleanor saw the OCD as a means for ensuring social welfare during the war, while La Guardia focused more narrowly on civilian defense. Taking his clue from the air raids abroad, he sought to recruit air raid wardens, install warning systems, and secure firefighting equipment. After receiving a blast of criticism from Eleanor, he offered her a job as assistant director. Initially she turned the offer down, fearing that as the wife of the president she would open herself and, indirectly, her husband to criticism, but with Hall's death, she needed a task to focus on. She became assistant director of the OCD in September.

Finding the office completely disorganized, she began immediately to set up systems and organize the staff, hiring Elinor Morgenthau as her assistant. La Guardia put her in charge of volunteer activities, giving her all of the "warm and fuzzy" assignments. She hoped to build up a cadre of volunteers who would work in day care centers, housing projects, and bomb shelters. Many of her ideas were based on her settlement house experience, but she showed poor judgment, hiring friends for tasks that Congress saw as irrelevant. She appointed Joseph Lash to an advisory committee on youth and an actor friend, Melvyn Douglas, to an arts council. Most notably, she hired Mayris Chaney, a dancer friend she had initially met through Earl Miller, to set up a dance program for children. Congress had a field day with the appointment, charging that Chaney was paid more than bomber pilots and voting not to provide funds for dancers teaching physical fitness.

In the midst of the furor, the nation went to war. On December 7, Japanese forces bombed Pearl Harbor, sinking 19 ships, decimating more than 200 planes, and killing over 2,000 soldiers. Declaring that "yesterday, December 7, 1941—a date which will live in infamy—the United States of America was suddenly and deliberately attacked . . . ," Franklin asked Congress for a declaration of war. After his speech, Eleanor and La Guardia flew to the West Coast, where people were in a state of panic. Many feared the Japanese would soon be on the West Coast. While Eleanor and La Guardia were en route, there were rumors of an attack on San Francisco. Hoping to quell fears and boost morale, Eleanor traveled by train from San Diego to Seattle, stopping along the way to meet with the public.

She and La Guardia were still at odds over the purpose of the OCD, however. The agency suffered from mismanagement and a negative image, and in January 1942 Franklin replaced La Guardia, appointing regional manager James Landis to head the OCD, an appointment Eleanor had recommended. Landis eliminated the physical fitness program, fired Mayris Chaney, and removed many of La Guardia's staff members. Recognizing that she would continue to be a liability, Eleanor offered her resignation, and Landis accepted it, although he personally liked Eleanor. It was "a perfectly impossible situation," he later wrote, "to have as an assistant director the wife of the President of the United States."[13] Attacked by the anti-Roosevelt press, Eleanor felt she was a scapegoat for the agency's failures.

ENTER "ROSIE THE RIVETER"

From farmers' wives to workers in the nation's shipyards, from West Virginia's coal miners to newly enlisted GIs, the nation came together after Pearl Harbor, heeding Franklin's challenge to let loose "the force of American democracy." Accepting shortages and, ultimately, the rationing of basic commodities, Americans put all of their resources into the war. Children grew up without candy as sugar was made into fuel for tanks. Adults adjusted their menus as coffee, butter, and meat were rationed. Cars became scarce as auto manufacturers made planes instead. Rubber, used for tires, went to the military, as did gasoline, and gas rationing kept people at home. Women's clothes lost their frills as the military used cotton and wool for uniforms, blankets, and socks. Children went without new toys. Parents bought war bonds. Two million women joined the workforce as men left for the military.

Posters of "Rosie the Riveter," a young, rosy-cheeked girl with a rivet gun, urged women to do their part. Posters reading "Uncle Sam Needs You!" showed Uncle Sam pointing his finger at them, and women heeded the call. Those with menial jobs as maids or seamstresses moved into higher-paying jobs as welders or equipment operators. Young high school graduates took jobs assembling B-17s in aircraft plants. Ultimately, married women with children joined the workforce as well. Leaving their children with whomever they could, they took jobs as welders, riveters, and assembly line workers, breaking with the long tradition of staying home to care for their families.

Having long held that women should have opportunities outside the home, Eleanor gave her full support to the new factory workers. Pointing to female war workers in England, she advocated the hiring of women and encouraged both married and single women to take defense jobs, writing that she would do so if she were younger. Seeking out women workers when touring defense plants with Franklin, she asked about their experiences and congratulated them in "My Day." Although she was thrilled to see women joining assembly lines, however, she was well aware of their problems, particularly the problems of working mothers.

Grocery stores closed as day shift workers were leaving work, and scarce items, such as meat, generally sold out early, making buying food a problem. Finding time to cook was difficult as well, and day care facilities were nonexistent. Women had to scramble for whatever childcare provisions they could find, often leaving an older child to tend to younger siblings or even leaving infants to sleep in a car outside the factory. Often women had to take time off to care for a sick child or just to buy food. Advocating possible solutions, Eleanor urged storekeepers to stay open later and suggested the creation of community kitchens, where women could get fully cooked meals to take home. She also began a crusade for day care centers, an idea she had advocated in peacetime.

Although she met with resistance from Frances Perkins as well as conservative critics, Eleanor convinced Franklin of the need for federal day care facilities, and the government funded several centers, the first of which opened in the summer of 1942. Considering them insufficient, Eleanor approached industry leaders as well, urging them to open private day care facilities. Arguing that day care centers would enhance production by reducing absenteeism, she convinced Henry Kaiser of Kaiser Shipyard in Portland, Oregon, to open a model day care facility. Building an attractive center with up-to-date equipment, Kaiser included play stations staffed by teachers, an infirmary with trained nurses, and a cafeteria that not only fed the children but also provided meals women could take home. Operating 24 hours a day to accommodate day and night shifts, the center was a great success, and other defense plants began to provide day care as well. By the end of the war well over a million children were cared for in day care centers.

JAPANESE AMERICANS

Triggering immediate hostility toward Japanese Americans, the attack on Pearl Harbor released long-held racial hatreds. Arriving at the turn of the century, Japanese immigrants had become successful farmers, living in farming and fishing communities along the coast, and anti-Japanese sentiment had infiltrated the West Coast long before the war. Pearl Harbor let it loose. An irrational hysteria swept across California. Anyone who looked oriental was suspect. Rumors of Japanese spies and saboteurs swept the coast. Responding to the hysteria, Franklin talked of moving Japanese Americans to relocation centers, or internment camps, and asked the military to investigate rumors of spies.

Eleanor abhorred the hostility. Considering Japanese Americans another minority about to be victimized, she spoke out against the hysteria and challenged Americans to be fair "to our citizens of every nationality." Visiting their communities as she traveled up the West Coast, she posed for photographs with Japanese Americans. Working with Attorney General Francis Biddle, she actively opposed evacuating Japanese residents, telling Franklin they are "good Americans" with "the right to live as anyone else,"[14] but only Biddle agreed with her. As Japan conquered Hong

Kong, Manila, and Singapore, hostility toward the immigrants increased. Vigilantes began attacking innocent victims. Afraid of being mistaken for Japanese, Chinese Americans began wearing signs, "Chinese, please!"

Accepting the advice of his military advisors, Franklin signed an executive order in February 1942, providing for the evacuation of Japanese Americans. To Eleanor, it was a violation of the Bill of Rights. By the end of the year, all but a few Japanese Americans were living in relocation centers. They "were not convicted of any crime," Eleanor wrote years later, "but emotions ran too high, too many people wanted to wreck vengeance on Oriental looking people. . . ."[15] At the time, however, she limited her comments, most likely at Franklin's insistence. While publicly silent, she worked behind the scenes to ensure that families were not separated and were treated humanely. Corresponding with internees, she took complaints about housing or ill-treatment to Dillon Myer, director of the War Relocation Authority (WRA). When internees found their bank accounts frozen, she helped them gain access to their money. Outside of the camps, she contributed money to Japanese American cultural organizations and sought to prevent discrimination against the few Japanese remaining in the workplace.

Initially accepting, then incredulous, the internees became increasingly bitter. Most had established good lives in their adopted country, and they had come to think of themselves as American. Their youngsters, for the most part, had been born in America and knew little of Japan. They resented their imprisonment, and in 1943 riots broke out in some camps. Afraid of pro-Japan elements, Harold Ickes became concerned about pockets of hostility. Franklin, still trusting Eleanor to give him a full and accurate report, sent her to assess the situation at the Gila River Camp in Arizona. Impressing Dillon Myer with her thoroughness, Eleanor toured the camp and reported on the industriousness of the Japanese even in an internment camp, on the community they created, the businesses they ran, and the gardens they grew. She also noted the disintegration of family life and the devastating impact of living behind barbed wire and recommended that the internees be released and allowed to return home. Harold Ickes and Dillon Myer agreed with the recommendation.

Franklin did not reject her recommendation out of hand, but Secretary of War Stimson resisted the idea. Believing there were small groups of pro-Japan residents in each camp, he wanted them isolated in a separate camp. Supporting Stimson, Franklin had the problematic internees moved to Tule Lake in California, but he also saw merit in Eleanor's view and looked into granting exit permits to individual internees. Although still banned from California, internees who had jobs or joined the army began receiving exit permits in 1943. After the 1944 presidential election, Franklin directed the WRA to start closing the internment camps. Eleanor openly criticized the evacuation of Japanese Americans after she left the White House.

AN UNEXPECTED OVERTURE

With her brother gone and all four of her sons in the military, Eleanor found personal life difficult. Afraid she would lose a son to the war, she worried about her boys. She also worried about Joe Lash, who was drafted in 1942. Joe was in love with a young married woman, Trude Pratt, who would eventually become his wife, and although Eleanor befriended Trude, she feared she was losing Joe as a confidant. Her friends Esther Lape and Elizabeth Read were moving to Connecticut, forcing her to give up her Greenwich Village apartment. Elizabeth, who was ill, would pass away in 1943. With Sara's death, Eleanor and Franklin sold the twin townhouses on 65th Street, residences that Eleanor did not miss, and she bought a new apartment on Washington Square, making it handicapped accessible in case Franklin wanted to visit. With only the two of them, Franklin asked Eleanor to spend more time at the Big House, but Eleanor did not want to move into Sara's home. Sara's furniture was to remain in place, as the house would eventually become a museum. Although Eleanor persuaded Franklin to let her convert a small area into a study if she noted Sara's placement of every piece, Eleanor still preferred Val Kill.

Although Franklin hid his feelings when Missy took ill, his mother's passing and Missy's absence left a void in his life. Grace Tully had taken over Missy's secretarial duties, but Grace never became a companion. Although Harry Hopkins still lived in the White House, he remarried in 1942 and was planning to move, as his wife, Louise, did not like vying with Eleanor over dinner arrangements. Bringing two of his unmarried cousins, Laura Delano and Margaret Suckley, into his life, Franklin sought a companion to replace Missy. Margaret was a quiet, unassuming woman whose letters suggest she liked to flirt with Franklin, but she was much too discreet to let others see. Laura was much showier. Typically adorned in red velvet slacks and a display of jewelry, she was openly flirtatious, witty, and sometimes nasty, leading Hall's daughter to suspect she was jealous of Eleanor's accomplishments. Although Franklin enjoyed their company, neither woman quite filled the void. Eleanor found their conversation tiresome and frivolous.

In September 1942, Franklin toured the country's military bases and defense plants, asking Eleanor, as well as Margaret and Laura, to join him.

While declining to stay for the entire trip, Eleanor joined Franklin for part of the tour. Together they viewed assembly lines and toured plants manufacturing tanks, guns, and planes. For Eleanor the trip was an opportunity to talk with female and African American workers, but for Franklin it was an opportunity to talk with Eleanor. Although they had grown apart, their marriage reduced to a political partnership, Eleanor and Franklin had never stopped loving each other. Eleanor, in James's words, "was the most remarkable woman [Franklin] had ever known, the smartest, the most intuitive, the most interesting, but because she was always going someplace he never got to spend time with her. . . . he was lonely and he needed her."[16] Perhaps in an effort to fill the void, perhaps with thoughts of their early years together, Franklin asked Eleanor to become his hostess again, to spend her time at the White House, to try resuming life as man and wife.

Eleanor could not answer immediately. Overcome with conflicting emotions, she needed time to think. Although she had long ago forgiven Franklin for his affair with Lucy Mercer, she had not forgotten the hurt. She still loved him. "That," Esther Lape claimed, "was why he always had the ability to hurt her."[17] Despite a deep-seated need for love, Eleanor could not be the frivolous type of hostess Franklin enjoyed. Nor would she be happy in that role. The very qualities that had attracted them—Eleanor's seriousness, her integrity, Franklin's light-hearted sociability, his ability to charm—had become sources of irritation. Ultimately, Eleanor decided she could not give up the life she had established for herself. Whatever regrets she may have had, she let Franklin know two weeks later at dinner. Eventually, their daughter Anna would become her father's closest companion. Eleanor would turn her attention to the soldiers abroad, experiencing some of the most emotionally draining moments in her career.

NOTES

1. Quoted in Goodwin, *No Ordinary Time*, p. 154.
2. Quoted in ibid., p. 245.
3. Quoted in Lash, *Eleanor and Franklin*, p. 830.
4. Joseph P. Lash, *Love Eleanor: Eleanor Roosevelt and Her Friends* (Garden City, NY: Doubleday & Co., 1982), p. 357.
5. Eleanor Roosevelt II, *With Love, Aunt Eleanor: Stories from My Life with the First Lady of the World* (Petaluma, CA: Scrapbook Press, 2004), p. 52.
6. Eleanor Roosevelt, *The Moral Basis of Democracy* (New York: Howell, Soskin, & Co., 1940), p. 48.
7. Quoted in Goodwin, *No Ordinary Time*, pp. 250, 252, 253.

8. Quoted in ibid., p. 253.

9. Quoted in Allida M. Black, *Casting Her Own Shadow: Eleanor Roosevelt and the Shaping of Postwar Liberalism* (New York: Columbia University Press, 1996), p. 92.

10. Quoted in David Emblidge, *My Day: The Best of Eleanor Roosevelt's Acclaimed Newspaper Columns, 1936–1962* (Da Capo Press, 2001), p. 80.

11. Quoted in Goodwin, *No Ordinary Time*, pp. 170, 171.

12. Ibid., p. 172.

13. Quoted in Beasley, Shulman, and Beasley, *Eleanor Roosevelt Encyclopedia*, p. 390.

14. Quoted in Black, *Casting Her Own Shadow*, p. 143.

15. Quoted in Goodwin, *No Ordinary Time*, p. 321.

16. Quoted in ibid., pp. 371–72.

17. Quoted in ibid., p. 629.

Chapter 8

THE FINAL WAR YEARS

Even as Eleanor worked for social justice at home, she longed to go abroad. She received letters regularly from American GIs and wanted to visit the troops and lend her moral support. As early as 1940 she had wanted to go to Europe with the American Red Cross, thinking she could give out blankets, food, or medicine as she had in World War I canteens. She envisioned helping either refugees or wounded soldiers, but the State Department denied her permission, believing she would be in too much danger. In the fall of 1942, however, shortly after she had rejected his overture, Franklin granted her request. Acknowledging her "fine way with people," he sent her abroad as a good-will ambassador.

WARTIME ENGLAND

Receiving the code name "Rover," Eleanor left for England in mid-October, staying at Buckingham Palace as the king and queen's guest and witnessing the destruction German bombs had inflicted on London. St. Paul's Cathedral, Buckingham Palace, and the shops and homes in working-class neighborhoods had all suffered bomb damage. Receiving bomb shelter instructions when she arrived, Eleanor found blackout curtains covering the palace windows and a black line in her bathtub, indicating how much water she could use for a bath. Water, like other items, was rationed. Writing her column daily, Eleanor brought the British experience home to Americans. "It is . . . appalling," she told her readers, "what one big bomb can do . . . a well-organized raid . . . can leave a city practically in ruins."[1] She also won the hearts of the British people speaking over the British broadcasting system.

With her usual energy Eleanor toured U.S. military bases and British defense plants, leaving reporters and guides scrambling to keep up. Talking with American soldiers, she noted especially the high morale of African Americans, who experienced less prejudice in England. Visiting London's Red Cross Club, she learned that soldiers' thin cotton socks did not keep their feet warm or prevent blisters, and she took their problem to General Eisenhower, who was in England preparing for an Allied invasion. Unearthing boxes of neglected socks in a warehouse, Eisenhower had warm woolen socks distributed to the soldiers. Touring England's defense plants, Eleanor took an interest in women fixing trucks, driving tractors, or digging ditches. Their children were in national day care centers, and Eleanor picked up several ideas she would pass along to the Kaiser center in Oregon. She also saw Elliott in London. He was stationed outside of Cambridge, and she visited his base as well, although her driver got lost and had to send out an alarm, "Rover lost her pup."

Welcomed by British dignitaries throughout her trip, Eleanor spent a weekend with the Churchills at their country estate, taking Elliott along with her. She had met Winston Churchill earlier, when he and Franklin held conferences in Washington. The two men had become great friends as well as allies. Although Eleanor enjoyed Mrs. Churchill, who joined her for part of her London tour, she and Winston were wary of each other. Eleanor did not approve of his views on British colonies in Asia and Africa or on the Spanish Civil War, and Churchill, who was not used to powerful women speaking their minds, found her hard to fathom. Eleanor had also fretted when Winston kept Franklin up late at night partying. Churchill, however, was enthusiastic about Eleanor's visit to England, writing after she left, "You certainly have left golden footprints behind you."[2] He would later describe Eleanor as having "a spirit of steel and a heart of gold."[3]

Eleanor was still in England on November 7, when Allied forces, under the command of General Dwight Eisenhower, invaded North Africa, driving German and Italian forces out of French North Africa in seven days. Exhilarated by the victory, Eleanor wrote of the excitement that swept through England, the joy that finally British and American forces were fighting together. She returned home on November 17. To her surprise, Franklin took time off to meet her plane, and in the days after her return, they spent more time together than usual.

AN INTERLUDE AT HOME

In January Franklin went to Casablanca, where he and Churchill planned an invasion of Sicily, the next step after the North African invasion. Resuming her hectic schedule, Eleanor traveled to military hospitals at home, visiting wounded soldiers, and toured the new Women's Army Auxiliary Corps in Des Moines, Iowa, where new recruits were being trained. In March she took time out of her schedule to visit Joe Lash, who was stationed in Illinois. Taking adjoining rooms in an Urbana hotel, they spent hours talking and had their meals in Eleanor's room. The following weekend Joe had a tryst with Trude Pratt, but two weeks later he and Eleanor met again in Chicago, where a hotel employee told Eleanor her room was bugged. Irate at the idea, Eleanor told Harry Hopkins, who investigated and found that indeed it was bugged.

Convinced that Joseph Lash was part of a communist conspiracy, the army Counter-Intelligence Corps (CIC) had him under surveillance, and when the Corps learned of his meetings with Eleanor and Trude, they bugged the women's rooms as well, learning quite a bit about Joe's affair with the married Mrs. Pratt. When Franklin heard of the surveillance, he was as angry as Eleanor, and he disbanded the CIC. The CIC turned its files over to the FBI. J. Edgar Hoover, head of the FBI, already considered Eleanor suspect because of her civil rights activities, and he had an extensive file on her. Shortly after the incident, Joseph Lash's unit was sent to the South Pacific. He always wondered if FDR was behind the order.

In July Eleanor visited Anna in Seattle. John had resigned his newspaper job and joined the military, leaving Anna to run the *Seattle Post-Intelligencer*, and although Anna took pride in her job, she did not get along well with William Randolph Hearst. Feeling especially close to her mother, Anna shared her feelings about the newspaper, and Eleanor, feeling close to her daughter as well, confided in Anna that she had trouble talking with Elliott, as she and Elliott had just had a tense Christmas visit at Hyde Park. Eleanor was also concerned about James's marriage, as James claimed Franklin always talked about his first wife, Betsey, in his wife's presence, but it was Elliott who would divorce in 1944.

THE SOUTH PACIFIC TOUR

Acting as ombudsman for American GIs, Eleanor continued to correspond with soldiers abroad and their families at home, passing their concerns along to military officials. In 1943 Franklin asked if she would visit the troops in the South Pacific and give him a report on their morale, their needs, and their concerns. Leaving in August, as Franklin went to Quebec to meet with Churchill, she anticipated the tour with some anxiety. She would be traveling without her secretary Tommy for the first time in years. She feared she would be in the way, a nuisance to military commanders who would give her so much protection she wouldn't be able to talk with the soldiers. Some commanders did, in fact, dread her visit.

Traveling as a special Red Cross delegate, she wore a Red Cross uniform and carried her typewriter in her suitcase. On most trips Tommy typed her columns, but in the South Pacific Eleanor would type "My Day" herself. Her first stop was on Christmas Island, a coral atoll in the Pacific. Her quarters were swarming with dreadful red bugs, and she had to suppress a desire to scream. Touring the island, she visited the military installations, barracks, and hospital, talking with soldiers, often promising to give messages to their families, a promise she always kept. Painfully aware, even at the age of 58, that she wasn't glamorous, Eleanor had feared the GIs, who knew only that a woman was coming, would be disappointed not to see a young, beautiful movie star. They were, however, overjoyed to see her. She was someone they hadn't seen for months, an American Mom!

Flying on to U.S. headquarters in New Caledonia, Eleanor met with William F. Halsey, commander of Allied naval forces in the South Pacific. An abrupt military man, he was not happy to see her. In one of the toughest battles in the Pacific, his forces had driven the Japanese from their base on Guadalcanal Island, a feat that would prove to be a turning point in the Pacific War, and his attention was now focused on a battle in New Georgia. Eleanor's presence was a distraction, and to his irritation, she wanted to see Guadalcanal. While she would write of the island's military significance, she also wanted to see Joe Lash, who was stationed there. When Eleanor gave Halsey a letter from Franklin, indicating he would leave the decision to Halsey but also saying, "She is especially anxious to see Guadalcanal and at this moment it looks like a pretty safe place to visit," Halsey told her "Guadalcanal is no place for you, Ma'am! . . . If you fly to Guadalcanal, I'll have to provide a fighter escort . . . , and I haven't got one to spare."[4] He agreed, however, not to make a final decision until after she had visited New Zealand and Australia.

Before leaving for New Zealand, Eleanor toured New Caledonia, impressing Halsey with her energy and her thoroughness, causing him to write, "When I say . . . she inspected these hospitals, I don't mean . . . she shook hands with the chief medical officer, glanced into a sun parlor, and left. I mean she went into every ward, stopped at every bed, and spoke to every patient. . . . She saw patients who were grievously and gruesomely wounded. But I marveled most at their expressions as she leaned over them. It was a sight I will never forget."[5] Eleanor found visiting the wounded difficult, however. She struggled not to flinch every time she smiled and bent over the severely wounded. She held back tears watching boys leave for the front, knowing not all of them would return. She found traveling without Tommy lonely and wondered many times if the trip had any value at all. Although she received cables from Franklin assuring her the trip was being received favorably at home, Eleanor knew she would sink into depression if she did not keep up a hectic pace.

In New Zealand and Australia she visited more hospitals, speaking to each and every one of the wounded soldiers. Entertained by dignitaries in Australia, she was popular in Canberra. GIs loved her as she spoke before large groups, telling them Franklin was keeping track of their movements. Accompanied by top brass, she saw military bases, visited Red Cross Clubs, and toured defense plants, learning as much as she could about the women workers. The military protection was suffocating, however. When she returned to U.S. headquarters, Halsey relented and let Eleanor go on to Guadalcanal. There she viewed the cemetery where American GIs were buried, dined with Admiral Halsey, and saw more military facilities. The highlight of Guadalcanal, however, was her reunion with Joseph Lash.

In five weeks Eleanor visited 17 islands, as well as Australia and New Zealand, and talked with some 400,000 soldiers. "She alone," Halsey wrote, "accomplished more good than any other person, or any other group of civilians, who passed through my area."[6] The trip took a heavy emotional toll, however. Eleanor would be haunted for years by images of brutally wounded boys and the graves, row after row, in the Guadalcanal cemetery. Her sorrow would turn to a lingering depression that would stay with her until the end of the war.

SHIFTING ROLES

Seeking emotional relief in her work, Eleanor pursued her vision for the postwar world. Embracing an idea proposed by Walter Reuther, a friend and leader in the labor movement, she told Franklin he should set up a Peace Production Board to oversee the transition from a war economy to a peacetime economy. Concerned about returning GIs, she advocated a government program to provide educational benefits for veterans, and she pursued her long-sought goal—an international organization to help nations settle their disputes and provide relief. The war was going well. The Allies had successfully invaded Sicily and were moving northward up the Italian peninsula. Mussolini had been toppled. Russians fighting

Germany on the eastern front were gaining ground, and Allied forces in the Pacific were island hopping toward Tokyo. With the future looking more hopeful, Franklin was receptive to Eleanor's efforts.

Partially accepting Reuther's idea, Franklin put Bernard Baruch in charge of an agency to monitor industry's conversion from war to peacetime production. The choice delighted Eleanor. Not only was Baruch a close friend, but he was highly respected by both Democrats and Republicans. In October Franklin asked Congress to pass a bill enabling returning GIs to attend school at government expense. Congress responded enthusiastically. Expanding on the original concept, both the House and the Senate unanimously passed the GI Bill of Rights, not only providing funds for education but also guaranteeing loans for home mortgages and new businesses as well as pay for up to a year for those looking for work. The bill also provided funds for new hospitals.

Although Franklin had shied away from the United Nations earlier, fearing lingering isolationist sentiment, he publicly supported the idea in the fall of 1943, partially in response to a book written by Wendell Willkie. At Franklin's direction, Secretary of State Cordell Hull took a first step at a Moscow conference, encouraging representatives from Great Britain, the Soviet Union, and China to pledge their support, and in August an international conference was held in Washington to consider the details. In November Franklin hosted a reception for the United Nations Relief and Rehabilitation Administration (UNRRA), prompting Eleanor to write, "The mere fact . . . this meeting is being held is a promise . . . we shall not repeat our past mistakes."[7] From 1944 to 1947 the UNRRA would provide relief to nations experiencing war or natural disasters.

Eleanor was not so happy, however, with Franklin's plans for his meeting in Teheran with Churchill and, for the first time, Joseph Stalin. Both she and Anna wanted to go along, Eleanor because she had never attended a summit conference, Anna because she wanted to see her husband, who was stationed in North Africa. Having already invited Elliott, Franklin Jr., and John Boettiger, Franklin told his wife and daughter that no women were allowed on naval ships, a reply Eleanor considered an insult. Rubbing salt into the wound, Churchill asked his daughter, Sarah, to accompany him, which made Eleanor furious when she found out. Anna got over the insult more rapidly than Eleanor, as Anna's primary concern was John's emotional health. Upset at having enlisted, John appeared to Anna to be having a nervous breakdown, and she wanted to help him get reassigned to Washington.

Knowing that Anna was upset over both John and her job, Eleanor encouraged her and the children to come east for the Christmas holidays.

Returning from Teheran, Franklin took great pleasure in Anna's visit. Seeing his exhaustion, she distracted him with gossip and jokes, while Eleanor interrogated him about the summit. Anna, like Missy, knew when Franklin wanted to be lighthearted and when he wanted to be serious. She could also tell a good story. Delighted at the attention her father was giving her, Anna spent much of her time with him, laughing and talking. Recognizing his fatigue, she started doing little things for him—greeting guests, reading his speeches and giving suggestions. Anna came closer to having Missy's dual talents—the ability to entertain and to handle administrative details—than either Margaret Suckley or Laura Delano. Almost casually, Franklin asked Anna if she would consider quitting her job and moving to the White House, where she could help him.

Anna liked the idea. Not only was she unhappy with her job, but John had gotten a transfer to the Pentagon and would be moving to Washington. She wanted her mother's approval, however, before saying yes, as she knew of Eleanor's conflicts with James's first wife, Betsey, and Louise Hopkins. Jealous of her role as mistress of the White House, Eleanor did not want anyone usurping it, even if she personally disliked the details. Eleanor told Anna categorically that she was not to assume the role of hostess when her mother was in Washington. With that understanding, however, she would be happy to have Anna at the White House. Anna agreed and moved to Washington.

Although she did not have an official title or receive a salary, Anna became Franklin's personal assistant, taking on more and more duties as Franklin would tell people, "Ask Anna to do that."[8] She spent the day helping with official business, taking time off only when her son first came home from school, and then she became Franklin's hostess at cocktail hour. Initially, her presence was a relief to Eleanor, as it enabled her to travel, write, and work, just as Missy's presence had. Traveling at an almost frenetic pace, she spoke at conferences and went on her usual speaking tours. In the spring, as Anna was taking on her duties, Eleanor visited the troops in Central and South America and the Caribbean, a less emotional trip than the one to the South Pacific, as troops stationed to protect the Panama Canal had seen no action. As Anna settled in, she and Franklin became closer, and Eleanor frequently did not know what Anna was working on. With time Eleanor came to resent being left out of the loop.

ANNA'S CONCERNS

Anna hadn't been at the White House long before she began to worry about her father's health. Although Dr. McIntire, Franklin's personal physician, tried to reassure her, telling her Franklin was recovering from the flu, Anna did not believe him. Her father had been steadily declining since his State of the Union address in January. He had dark rings under his eyes, headaches, and a steady cough. His color was not good, and he couldn't sleep. He had little energy. Losing confidence in Dr. McIntire, Anna wanted her father sent to the hospital for a checkup, and although Dr. McIntire resisted, he acceded to her wishes and sent Franklin to Bethesda Naval Hospital in March.

A young, junior-level cardiologist, Dr. Howard Bruenn, examined the president and quickly diagnosed his condition as congestive heart disease, noting that Franklin's blood pressure had been high for years. Perhaps a bit resentful, Dr. McIntire protested, claiming Dr. Bruenn couldn't possibly be right. When his colleagues examined the president, however, they confirmed the diagnosis, and Franklin was put on a new "miracle drug," digitalis, which stabilized his heart. He was also put on a low-fat diet and told to cut down on cigarettes. Although the digitalis improved his immediate condition, the doctors also wanted him to rest, and Franklin spent a month sleeping and relaxing at Bernard Baruch's summer home in South Carolina. With rumors about the president's health flying, Dr. McIntire assured the public he was recovering from a touch of bronchitis.

Eleanor returned from her South American trip when Franklin was entering the hospital. She attributed his fatigue to anxiety over an upcoming battle—the invasion of France planned at Teheran—and did not realize how ill Franklin was. Having never experienced any fatigue other than that brought on by depression, Eleanor had little sympathy for sickness, and she expected Franklin to snap out of it. Franklin could muster his strength when he had to, and after his month of rest, he did appear to be better. His health would decline over the coming year, however. Seemingly oblivious to his worsening condition, Eleanor would continue to badger him with political issues, causing Anna to lose her temper at a dinner party and snap, "Mother, can't you see you are giving Father indigestion?"[9]

Unwittingly Anna became caught between her parents. Soon after his month of rest, Franklin asked her for a favor. Would she discreetly invite an old friend, Lucy Mercer Rutherford, to dinner when Eleanor was away? Well aware of her father's affair, Anna's first reaction was anger. Eleanor had told her of the affair years ago, a confidence that had helped her understand her parents' marriage and made her feel closer to her mother, and she resented her father's request. She did not know Lucy had visited Franklin in South Carolina. Widowed shortly before Franklin's illness, Lucy had called Franklin, and he was eager to renew the friendship. Doris Kearns Goodwin believes Franklin saw Lucy in 1941 as well, when a

"Mrs. Johnson," identified in Secret Service records as Mrs. Rutherford, visited the White House. Other writers have reported earlier meetings, but Goodwin notes there is little evidence they actually occurred.

Torn between loyalty to her mother and concern for her father, Anna had to choose. Although painfully aware of the hurt it could cause her mother, she felt seeing Lucy might help her father relax, and she was, first of all, worried about his health. She also remembered Lucy from her childhood and liked her. With some reluctance, Anna agreed. If Lucy's visit was kept off the record and classified as top secret, she rationalized, her mother would never have to know. In July, while Eleanor was in Hyde Park celebrating the desegregation of military buses, Lucy dined with Franklin and Anna at the White House. Mixed as her emotions were, Anna could not help but like Lucy, and the two women became friends. Franklin would see Lucy several more times, meeting her at Warm Springs, her home in New Jersey, and the White House.

THE END OF AN ERA

On June 6, 1944, British and American forces crossed the English Channel and invaded France, ultimately liberating France from German occupation. Rallying to the occasion, Franklin kept in touch with Churchill all night, told his cabinet of the invasion at 4:00 A.M., and delivered a simple speech to the nation. Rejoicing that the invasion had gone well, Franklin was elated, but when it was over, he was exhausted. Telling Eleanor in a rare outburst, "I cannot live out a normal life span. I can't even walk across the room to get my circulation going,"[10] he felt weary and longed to retire to the Hudson.

In July, however, he was nominated to run for a fourth term. Although dreading the thought of four more years, Eleanor supported his decision to run. Like the majority of the Democratic Party, she believed Franklin should see the war through to its conclusion. His running mate was in question, however. While Franklin had insisted on Wallace four years earlier, he no longer felt strongly about the vice-presidential candidate. Several candidates, including Wallace, believed they were his first choice, but he gave a nod of approval when colleagues selected a compromise candidate, Senator Harry Truman of Missouri. A New Deal liberal, Truman could presumably carry on Roosevelt's domestic policies. Eleanor was disappointed, as she had come to respect Wallace, but he had never had the party's support. Nominated without ceremony, Franklin was not at the convention. Secretly traveling across the country by train, he was en route to Hawaii, where he would meet with Admiral Chester Nimitz and General Douglas MacArthur about the Pacific War. In October, two weeks before the election, MacArthur would invade the Philippines.

During the summer Eleanor began to realize how ill Franklin was. Spending time with him at Hyde Park and joining him on a trip to Quebec, where he met with Churchill, she saw how old and frail he looked and became worried. His braces no longer fit properly, making it impossible for him to stand. From a sitting position, however, he made several rousing speeches, summoning the strength to campaign against the Republican candidate, Thomas E. Dewey. Campaigning in New York, he stopped at Eleanor's Washington Square apartment to rest, the only time he ever visited her hideaway. Rumors about his health abounded. Some questioned his ability to continue a president's rigorous schedule, but he was elected with 53.3 percent of the popular vote and 432 electoral votes. Dewey received 99 electoral votes.

Eleanor's spirit was depleted after the election. She spent Thanksgiving alone, her plans with Joseph Lash having fallen through. Although Franklin enjoyed the holiday in Warm Springs, where he saw Lucy, he revealed his feelings for Eleanor at Christmas, telling Elliott she was "the most extraordinarily interesting woman" he had ever met and expressing a desire to spend more time with her, saying "I only wish she wasn't so darned busy."[11] In January, with all of his grandchildren present, Franklin was inaugurated president for the fourth time.

Although he was clearly failing, his lips blue, his attention span short, Franklin went to Yalta to meet with Churchill and Stalin. Eleanor wanted to go, just as she had wanted to go to Teheran, but Franklin, recognizing his need for care, took Anna with him instead. Both Dr. McIntire and Dr. Bruenn accompanied him as well. Harry Hopkins, who was succumbing to cancer, met them in Yalta. Franklin celebrated his 63rd birthday on shipboard, while Eleanor attended a series of birthday balls, annual events held to benefit polio victims. At Yalta the three world leaders, Churchill, Stalin, and Roosevelt, discussed the makeup of the postwar world, the conclusion of the Pacific War, and the United Nations.

Spending a weekend together at the end of March, Eleanor and Franklin talked of traveling to San Francisco for the first session of the United Nations. Denying the reality of Franklin's health, they also talked of going to Europe and of traveling around the world together. Soon thereafter, Franklin went to Warm Springs, vacationing with Margaret Suckley, Laura Delano, and Grace Tully. Although Anna stayed in Washington, she arranged for Lucy Rutherfurd and an artist friend, Elizabeth Shoumatoff, to join them. Elizabeth had agreed to paint the president's portrait. On April 12 Franklin was posing for his portrait while Lucy, Margaret, and Laura watched, when he suddenly turned to Margaret, saying "I have a terrific pain in the back of my head,"[12] and collapsed. He died later that day of a brain hemorrhage. In the ensuing confusion, Lucy and Elizabeth quickly packed their bags and slipped out.

Eleanor was attending a fundraiser in Washington when Franklin died. Dr. McIntire had called her earlier in the day, telling her only that Franklin had fainted and advising her not to cancel the fundraiser. She had just given a short speech and was sitting down when she was called to the telephone. Steve Early told her only to return to the White House, but she knew immediately what had happened. Her emotions in check, she remained calm throughout the ordeal. Returning to the White House, she put on a black dress, cabled her sons, and summoned Harry Truman, telling him simply, "Harry, the president is dead." When Truman, in a state of shock, asked Eleanor if there was anything he could do for her, she asked him, "Is there anything *we* can do for *you*? For you are the one in trouble now."[13] Once Truman was sworn in as president, Eleanor left for Warm Springs. Anna stayed behind to make funeral arrangements.

Arriving in Warm Springs, Eleanor asked the women about Franklin's death. Grace said she wasn't in the room, and Margaret talked discreetly about Franklin's collapsing without mentioning Lucy. Laura, however, had no such reservations. She gave Eleanor all of the details, including Lucy's presence. Eleanor showed no emotion, then or later. Without saying a word, she got up, went into the other room, and viewed Franklin's body. Upon questioning, Laura went on to tell Eleanor that with Anna's help Franklin had seen Lucy several times in the past few months. When Eleanor eventually confronted Anna, her anger was so great that Anna feared they would never be friends again.

The entire nation mourned Franklin's death. In London Churchill was devastated, as was Harry Hopkins in the Mayo Clinic. Thousands watched the train pass by as Franklin's body was carried to Washington, where he lay in state. Eleanor rode on the train as well. Following a funeral procession and service in Washington, Franklin was buried in Hyde Park. Within a week, Eleanor packed their furniture, held a tea for women reporters, and moved out of the White House. Finding a reporter outside her apartment in New York, she said simply, "The story is over."[14] For Eleanor, however, the story would not be over.

NOTES

1. Quoted in Rochelle Chadakoff, ed., *Eleanor Roosevelt's My Day, Her Acclaimed Columns, 1936–1945* (New York: Pharos Books, 1989), p. 264.

2. Quoted in Beasley, Shulman, and Beasley, *Eleanor Roosevelt Encyclopedia*, p. 27.
3. Quoted in Goodwin, *No Ordinary Time*, p. 457.
4. Quoted in Lash, *Eleanor and Franklin*, p. 882.
5. Quoted in ibid., p. 883.
6. Quoted in Purcell and Purcell, *Eleanor Roosevelt*, p. 208.
7. Quoted in Chadakoff, *Eleanor Roosevelt's My Day*, p. 316.
8. Quoted in Goodwin, *No Ordinary Time*, p. 490.
9. Quoted in ibid., p. 504.
10. Ibid., p. 516.
11. Ibid., p. 568.
12. Ibid., p. 602.
13. Quoted in Lash, *Eleanor and Franklin*, pp. 928–29.
14. Quoted in Joseph P. Lash, *Eleanor: The Years Alone* (New York: W. W. Norton, 1972), p. 15.

Chapter 9

ALONE AND ON HER OWN

Plagued initially with doubts about her influence as a private citizen, Eleanor faced the future with some uncertainty, even telling friends she might retire to a rocking chair and sit by the fire knitting, but she was much too involved, too concerned with Democratic politics to sit back and relax. Eleanor Roosevelt would not retire from the limelight. While remaining a force in the Democratic Party, she would take on new roles in the United Nations and, in the eyes of many, become the first lady of the world.

Her most immediate concerns, however, were in Hyde Park, as she and the children went through Franklin's belongings, distributing his books, stamp collection, and memorabilia. Although the Big House would go to the government for a museum, Eleanor planned to stay at Val Kill, and she bought her cottage, along with some 825 acres of land, from Franklin's estate, also buying out Nancy and Marion's share in their cottage. Elliott and his third wife, actress Faye Emerson, moved into Top Cottage, a small cottage Franklin had hoped to use as a retirement retreat. Feeling secure with Elliott nearby, Eleanor helped him buy a small farm located on the property, and he began to oversee the farm, hiring local farmers and increasing both the livestock and the crops.

Five days after Franklin's death, Eleanor resumed writing "My Day," issuing a call to carry on Franklin's legacy and "build a peaceful world with justice and opportunity for all."[1] Along with wanting to continue writing and radio broadcasting, Eleanor was dedicated to preserving Franklin's legacy. Signing a contract for a second autobiographical volume, *This I Remember*, she saw the new book as a way to shed light on FDR's legacy as much as on her own life. Harold Ickes, who had once thought she should mind her own business, tried to persuade Eleanor to run for the Senate, as would others in coming years, but she flatly rejected the idea of public office. No longer restricted by her role as first lady, she wanted to write and say what she thought without constraints. Wielding her influence in the Democratic Party, she sought to keep the party on a liberal track. Often she was at odds with the new president, Harry Truman, even as he sought to keep her loyalty by offering her a position on the U.S. delegation to the newly formed United Nations.

THE UNITED NATIONS

When Germany surrendered to the Allies in May 1945, Eleanor spoke to the nation, expressing Franklin's gratitude and urging her audience to go on to "win . . . a permanent peace. That was the main objective my husband fought for."[2] She had been advocating an organization like the United Nations since the 1930s and considered it an important part of Franklin's legacy. Yet when Truman offered her a place on the U.S. delegation, she hesitated, claiming she had no foreign policy or diplomatic experience. Her family and friends encouraged her to accept, however, telling her that she had firsthand knowledge of the war's devastation. Ultimately she joined the delegation. Her suitcase loaded with State Department documents, Eleanor boarded the *Queen Elizabeth* late in December 1945 and left for London, where the first meeting of the General Assembly would be held in January. While on board ship, she spent much of her time studying State Department reports, and she attended all State Department briefing sessions. By the time she arrived in London, Eleanor had a good knowledge of State Department policy and the technicalities of diplomacy.

Committee III

Headed by Secretary of State James Byrnes and former Secretary of State Edward Stettinius, the U.S. delegation consisted of five main delegates and five alternates. Eleanor was the only woman. Not all of her colleagues were happy about her presence. Aware perhaps that her appointment stemmed in part from Truman's desire to retain African American support, the delegates doubted her qualifications and, without consulting her, appointed Eleanor to Committee III, causing her to speculate that the gentlemen must have decided, "Ah, here's the safe spot for her— Committee 3. She can't do much harm there!"[3] While other committees were to deal with budgetary, political, and legal questions, Committee III dealt with humanitarian, social, and cultural issues. Without realizing it, the delegates had thrust Eleanor into a critical position. Committee III would be charged with solving Europe's refugee problem.

World War II had displaced over a million people. Their lives torn apart, their homes gone, they were living in makeshift refugee camps. Many were former prisoners of war, others concentration camp survivors. Vast numbers had fled from Eastern Europe as postwar communist regimes took over their homeland. Western Europe, barely on its way to recovery, was unable to help. Eleanor, as spokesperson for Committee III, soon found herself at odds with the Soviet Union. Advocating a policy enabling refugees to choose a new homeland, Eleanor believed the United Nations should resettle the refugees, setting up an international refugee organization. Most Western nations accepted the principle, but the Soviet bloc did not. In Soviet eyes, those who chose not to return to Eastern Europe could only be traitors or war criminals. They should be forced to return and dealt with accordingly. For many, that would mean certain death. While Eleanor opposed repatriation, both Soviet and Yugoslav delegates opposed resettlement. Seeking to draft a resolution acceptable to both sides, Committee III struggled with Russian demands to place refugees in camps supervised by the countries they had fled. Trying to befriend the Russians while challenging their demands, Eleanor found the task close to impossible.

Eventually, Committee III submitted a resolution recommending tolerance, resettlement, and asylum for political refugees. The Russian response was swift. Challenging the resolution, Andrei Vishinsky, head of the Soviet delegation, announced he would speak before the General Assembly, catching the U.S. delegation off guard and forcing John Foster Dulles, a Republican delegate, to ask Eleanor if she would respond to Vishinsky. Speaking without notes, she faced a formidable opponent. In the 1930s, when Stalin was murdering those who opposed him, Andrei Vishinsky was the lead prosecutor in the Moscow purge trials. An accomplished debater, he attacked the idea of political asylum, equating it with early Western efforts to appease the Nazis, and denounced resettlement. Eleanor, in turn, raised the likelihood of Spanish Loyalists being forced to return to fascist Spain, concluding that the United Nations should "frame things . . . which . . . consider first the rights of man, . . . not governments but man!"[4] Despite Russian objections, the General Assembly passed the committee's resolution.

Eleanor did not limit her activities in London to Committee III. She gave the welcoming speech when the General Assembly opened, and, seeing fewer than 20 women in the entire assembly, she hosted teas for the women, enabling them to discuss issues relevant to women. She also spoke over the British radio, dined with the king and queen, and checked on American GIs still in London. Although Republican delegates John Foster Dulles and Arthur Vandenberg had scorned Eleanor's appointment, she won their respect, and they came to consider her "one of the most solid members of the delegation."[5]

The Universal Declaration of Human Rights

Prior to World War II, nations rarely interfered with persecutions in other countries, leading most of the world to ignore Germany's slaughter of the Jews. The horror of that tragedy changed attitudes, bringing a new concept to international relations—universal human rights. Unlike the earlier League of Nations, the UN Charter provided for a commission to promote human rights, and in April 1946 Eleanor became chair of a temporary committee charged with setting up the commission. Under her oversight, the UN Commission on Human Rights was born, holding its first meeting in January 1947. Truman asked Eleanor to represent the United States on the commission, and as an American authority on human rights, she was soon elected chair of the 18-member commission.

As its first task, the commission set out to draft a document defining human rights, a declaration that would serve as an international bill of rights. The task was not an easy one. Eleanor and other Western leaders envisioned a declaration modeled after the American Declaration of Independence and the U.S. Bill of Rights, a document focusing on individual civil rights. Soviet bloc leaders had an entirely different concept of human rights. To them, the individual was subordinate to the state. Individual civil rights had no place in their ideology. The Soviets focused instead on economic rights, on guarantees that all individuals would have jobs and thus contribute to the communist state, and on social rights, including universal health care and guaranteed housing. The developing nations had still other concerns, and their leaders might vote with either the East or the West.

Taking charge of drafting the document, Eleanor let others debate political philosophy. She saw her role as that of writing a declaration that lay people could understand and both the U.S. State Department and other nations would approve. Initially meeting with a small drafting committee in her Washington Square apartment, she circulated working drafts to members of the commission and submitted completed drafts to the General Assembly for comments. Holding meetings in New York, Geneva, and Paris, Eleanor worked the commission hard and put in long hours, studying drafts late into the night. As diplomatically as she could, she negotiated phrasing with Asian, Eastern European, and Western delegates and with the U.S. State Department. As Soviets sought a clause to "enforce" jobs for everyone, she urged the State Department to accept a provision "promoting" full employment. To placate women delegates, she eliminated the phrase "all men," using instead "all human beings," "everyone," or "no one." Bowing to communist objections, she removed implied references to a god, changing "created free and equal" to "born free and equal."

As the world moved into the cold war era, America became less enthusiastic about the United Nations, questioning its value as tensions arose between the United States and the Soviet Union. In the General Assembly, Westerners criticized the Soviets for subjugating their citizens, while Soviet delegates attacked Eleanor for America's treatment of African Americans, demanding an investigation into human rights in the United States. Eleanor persevered, however, and late in 1948, a year and a half after its initial meeting, the UN Commission on Human Rights completed a final draft and submitted its declaration to Committee III, where the Soviets continued to debate each and every point. Finally, in December, the commission presented the Universal Declaration of Human Rights to the General Assembly. With eight Soviets abstaining, the General Assembly voted unanimously on December 10 to accept the declaration, and the entire hall rose to give Eleanor a standing ovation. The declaration would become the international standard for human rights.

The declaration alone, however, did not provide a means for enforcing human rights. It did not have any legal teeth. For that, the commission had to draw up covenants, legally binding contracts to be ratified, like treaties, by member nations. Knowing that drafting and getting approval of such covenants would take considerable time, Eleanor had pushed the commission to write the declaration first. Once it was approved, the commission worked on two covenants, an International Covenant on Civil and Political Rights and an International Covenant on Economic, Social, and Cultural Rights, but the General Assembly would not approve the covenants until 1966, four years after Eleanor's death.

POLITICS AT HOME

Although Eleanor would have preferred Henry Wallace as Franklin's successor, she supported Truman when he took office, giving him tips on how to win over Churchill or handle the Russians, providing him with information on Franklin's staff, and sending letters of advice. In August, when Truman decided to bring an end to the Pacific War by dropping an atomic bomb on Hiroshima, she supported the decision, believing, as others did, that more lives would have been lost in an extended conflict. She did not always agree with Truman, however, and she doubted his commitment to liberal domestic policies. She encouraged him, for instance, to appoint women to his administration, giving him a list of highly qualified candidates, and he did not heed her advice, appointing only men to high-level positions. Although he always replied graciously to Eleanor, even encouraging her to write, Eleanor and Truman were, in fact, leery of each other.

In Eleanor's eyes, Truman had yet to prove himself, and she did not hesitate to criticize his policies. Although he voiced support of Franklin's postwar plans, she questioned his ability to carry them out, writing to a friend, "He's not accustomed to night work or reading and contemplation and he doesn't like it. . . . I am sorry for him & he tries so hard."[6] When he appointed conservative Democrats to his cabinet, replacing Henry Morgenthau and Frances Perkins, Eleanor doubted his commitment to New Deal liberalism, and when he bowed to conservatives in Congress, she saw him as weak and lacking in leadership. Truman, however, was a pragmatic politician, not a liberal idealist. While Eleanor worried that the liberal Democratic coalition of women, African Americans, farmers, and working people would disintegrate, causing the party to lose direction, Truman acted to hold the party's base, appointing Eleanor to the United Nations to keep African American and female support and retaining Franklin's secretary of commerce, Henry Wallace, to cement labor's support.

Having called for "a century of the common man" in 1942, Wallace, like Eleanor, wanted a postwar economy that provided job opportunities for all Americans, and he sought congressional passage of a Full Employment Bill. For America to thrive, he believed, government should use wage and price controls and government spending to ensure jobs and decent wages. Truman, in contrast, did not support government spending to provide job opportunities. While including a Full Employment Bill in his agenda and telling Eleanor he sought its passage, he told the House majority leader that he wasn't committed to any specific employment bill. Watching him switch from one position to another, Eleanor tried to influence the bill's fate, talking with Democratic leaders and promoting the bill in "My Day."

Despite Wallace's appointment, unrest developed in the automobile and steel industries. Walter Reuther, head of the auto workers' union, called for a strike at General Motors, and Eleanor supported the striking workers, joining a citizens' committee to help their families. By

January 1946 steelworkers, meatpackers, and electrical workers were also on strike, soon to be followed by coal miners and railroad workers. Truman chose not to negotiate and sought instead to arbitrate the General Motors strike, seize the coal mines, and draft striking railroad workers into the military. Writing of the strikes, Eleanor criticized Truman's failure to negotiate and accused Congress of catering to lobbyists. Pointing to the threat of Communism abroad, she claimed the world was watching and urged labor, business, and government leaders to consider "the world point of view"[7] and set an example for democracy.

In September 1946 Wallace resigned as secretary of commerce. Not only did he and Truman disagree on employment issues, but Wallace thought Truman was too tough on the Soviet Union. While Eleanor had considered Wallace an ally, she quickly became disillusioned with him as well. She disagreed with his approach to foreign policy. Once Germany had surrendered, Truman found the Russians impossible to deal with, and he took a tough stand on communism. Initially Eleanor, like Wallace, thought he should try harder to talk with the Russians, but Eleanor was more aware of Soviet guilefulness than Wallace. Working with the Soviets at the United Nations, she came to realize that true cooperation was impossible, and with some reluctance, she too came to take a tough anti-communist stand. As Wallace came to lead the Progressive Citizens of America (PCA), a group purporting to support New Deal policies while also welcoming communists, Eleanor felt he was falling prey to the same sort of Soviet subterfuge she had experienced in the 1930s, when she supported the American Youth Congress.

While she disliked the PCA, Eleanor liked the idea of a group dedicated to New Deal liberalism. Along with Joe Lash and other leading liberals, she helped to form the Americans for Democratic Action (ADA), an organization that would play a role in Democratic politics for the next 20 years. Comprised of liberal politicians, intellectuals, and labor leaders, the ADA excluded communists, a policy Eleanor endorsed. Giving the keynote address at the ADA's founding meeting, she set the group on a liberal, anti-communist path while also encouraging efforts to "make peace with the Russians." Still an effective fundraiser, she told the group "there's plenty of people . . . here who can make a substantial contribution to getting this thing going"[8] and elicited an enthusiastic outpouring of contributions. Over the years she would continue to attend ADA functions and advise its leaders, but she never took an active role in running the organization. Franklin Jr. also joined and supported ADA.

When Truman issued a plan to give Greece and Turkey military and economic aid, Eleanor wished he had approached the United Nations

instead and sought relief for Poland, Czechoslovakia, and Yugoslavia as
well. Sympathizing in particular with Yugoslavia, she became honorary
chair of the American Committee for Yugoslav relief. She applauded Truman's action, however, when he appointed former Army Chief of Staff
George Marshall secretary of state. Marshall proposed a comprehensive
European Recovery Plan, and Eleanor fully endorsed his plan. She became one of its most outspoken proponents at the United Nations, eliciting Marshall's praise, and she was pleased when Truman endorsed the
Marshall Plan.

Eleanor also began to feel better about Truman when he proposed a
10-point African American civil rights program. Incorporating many of
Eleanor's goals, he recommended the elimination of poll taxes, a federal
anti-lynching law, and the creation of a civil rights division within the
Department of Justice. He also desegregated the military and became the
first president to address the annual convention of the National Association for the Advancement of Colored People (NAACP), a symbolic
move that Eleanor applauded. Still, she did not believe he could win the
1948 election. Unable to suggest a better candidate, she did not endorse
anyone initially, telling reporters she hadn't decided whom to support.
Franklin Jr. and Elliott joined a movement to draft Eisenhower as a Democratic candidate, but Eleanor did not like that idea. Eisenhower was not
interested in running, and his political views were unknown.

Eleanor found the prospects for 1948 discouraging. Although the nation was clearly shifting to the right, she urged Democrats to remain the
liberal party, claiming Democrats could not be elected "by appealing to
the conservatives. The Republicans are better conservatives than we are."[9]
While she praised local candidates, she remained silent on Truman's candidacy. In October, when she was attending a UN session in Paris, Frances
Perkins called and asked her to endorse Truman to show her support of
the Democrats. In reply Eleanor wrote, "I haven't actually endorsed Mr.
Truman because he has been such a weak and vacillating person and made
such poor appointments. . . . I can not have much enthusiasm for Mr. Truman. . . . Nevertheless, since you asked me to [I am sending] . . . you the
enclosed letter . . . because you are quite right. . . ." She addressed her
endorsement to Truman, giving him permission to release it and saying,
"I am unqualifiedly for you as the Democratic candidate for the Presidency."[10] The night before the election, she spoke to the nation from
Paris, endorsing Truman in a radio address.

Few people expected him to beat the Republican candidate, New York
Governor Thomas Dewey, but Truman ran an effective campaign and
won by a narrow margin. Although he and Eleanor would continue to vie

over policy, they would work together for another four years. Well aware of her contribution, Truman reappointed Eleanor to the United Nations. He was the first person to tell her she was the first lady of the world.

ONGOING CONCERNS
African American Civil Rights

Joining the NAACP's board of directors soon after Franklin's death and the Congress of Racial Equality (CORE) later in the year, Eleanor continued to advocate African American civil rights. She used her column to discuss segregation in schools and housing, discrimination at work, and voting rights. She pressured Truman for reforms that ultimately appeared in his 10-point civil rights program. The guiding force behind his decision to speak before the NAACP, she appeared with him on the steps of the Lincoln Memorial as he spoke. In 1946, when a racial conflict in Tennessee threatened to erupt into a full-scale riot, Walter White asked her to head an NAACP investigative committee. Working with Thurgood Marshall, who was then an NAACP lawyer, she helped to bring justice to black victims and peace to the Tennessee community. Shortly thereafter, she became a member of the NAACP's legal affairs committee.

She did not always agree with NAACP members, however. Although she pressured Truman to establish a permanent Fair Employment Standards Commission, an issue the NAACP considered its own, Eleanor did not believe fair employment was strictly an African American issue, arguing that others also suffered from unfair employment practices. When the NAACP prepared an appeal to the United Nations to redress the grievances of blacks in America, Eleanor refused to introduce the petition, threatening to resign from the NAACP if they persisted. Although Walter White persuaded her not to resign, she told board members early in 1948 that she would be devoting her time to the United Nations and would not be able to attend meetings regularly. Her presence on the board had great symbolic significance, however.

Jewish Refugees and the Creation of Israel

Among those living in Europe's makeshift refugee camps were Jews who had survived Hitler's mass slaughter, and they weighed heavily on Eleanor's mind. She had not supported the idea of a Jewish homeland during the war, as she believed Jews could live happily outside of a Jewish state. She had sought, instead, to bring Jewish refugees to the

United States. As she watched America close its doors, however, she was forced to reconsider. Much of the world shut its doors to Jewish refugees. When the war came to an end, the true horror of Germany's concentrations camps came to light. Visiting German refugee camps after the London General Assembly in 1946, Eleanor witnessed the sorrow and despair of Jewish survivors, writing years later of "an old woman whose family had been driven from home by the war madness and brutality. . . . We could not speak each other's language, but she knelt in the muddy road and simply threw her arms around my knees. 'Israel,' she murmured, over and over. 'Israel! Israel!' As I looked at her weatherbeaten face and heard her old voice, I knew for the first time what that small land meant to so many, many people."[11]

Shortly thereafter an Anglo-American Committee of Inquiry, established in 1945, recommended that 100,000 Jews be admitted immediately to Palestine, a territory mandated to Great Britain after World War I. Eleanor supported the recommendation, as did Truman, but Great Britain sympathized with Palestinian Arabs and denied the Jews access to Palestine. Taking up the issue at a special UN session in 1947, the General Assembly considered partitioning Palestine into a Jewish state and an Arab state, and once the United Nations voted for partition, Eleanor supported the idea wholeheartedly. She urged both Truman and Secretary of State George Marshall to work for it and to recognize Israel, but Marshall was vehemently opposed, causing Truman to waiver. Marshall was afraid Arab retaliation would affect America's access to Middle Eastern oil reserves.

Eleanor saw the recognition of Israel as a test of UN strength. When Truman hesitated, she put her career on the line, threatening to resign, but he did not accept her resignation. Without alerting the U.S. delegation, the United States recognized the state of Israel in May 1948, causing Eleanor to chastise Truman for not giving the delegates a heads up. She believed his unilateral action weakened the United Nations. Eleanor would become one of Israel's staunchest supporters, visiting the new nation several times in the coming years.

WRITING, RADIO, AND TELEVISION

Although writing about her years in the White House was harder than anticipated, Eleanor completed the manuscript for *This I Remember* in 1949. She was writing a monthly column for the *Ladies' Home Journal*, albeit without a long-term contract, and she expected the *Journal* to serialize the new book, just as it had serialized *This Is My Story*. She had put considerable effort into the book, even asking Hick to help her pick anecdotes for inclusion, but the *Journal's* new editor, Bruce Gould, didn't like the book. Finding it dull, he told Eleanor, "You have written this too hastily—as though you were composing it on a bicycle while pedaling your way to a fire."[12] Even after she did some revising, he didn't like it, and he wanted her to bring in a collaborator. Eleanor refused. Discharging her literary agent, she asked Elliott to find her a publisher, and he approached *McCall's* magazine. *McCall's* bought the serial rights without reading the manuscript and offered Eleanor a five-year contract for her column. Sales of *McCall's* soared, and *This I Remember* became a Book of the Month Club selection. Eleanor would write for *McCall's* until her death in 1962.

Continuing her radio career, Eleanor frequently spoke on U.S. foreign policy for the Voice of America, doing broadcasts in French, German, Italian, and Spanish. In 1948–49, she cohosted a 15-minute daytime show, *The Eleanor and Anna Show*, with her daughter. The two women had resolved their differences after Franklin's death, and Anna, who had divorced John, was having financial problems. All of the show's income went to Anna. Covering serious topics, Eleanor interviewed such guests as George Marshall and UN diplomat Ralph Bunche, while Anna talked about fashion trends, theater, and the movies. Although praised as "the first network recognition of female intelligence in daytime programming,"[13] the show was short-lived, as it lacked a sponsor. In 1950 Eleanor undertook another talk show, *The Eleanor Roosevelt Show*, to help Elliott with his financial problems. Elliott negotiated the contract, coproduced the show, and appeared on it, asking his mother questions before she interviewed her guests. Elliott also gave the commercials, eliciting criticism because he was using his mother's name to sell soap. It was another short-lived show.

After making her television debut on *Meet the Press*, Eleanor began hosting her own Sunday afternoon television show, *Mrs. Roosevelt Meets the Public*, in 1950. Packaged by Elliott, the show was another venture to ease Anna's and Elliott's financial problems. Eleanor's share of the income went to Anna. Taking the form of a tea party, the show featured Eleanor sitting in a living room and serving tea as she interviewed her guests. Elliott had promised NBC she would include such celebrities as Winston Churchill and Andrei Vishinsky. Although neither of them agreed to appear, she interviewed some notable people, including heads of state and Albert Einstein. Lasting only a year and a half, the show was controversial, as Eleanor's liberal stance was suspect in the cold war era. Throughout the 1950s, however, she continued to make guest appearances on *Meet the Press*, *Person to Person*, and other talk shows.

COLD WAR HYSTERIA

After World War II, America succumbed to an anticommunist, cold war hysteria fueled by the House Un-American Activities Committee (HUAC) and the Republican Senator from Wisconsin, Joseph McCarthy. As America watched communist regimes spread first into Eastern Europe and then into China, a deep, unreasoning fear permeated the country, culminating in a virulent anticommunist witch hunt. Led by self-appointed communist haters, HUAC sought to weed out spies and communist sympathizers, subjecting Hollywood filmmakers, civil rights workers, and liberal intellectuals to investigation, often without factual evidence. Accusing anyone who knew or had ever known a communist, the committee blacklisted actors, film directors, and writers believed to have communist leanings. Even ordinary citizens became hesitant to voice their opinions or acknowledge friendships with suspected individuals.

While well aware of the communist threat abroad, Eleanor was equally afraid of America's witch hunt at home. Having opposed HUAC as early as the late 1930s, when Martin Dies led the committee in an attack on the Federal Theatre Project, she told the nation, "I have never liked the idea of an Un-American Activities Committee. . . . A strong democracy should stand by its fundamental beliefs and . . . a citizen of the United States should be considered innocent until he is proved guilty. . . . The . . . Committee seems to me to be better for a police state than for the USA."[14] When Truman established a loyalty program for government employees, Eleanor expressed her dismay early on, writing that "if a wave of hysteria hits us, there will be very little protection for anyone who even thinks differently."[15]

Although her stance was not a popular one, Eleanor spoke out in support of anyone she believed was being accused unfairly, including her friends Aubrey Williams, Mary McLeod Bethune, and Walter White. By doing so she opened herself to criticism from the left and the right. Even liberal friends questioned her judgment when she stood behind Alger Hiss. Charged with being a Soviet spy, Hiss was a former member of Franklin's State Department and head of the Carnegie Endowment for International Peace. Initially charged by HUAC and prosecuted by California Senator Richard Nixon, he was ultimately convicted of perjury. Eleanor never believed he was a spy and continued to defend Hiss even as his friends deserted him. Taking an intense dislike to Nixon, Eleanor believed Hiss was a victim of HUAC's witch hunt and Nixon's political ambitions.

In the 1950s Joseph McCarthy's anti-communist crusade came to dominate the scene, overshadowing HUAC as McCarthy attacked colleges

and universities, labeling their faculty members as communists, and accused the State Department of harboring communists. Rarely did he have
evidence for his accusations. Although Eleanor initially considered Mc-
Carthy a silly, frivolous man, not nearly as dangerous as Richard Nixon,
she became alarmed when she realized the extent to which McCarthyism was poisoning the nation. High school teachers hesitated to assign
controversial reading. School librarians saw books removed from their
shelves. College students were afraid to attend political meetings for fear
of being identified as communists. She abhorred McCarthy's attacks on
the Voice of America.

Speaking to the ADA, Eleanor told her audience, "The day I'm afraid
to sit down with people who I do not know because five years from now
someone will say five of those people were Communists and therefore you
are a Communist—that will be a bad day."[16] Urging ADA not to let its anti-
communist membership policy play into McCarthy's hands, she encouraged
members to speak out against his tactics, and she held that communists had
the same right to free speech as everyone else. When ADA itself became
subject to attack, Eleanor became its honorary chair, lending her name and
prestige to the organization. Although a few McCarthy supporters suggested
Eleanor should be brought before the committee, conservative politicians
were generally leery of confronting the former first lady, and McCarthy
never attacked her directly. Nevertheless, she considered McCarthy "the
greatest menace to freedom we have in this country."[17]

PERSONAL LIFE
A Kindred Spirit

While nursing Joe's wife, Trude Lash, as she recovered from an illness,
Eleanor met the handsome Dr. David Gurewitsch in 1944, and his sen-
sitivity impressed her. After leaving the White House, she asked him to
become her physician, telling him she was very healthy and wouldn't take
much of his time, and until November 1947 they had a straightforward
doctor–patient relationship. That changed when Eleanor invited David
to join her flight to Europe. His childhood tuberculosis had reoccurred,
and he would be spending a year convalescing in Davos, Switzerland, as
rest was the only cure available in 1947. Eleanor was flying to Geneva to
meet with the UN Commission on Human Rights.

A Russian Jew whose father had died before he was born, David was
a man without a country. He spent his first five years in Russia, living
with his grandmother while his mother went to medical school. When his

mother set up medical practice in Berlin, he went to live with her, fleeing to Switzerland when Nazism began to take hold. After graduating from a Swiss medical school, he moved to Palestine, where he practiced medicine in a Jewish kibbutz, and when the United Nations voted to partition Palestine, just as he and Eleanor were leaving for Switzerland, David was as intensely interested as Eleanor. He had been living in the United States since the 1930s.

The flight to Switzerland took four days, as the plane was delayed in Newfoundland, where the engine needed repair, and in Ireland, where they waited three days for fog to lift. During the flight, David shared his life story with Eleanor, and she shared hers with him. They had much in common. Raised as young children by their grandmothers, they had both grown up feeling like outsiders and developed the same ability to feel compassion for others. David's medical specialty was polio, a disease Eleanor knew only too well, and he was as deeply interested in politics as she. They both wanted to help, David through medicine, Eleanor through politics. Though they came from very different worlds, they were, in Edna Gurewitsch's words, "kindred souls."

Charming yet reserved, urbane yet vulnerable, David was attractive to women, and Eleanor, like other women, was drawn to him. Over four days they formed the beginnings of a truly deep friendship. Eleanor was 63, and David was 45. They talked every day while Eleanor was in Geneva, and in the following year they met twice in Europe, staying in hotels in Geneva and Paris, where Eleanor showed him drafts of *This I Remember*, asking for his comments. When she was home, Eleanor befriended his wife, Nemone, and daughter, Grania, inviting them to Val Kill, though she knew the marriage was in trouble. Just as she had with Earl Miller, Eleanor would watch David court younger women, often listening to his relationship problems.

As the friendship grew, David became as special to Eleanor as Earl Miller, Lorena Hickok, or Joe Lash had ever been, and in the mid-1950s, she wrote to him, "You know without my telling you that I love you as I love and have never loved anyone else."[18] She kept his photograph on her bedside stand in Val Kill and in New York, to the dismay of her children, and carried his photo wherever she went. As his wife Edna later noted, Eleanor's love for David was multilayered. "Her letters reveal thoughts of David as a lover; she revered him at times as a father, and protected him as a son." David found the love of a former first lady "inspiring." It gave him "a sense of stability." "He didn't have to earn Mrs. Roosevelt's love. He had it."[19] Although he loved her as well, his love was not a romantic love. He was not in love with her, as she was with him, but he gave her the kind of sympathetic, understanding friendship she had never known from her husband. They would remain friends for the rest of her life.

Loss and Worry

In 1949 Eleanor sold her Washington Square apartment and moved to the Park Sheraton Hotel in midtown, within easy walking distance of the United Nations. Although her secretary Tommy moved with her, Tommy's health began to fail in the early 1950s, forcing her to give up some of her duties, and Maureen Corr began to take over, becoming Eleanor's travel companion in 1952. Tommy passed away in 1953, and her death left Eleanor bereft. She had been Eleanor's most constant companion for 30 years.

Eleanor worried about her children as they switched careers and went from one marriage to another. Anna's marriage had begun to deteriorate during the war, and the couple separated in 1947, divorcing in 1949. Eleanor found the divorce upsetting and was distraught a year later, when John committed suicide, as she had always liked him. After struggling for a few years, Anna remarried in 1952, moving with her husband, Dr. James Halsted, from one city to another and living for a while in Iran. Elliott divorced Faye Emerson in 1950. Having held a variety of jobs, he was staying afloat financially by acting as his mother's literary agent. In 1952 he remarried, sold Franklin's cottage, which made Eleanor unhappy, and left Hyde Park.

Franklin Jr. divorced his wife, Ethel du Pont, in 1949 and remarried that same year. Defeating a Tammany Hall candidate, he also ran successfully for Congress, becoming a representative from Manhattan's Upper West Side. Eventually he would serve three terms in Congress. Although James would eventually serve in Congress as well, he ran unsuccessfully for governor of California in 1950, failing to get Truman's endorsement and giving Eleanor yet another reason to resent Truman. After divorcing his wife Betsey, James had remarried in 1941.

The only son never to run for public office, John was a businessman. Switching parties in 1947, he was also a Republican. He and his wife, Anne, moved into Nancy and Marion's old cottage in 1952 and lived in Hyde Park until after Eleanor died, enabling her to stay at Val Kill and giving her an opportunity to enjoy his children. Although both Elliott and John lived in Hyde Park for a while, they did not get along well. In later years, Eleanor stopped having family get-togethers, as she found her children's quarreling difficult to deal with and preferred to see them separately.

STEPPING DOWN

In 1952 Dwight Eisenhower, a man Eleanor disliked intensely, ran for president as the Republican candidate, and she was quick to criticize him. Her feelings were personal as well as political. Although his politics were in opposition to hers, she felt most strongly that he was too silent on McCarthyism. When Secretary of State George Marshall, a man who had supported Eisenhower's military career, came under attack, Eisenhower did not come to his defense, preferring instead to distance himself. Eleanor, who held Marshall in high esteem, would never forgive Eisenhower for his silence, although as president he would denounce McCarthy. Adlai Stevenson replaced Truman as the Democratic candidate, and Eleanor supported him. She agreed with his views on foreign policy and was happy to make appearances for him, although she did not take an active part in the 1952 election.

A national war hero, Eisenhower won the election with ease, and as members of Truman's administration offered their resignations, he was quick to accept Eleanor's. Stepping down from her official role at the United Nations, she began to devote her time to the American Association for the United Nations (AAUN), an organization dedicated to promoting an understanding of the UN. She had first joined the group in 1947, volunteering as an administrator, speaker, and fundraiser. Working from the New York office, Eleanor helped the AAUN set up chapters throughout the country, increasing the number of local chapters from 30 to 200. She also embarked on a nationwide speaking tour, encouraging Americans to support U.S. membership in the United Nations, and in 1961she was named chair of the AAUN board.

VISITING THE REST OF THE WORLD
The Middle East and India

Although Eleanor traveled regularly to Europe, she wanted to visit new places. She was eager to see Israel, and Prime Minister Nehru had invited her to India. In February 1952, after a UN session in Paris, she and Maureen Corr set off for the Middle East, visiting Lebanon, Syria, and Jordan as well as Israel. Eleanor found the Arab nations upsetting. Many Arabs lived in poverty, without hope, and when she visited refugee camps for displaced Palestinians, she found them "distressing beyond words." Moving from Arab countries into Israel was almost a relief, "like breathing the air of the United States again."[20] Impressed by the industriousness of the Israelis, Eleanor felt an affinity for Israel that she did not have for the Arab nations.

Her friend David met them in Israel, as he had been advised to stay away from Arab countries, and they traveled together to Asia. After a short visit to Pakistan, they spent a month in India, staying at Nehru's residence as the guests of his sister, Madame Vijaya Pandit, head of the Indian UN delegation. Although Indian roads with their mixture of camels, hand-drawn carts, and automobiles were a revelation, Eleanor visited both rural areas and cities, meeting people from all castes and backgrounds and seeking out women's groups. Speaking to groups of students, she visited schools and universities, receiving several honorary degrees, and with David at her side, she visited hospitals, observing Indian health care. Her only indulgence was a visit to the Taj Mahal in moonlight, a sight her father had described in his letters from India.

Having won its independence from Great Britain just five years earlier, India was trying to walk a fine line between the United States and the Soviet Union. Many Americans feared India would turn communist. As she spent time with Nehru, Eleanor talked of India's relation with the United States and came to understand the country's need to remain neutral. In her book *India and the Awakening East*, she would tell America that India needed economic help, not military aid, to fight communist propaganda. Speaking to the Indian Parliament, she won over an initially hostile audience with her conversational tone and a reference to America's having once been a British colony.

Japan and Yugoslavia

In the spring of 1953 Eleanor spent five weeks in Japan as part of a cultural exchange program, traveling with Maureen and Elliott's current wife, Minnewa. Visiting Hiroshima, she witnessed the devastation wrought by the atomic bomb and tried to explain America's decision to the Japanese people. She learned about Japan's emergence from a feudal society as she talked with Japanese scholars and government officials. Speaking with Japanese women, she learned of their difficulty adjusting as old norms broke down, leading to conflicts between young people and their parents. She also had an audience with the emperor and empress. Leaving Japan, Eleanor made quick stops in Hong Kong, Turkey, and Greece, joining David in Athens before flying to Yugoslavia. Witnessing communist life firsthand, she and David traveled in the Yugoslav countryside as well as the cities and spent a day with President Tito at his island retreat in the Adriatic, where she asked him about communism in Yugoslavia.

The Soviet Union

Eleanor made the first of two trips to the Soviet Union in 1957 as a journalist for *The New York Post*. Traveling with David, who spoke fluent Russian, and Maureen, she visited Russian schools, observing the country's educational system, while David learned about Russian medicine, visiting hospitals, talking with Russian doctors, and joining Eleanor on her visits to medical schools. Although they saw Lenin's tomb and other approved attractions, the Russian guides, who tried to limit their itinerary, caused them some frustration. In Yalta Eleanor interviewed Nikita Khrushchev, who had replaced Stalin as Soviet dictator. The only American reporter to gain access to Khrushchev, Eleanor became an instant authority on Soviet affairs as she wrote articles about the trip and reprinted her interviews with Khrushchev in "My Day." While she wrote later, "I think I should die if I had to live in Soviet Russia," she found the trip "one of the most important . . . and . . . most informative [she] ever made."[21]

Traveling for her own pleasure, Eleanor also visited Indonesia, Thailand, Cambodia, and Morocco in the 1950s, often accompanied by David or her family members. She took two of her grandchildren to the Middle East, showing them Israel and visiting Anna in Iran, and she made several family trips to Europe.

BACK INTO POLITICS

After limiting her participation in the 1952 presidential election, Eleanor reentered politics in 1956, putting all of her support behind Adlai Stevenson. Several Democrats sought the nomination, and Stevenson's candidacy was not a certainty. Helping him to raise funds, Eleanor gave him names of potential donors, and she provided tips on strategy, suggesting, for instance, that he make his speeches more down to earth. With presidential primaries gaining in importance, she campaigned vigorously in California, and she spoke at the Democratic National Convention. The leading lady of the party, she was as forceful as ever. Once Stevenson was nominated, she traveled throughout the country on his behalf, helping particularly to keep African American voters, as young blacks considered Stevenson too cautious on desegregation. Eisenhower could not be beaten, however, and he was reelected with Richard Nixon as his vice president.

Although Eleanor sought Stevenson's nomination again in 1960, Massachusetts Senator John F. Kennedy was the Democratic favorite, and he got the nomination with ease. Eleanor's feelings about Kennedy were decidedly lukewarm, at times overtly negative. She disliked his father, Joseph Kennedy, who had served in Franklin's administration, and distrusted the entire family. John had angered her in the early 1950s because he, like Eisenhower, refused to denounce McCarthy, taking the safer road of distancing himself. She also thought he failed to pursue African American civil rights vigorously enough. James, Elliott, and Franklin supported Kennedy, however. When Kennedy asked Eleanor for her support, she told him, "You have a son of mine on the East Coast, a son on the West Coast, and a third son, Elliott, working for you. You do not need me."[22] But he did. Eleanor's endorsement would bring out the liberal Democratic vote, and Kennedy knew he needed that if he was to beat his Republican opponent, Richard Nixon.

When a small group of senior citizens planning a trip to Hyde Park asked Kennedy to speak, he jumped at the opportunity, and Eleanor, of course, invited him to lunch at Val Kill. She was already softening toward him. Liberal Democrats as well as her sons were urging her to support Kennedy, and Franklin Jr. hoped for a position in his administration. Two days before the luncheon, David asked her, "You *really* don't want Mr. Nixon, do you?"[23] After a lengthy conversation over lunch, Eleanor wrote in "My Day," "I have come to the conclusion that the people will have in John F. Kennedy, if he is elected, a good President."[24] In exchange for her support, Kennedy had agreed to give Adlai Stevenson a role in foreign policy, and he would appoint Stevenson ambassador to the United Nations. Although her energy was waning, Eleanor supported Kennedy throughout the campaign, traveling on his behalf and appearing in television commercials for him. She was delighted when he beat Nixon.

IN THE FINAL YEARS

In 1958 Eleanor's friend David Gurewitsch remarried. Although initially troubled by his engagement, Eleanor "was prepared to love whom David loved,"[25] and she quickly befriended his fiancée, Edna Perkel, an art historian David had known since 1956. After the marriage, Eleanor and the Gurewitsches bought a townhouse on East 74th Street, and Eleanor moved into the building, an arrangement Edna had suggested. While living in a separate apartment, Eleanor frequently had dinner with her two friends and went to the theater and concerts with them. While her children resented Eleanor's devotion to David, they were relieved to have their mother living near her physician. At the end of 1958, David and Edna joined Eleanor on her second trip to the Soviet Union.

Eleanor continued to be busy well into her seventies, entertaining family, friends, and such notables as Tito and Khrushchev. In addition to her travels, newspaper columns, and speaking tours, she continued to work for the AAUN and was active on behalf of the NAACP, the United Jewish Appeal, and other organizations. She moderated a public television series, *Prospects of Mankind*, inviting Martin Luther King to be her first guest, and at the age of 75, took a job as lecturer at Brandeis University. Writing about her life after Franklin's death, she published a third autobiographical volume, *On My Own*, in 1958 and coauthored two small works on the United Nations. In 1960 she summarized her views on life in *You Learn by Living*, and in her final year she wrote a book about the dangers of the cold war, *Tomorrow Is Now*, which was published after her death. In 1961 President Kennedy named her chair of the President's Commission on the Status of Women and reappointed her to the UN delegation, but her health was failing, precluding her being active in either role.

One day in 1960 Eleanor called the Gurewitsches and asked Edna, "May I come up, dear? I was just hit by a car." As she stepped off the curb, a taxi had backed into her, hitting her leg and knocking her down. Feeling she was partly to blame and afraid the driver, an African American, would be arrested, Eleanor wouldn't let him help, telling him to leave "before the police come."[26] Although David wanted her to have X-rays immediately, she refused, insisting she had to speak at a fundraiser and telling him afterwards that her condition had prompted more generous giving. Visiting the hospital the next day, largely to make David happy, she was released after X-rays showed a sprain and she promised to stay off her feet.

When David followed up with an exam, however, Eleanor's leg showed signs of edema, or a buildup of fluid, and her pulse was abnormal. A complete physical revealed she was suffering from anemia, although doctors couldn't find a cause. Eleanor tried to keep up her schedule, but her energy began to wane. Over the next two years she had spells of weakness, shortness of breath, and unexplained bleeding. Her anemia had leukemia-like symptoms, but no traces of leukemia could be found. Although David consulted with a variety of physicians, including Anna's husband, James Halsted, no one could provide answers. With no real diagnosis, Eleanor had regular blood tests, and increasingly, she needed blood transfusions.

Nevertheless, she traveled to Israel with Edna Gurewitsch in February 1962 and spent time in Europe with Edna and David. Twice during the trip Eleanor felt weak and short of breath, scaring her friends, but she rallied after the episodes passed. In August, although she could barely walk, Eleanor made a final trip to Campobello. Taking David and Edna along, she showed them her favorite spots, even as they had to carry her. On the drive back to New York, she stopped to say goodbye to Esther Lape and other old friends.

With her return to the city, David insisted she go to the hospital. Trying to determine the source of her anemia, he brought in another specialist, who diagnosed Eleanor as having a rare form of tuberculosis in her bone marrow, most likely resulting from a misdiagnosed case of tuberculosis years earlier. David's spirits lifted for a moment, as he believed they could cure tuberculosis, but Eleanor was ready to let go. Although David wanted to continue treatment, Eleanor wanted to return home, and she left the hospital on October 18. James Halsted supported her wish to discontinue treatment, and Anna took over her mother's care, coordinating doctors' visits, nurses' schedules, and her brothers' activities. As her underlying resentment came to the surface, she also limited David's visits as well as visits from Edna and the Lashes.

On November 7, 1962, Eleanor Roosevelt passed away. After a simple service attended by President Kennedy, former presidents Truman and Eisenhower, Vice President Johnson, Franklin's cabinet members, and her family and friends, Eleanor was buried next to Franklin in Hyde Park. Delegates at the United Nations stood for a moment of silence. Some 10,000 people attended a memorial service in New York City. John F. Kennedy called her "one of the great ladies in the history of this country," while Adlai Stevenson eulogized, "She would rather light candles than curse the darkness."[27] Perhaps, however, her spirit is best captured in Eleanor's own words: "Life was meant to be lived. . . . One must never, for whatever reason, turn his back on life."[28]

NOTES

1. Quoted in Emblidge, *My Day*, p. 99.

2. Quoted in Lash, *Eleanor: The Years Alone*, p. 23.

3. Eleanor Roosevelt, *On My Own: The Years Since the White House* (New York: Dell Publishing Co., 1958), p. 56.

4. Quoted in Lash, *Eleanor: The Years Alone*, p. 54.

5. Quoted in ibid., p. 53.

6. Quoted in Black, *Casting Her Own Shadow*, p. 65.

7. Quoted in ibid., p. 74.

8. Quoted in Beasley, Shulman, and Beasley, *Eleanor Roosevelt Encyclopedia*, p. 21.

9. Quoted in Lash, *Eleanor: The Years Alone*, p. 144.

10. Quoted in ibid., p. 153.

11. Roosevelt, *On My Own*, p. 70.

12. Quoted in Lash, *Eleanor: The Years Alone*, p. 187.

13. Quoted in Maurine H. Beasley, *Eleanor Roosevelt and the Media: A Public Quest for Self-Fulfillment* (Urbana: University of Illinois Press, 1987), p. 172.

14. Quoted in David Emblidge, *Eleanor Roosevelt's My Day: Her Acclaimed Columns*, vol. II, *The Post-War Years, 1945–1952* (New York: Pharos Books, 1990), pp. 115–6.

15. Quoted in ibid., p. 94.

16. Quoted in Lash, *Eleanor: The Years Alone*, p. 234.

17. Quoted in Black, *Casting Her Own Shadow*, p. 168.

18. Quoted in Gurewitsch, *Kindred Souls*, p. 12.

19. Gurewitsch, *Kindred Souls*, p. 43.

20. Roosevelt, *On My Own*, pp. 122, 123.

21. Ibid., p. 229.

22. Quoted in Gurewitsch, *Kindred Souls*, p. 219.

23. Quoted in ibid., p. 220.

24. Quoted in Emblidge, *My Day*, p. 287.

25. Quoted in Beasley, Shulman, and Beasley, *Eleanor Roosevelt Encyclopedia*, p. 220.

26. Gurewitsch, *Kindred Souls*, p. 211.

27. Quoted in Beasley, Shulman, and Beasley, *Eleanor Roosevelt Encyclopedia*, p. 122.

28. Roosevelt, *Autobiography*, p. xix.

EPILOGUE

At the service for Franklin's burial, his former secretary of the treasury, Henry Morgenthau, told Eleanor the security guards didn't want to let him in. They didn't know who he was. Eleanor told him to sit down, asking if he thought she would be remembered. She didn't think so. Never seeking credit for herself, she characteristically denied her influence and in later years often told friends she would be forgotten in 10 years. Quite possibly, she would be astonished at the attention her life receives today. Yet much of what Eleanor Roosevelt fought for is now an integral part of American life.

Her style was to work with others when fighting for a cause. Moving into the world of politics when Franklin took ill, Eleanor not only kept the Roosevelt name alive, helping to ensure his career, but also became a force in the Women's Division of the Democratic Party, bringing women into the mainstream of Democratic politics. Joining forces with early women reformers, she adopted their causes—an eight-hour workday, decent wages, the prohibition of child labor, safety in the workplace, workers' compensation—and brought them to her work in the Democratic Party. With guidance from Louis Howe, she became a politician in her own right.

When Franklin was elected governor of New York, Eleanor became a new kind of helpmate, forming a unique political partnership with her husband and traveling as his "eyes and ears." Ultimately, when Franklin moved into the White House, she played a major role in the shaping of the New Deal. Finding women, African Americans, and youth excluded from early New Deal programs, she agitated for their inclusion, leading to the creation of the National Youth Administration (NYA), a Women's Division within the Federal Emergency Relief Administration and the Works Progress Administration, and the appointment of Mary McLeod Bethune to the NYA, where she provided work for more African Americans than any other New Deal agency did. Working with Louis Howe and Harry Hopkins, Eleanor brought decent housing to West Virginia's destitute coal miners and introduced them to a new way of life.

Committed to women's rights and African American rights, Eleanor kept both issues alive throughout Franklin's presidency. Playing a major role in bringing women into his administration, she ensured that they were given responsible positions. Holding women-only press conferences, she compelled newspapers to hire female reporters and brought women's issues into the limelight, and she was the force behind New Deal programs aiming to help impoverished women as well as married men. Speaking out for African Americans' rights even as her husband and his administration preferred to dodge the issue, she sought to bring their issues to Franklin's attention, giving Walter White, Mary McLeod Bethune, and other black leaders access to the president's ear. Entertaining blacks at the White House, traveling to black communities, and working to bring blacks into New Deal programs, she chipped away at prejudice, and in the process helped to bring the black vote to Franklin when he ran for reelection in 1936.

Working to earn money for her various charity projects, Eleanor also had a lucrative career as a journalist, radio commentator, and public speaker. Initially teaching at the Todhunter School, a job she loved but had to give up when she moved into the White House, she soon turned to writing and radio broadcasting. While beginning her writing with the *Women's Democratic News*, she soon had assignments for magazine articles and a monthly column for the *Woman's Home Companion*. She appeared on a number of radio talk shows, giving, for instance, weekly commentaries on the news and on education, and she began to make speaking tours to colleges and community centers. While earning a sizable income, Eleanor used these vehicles to advocate her views as well. She would speak and write on topics as varied as world peace, bringing women into politics, and, somewhat ironically, how to have a successful marriage.

In 1936 she began one of her most successful writing endeavors, her highly popular "My Day" column. The daily column took off immediately, and Eleanor wrote it for the rest of her life. Covering a variety of topics, from her family's activities to politics, she ultimately used the column to promote her goals, take political stands, and bring issues to the public's attention. In 1937 she published her first autobiographical volume, *This Is*

My Story, selling serial rights to the *Ladies' Home Journal*. Eventually she would write about her years in the White House in *This I Remember* and the years after Franklin's death in *On My Own*, as well as books of advice, books on political topics, and children's books. By 1937, with the income from her writing, her radio shows, and her speaking tours, Eleanor's income exceeded Franklin's. She gave a good portion of it to charity.

Although her power waned in the late 1930s, Eleanor's activism continued during World War II. She applauded women who joined the workforce and spearheaded the creation of day care centers for their children. Fighting for racial justice, she did what she could, albeit behind the scenes, for interned Japanese Americans and publicly supported the rights of blacks. As she had before the war, Eleanor sought to eliminate slums and provide decent housing for blacks, initiating the Sojourner Truth Project in Detroit, just as she had initiated an African American homestead under the New Deal and fought for new housing to replace Washington's alley slums. Acting as a conduit between A. Philip Randolph and Franklin, she helped to facilitate FDR's issuing of an executive order banning discrimination in the defense industry, and, again working with black civil rights leaders, she chipped away at prejudice in the military, ultimately opening the way for blacks to serve in the same capacities as white GIs.

Giving moral support to GIs abroad, Eleanor visited the troops in England, the Pacific, and the Caribbean. Promising to deliver messages to their families or take their concerns to military authorities, promises she always kept, Eleanor talked with soldiers, inspected their barracks, and met with commanders. As she visited military hospitals, she saw each and every patient, however difficult she found it to smile at deformed and seriously wounded boys, bringing a ray of hope to them. Writing of her travels, she brought the GI experience home to America.

Accepting Harry Truman's offer, Eleanor became a delegate to the United Nations after the war, ultimately playing a significant role in international politics. Finding herself in direct confrontation with the Soviet bloc, she navigated difficult political waters and helped to create a fair and humane resettlement policy for European refugees. She actively promoted the creation of an Israeli state and the Marshall Plan for European Recovery. As chair of the UN Commission on Human Rights, Eleanor was the major force behind the Universal Declaration of Human Rights, an international bill of rights that remains the accepted standard for human rights.

Upon leaving the UN delegation, Eleanor volunteered for the American Association for the United Nations and became a founding member of Americans for Democratic Action. She continued to speak out on political issues, taking a strong stand against cold war hysteria during the McCarthy era, and to play a role in Democratic politics, campaigning for Adlai Stevenson and giving her support to John F. Kennedy. She also continued her journalism career, writing new books and articles for *McCall's* magazine, talking on new radio shows, and making her television debut. The only American journalist to gain access to and interview Soviet dictator Nikita Khrushchev, she wrote extensively on the Soviet Union after a visit there, becoming the nation's leading authority on that communist nation.

Born at the end of the nineteenth century, Eleanor Roosevelt was very much a product of the Victorian era. Yet she was also a woman ahead of her time, a woman at the forefront of the labor movement, the civil rights movement, and the women's movement. She was a new kind of first lady, an activist and a politician. Often working behind the scenes, she played a major role in the history of the twentieth century. Although not a saint, as some have portrayed her to be, Eleanor Roosevelt was an extraordinary woman.

BIBLIOGRAPHIC ESSAY

Much has been written about Eleanor Roosevelt. Readers who wish to learn more about her might want to begin with her own work. A good place to start is her single-volume book *The Autobiography of Eleanor Roosevelt* (New York: Harper & Brothers, 1961; repr., Da Capo Press, 1992). That book condenses her three original autobiographies—*This Is My Story* (New York: Harper & Brothers, 1937), *This I Remember* (New York: Harper & Brothers, 1949; repr., Westport, CT: Greenwood Press, 1975), and *On My Own: The Years since the White House* (New York: Dell Publishing Co., 1958)—and includes an additional section on the years from 1958 to 1961. Although only the *Autobiography* is still in print, other books by Eleanor Roosevelt can be obtained through interlibrary loan, including *If You Ask Me* (New York: Appleton-Century, 1946), *It's Up to the Women* (New York: Frederick A. Stokes, 1933), *The Moral Basis of Democracy* (New York: Howell, Soskin, & Co., 1940), *India and the Awakening East* (Harper & Brothers, 1953), *You Learn by Living* (New York: Dolphin Books, 1960), and *Tomorrow Is Now* (New York: Harper & Row, 1963).

Eleanor's "My Day" columns provide a wealth of information about her thoughts and opinions, both personal and political. David Emblidge's *My Day: The Best of Eleanor Roosevelt's Acclaimed Newspaper Columns, 1936–1962* (Da Capo Press, 2001) is a single-volume sampling of her columns. A larger collection appears in the three-volume *Eleanor Roosevelt's My Day: Her Acclaimed Columns*, vol. I, *1936–1945*, edited by Rochelle Chadakoff, vol. II, *The Post-War Years, 1945–1952* and vol. III, *1953–1962*, edited by David Emblidge (New York: Pharos Books, 1989, 1990, 1991). The website for The Eleanor Roosevelt Papers Project, www.gwu/~erpapers/, provides "My Day" columns electronically, and the columns can be searched there.

Allida M. Black's *Courage in a Dangerous World: The Political Writings of Eleanor Roosevelt* (New York: Columbia University Press, 1999) provides a sampling of Eleanor's political writing in magazines, speeches, and columns. Black collected Eleanor's essays in *What I Hope to Leave Behind: The Essential Essays of Eleanor Roosevelt* (Brooklyn, NY: Carlson Publishing, 1995). Eleanor's press conferences are available in *The White House Press Conferences of Eleanor Roosevelt*, edited by Maurine H. Beasley (New York: Garland, 1983).

Several books provide collections of Eleanor's letters to friends, family, and political figures. In *It Seems to Me: Selected Letters of Eleanor Roosevelt* (Lexington: University of Kentucky Press, 2001), Leonard C. Schlup and Donald W. Whisenhunt, eds., focus on her political letters, including correspondence with such figures as Walter White, George G. Marshall, and Winston Churchill. Her correspondence with Harry S Truman appears in Steve Neal, ed., *Eleanor and Harry: The Correspondence of Eleanor Roosevelt and Harry S Truman* (New York: Scribner, 2002). Robert Cohen's collection, *Dear Mrs. Roosevelt: Letters from Children of the Great Depression* (Chapel Hill: University of North Carolina Press, 2002), shows the distress children, as well as adults, felt during the Great Depression. Other collections show Eleanor's interaction with her family and friends. These include Bernard Asbell, ed., *Mother and Daughter: The Letters of Eleanor and Anna Roosevelt* (1982; repr., New York: Fromm International, 1988) and Joseph P. Lash's *Love Eleanor: Eleanor Roosevelt and Her Friends* and *A World of Love: Eleanor Roosevelt and Her Friends, 1943–62* (Garden City, NY: Doubleday & Co., 1982, 1984). Letters from Robert Cohen's book also appear on the New Deal Network website, www.newdeal.feri.org/eleanor/index.htm, under the heading "Dear Mrs. Roosevelt."

A multivolume collection of Eleanor Roosevelt's papers is currently being compiled, and the first volume has been published: John F. Sears and Allida M. Black, eds., *Eleanor Roosevelt Papers: The Human Rights Years, 1945–1948*, vol. I (Detroit: Thomson Gale, 2007). The website for the Eleanor Roosevelt Papers project, www.gwu/~erpapers/, provides information about this project as well as a bibliography of works about Eleanor Roosevelt, links to related websites, copies of selected documents, and her "My Day" columns.

The earliest biographies of Eleanor include Ruby Black's *Eleanor Roosevelt: A Biography* (New York: Duell, Sloan, and Pearce, 1940), Tamara K. Hareven's *Eleanor Roosevelt: An American Conscience* (Chicago, Quadrangle Books, 1968), and James R. Kearney's *Anna Eleanor Roosevelt: The*

Evolution of a Reformer (Boston: Houghton Mifflin Co., 1968). In 1962, Lorena A. Hickok wrote *Eleanor Roosevelt: Reluctant First Lady* (repr., New York: Dodd, Mead, & Co., 1980), an interesting firsthand account of her friendship with the first lady.

Joseph P. Lash wrote the first comprehensive biography of Eleanor: *Eleanor and Franklin: The Story of Their Relationship Based on Eleanor Roosevelt's Private Papers* and *Eleanor: The Years Alone* (New York: W. W. Norton, 1971, 1972). The Roosevelt family invited Lash to write these two books, and for many years, they comprised the definitive work on Eleanor Roosevelt. Blanche Wiesen Cook's more recent biographies, *Eleanor Roosevelt*, vol. I, *1884–1933* and *Eleanor Roosevelt*, vol. II, *The Defining Years, 1933–1938* (New York: Viking Penguin, 1992, 1999) provide new perspectives on some aspects of Eleanor's life. Doris Kearns Goodwin's *No Ordinary Time, Franklin and Eleanor Roosevelt: The Home Front in World War II* (New York: Simon & Schuster, 1994) gives a comprehensive, readable account of both Eleanor and Franklin during the war years.

Shorter biographies include Sarah J. Purcell and L. Edward Purcell, *Eleanor Roosevelt* (Indianapolis, IN: Alpha, a Pearson Education Co., 2002) and J. William T. Youngs, *Eleanor Roosevelt: A Personal and Public Life* (New York: Longman, 2000). Lois Scharf, in *Eleanor Roosevelt: First Lady of American Liberalism* (Boston: Twayne, 1987), focuses on Eleanor's political life, while Allida M. Black, in *Casting Her Own Shadow: Eleanor Roosevelt and the Shaping of Postwar Liberalism* (New York: Columbia University Press, 1996), considers her role in postwar politics. In *Eleanor Roosevelt and the Media: A Public Quest for Self-Fulfillment* (Urbana: University of Illinois Press, 1987), Maurine H. Beasley writes about Eleanor as a journalist. Edna P. Gurewitsch writes of Eleanor's friendship with her husband, David Gurewitsch, in *Kindred Souls: The Devoted Friendship of Eleanor Roosevelt and Dr. David Gurewitsch* (New York: Plume, 2002). In *Sara and Eleanor: The Story of Sara Delano Roosevelt and Her Daughter-in-Law, Eleanor Roosevelt* (New York: St. Martin's Griffin, 2004), Jan Pottker takes a second look at the relationship between these two women, painting a very different picture of Sara from the one initially given by Joseph Lash and often repeated by other biographers.

A good source of quick factual information about Eleanor Roosevelt is Maurine H. Beasley, Holly C. Shulman, and Henry R. Beasley, eds., *The Eleanor Roosevelt Encyclopedia* (Westport, CT: Greenwood Press, 2001).

An Internet search will pull up a good many sites with information on Eleanor Roosevelt, often a capsule biography. In addition to the site for the Eleanor Roosevelt Papers Project, the following sites are particularly worthwhile: PBS's "American Experience," www.pbs.org/wgbh/amex/eleanor/; the Franklin D. Roosevelt Presidential Library and Museum, www.fdrlibrary.marist.edu/index.html/; the Franklin & Eleanor Roosevelt Institute, www.feri.org; the New Deal network, www.newdeal.feri.org; and the Eleanor Roosevelt Institute at Val Kill, www.ervk.org.

INDEX

About the Author

CYNTHIA M. HARRIS retired from Greenwood Press in 2003. She worked for Greenwood for 27 years in various editorial capacities and was director of developmental editing when she retired.

pg 92
rainbow flyers

pg 85 —
Alley Housing Bill —